Great Lakes CRIME

Murder, Mayhem, Booze & Broads

Frederick Stonehouse

Avery Color Studios, Inc.
Gwinn, Michigan

ISBN: 978-1-892384-25-6

Library of Congress Control Number: 2003116653

First Edition–2004

10

Published by Avery Color Studios, Inc.
Gwinn, Michigan 49841

TABLE OF CONTENTS

INTRODUCTION

The topic of this book is Great Lakes crime including murder, mayhem, piracy, rum running, red lights, etc., all the "normal" nefarious activities that add a bit of spice to life.

The book certainly isn't all-inclusive. There is just too much criminal activity to cover it all in a single volume! But it is a fair sample of the kinds of illegal goings-on common to the Great Lakes.

Some is certainly expected. People are always murdering each other and it makes little difference where it happens. Barratry, defined as the "willful casting away of a ship by her master," is a different story. It can only be done on water. While countless businesses ashore were "sold" to insurance companies when they mysteriously burned to the ground, on the Great Lakes many ships inexplicably suddenly sank in deepwater when economic times were hard, forcing an insurance payoff. As with land-based business, proving criminal action was difficult and there is the feeling only the truly incompetent or unlucky ever were caught. While barratry is not a major problem on the Great Lakes today, on salt water it is a different story.

I was surprised by the amount of Prohibition rum running, both "illegal," when the authorities genuinely tried to prevent delivery and "legal," when bootlegger payoffs had cleared the way for an uncontested delivery. If all the old stories and government reports are true, the illegal booze rivaled iron ore as the major product hauled on the lakes.

The wide spread actions of the thieving timber pirates was another surprise. While I knew about the cutting of "round forties" I thought such actions were comparatively rare, the action of a few small time timbermen. Instead I discovered the activity was widespread and the basis for the fortunes of many now respected lumbermen. Before I did the research for the book, I thought the now sleepy and picturesque little Lake Michigan town of Manistee had come by it's lumber town reputation honestly. Instead I found it was a nest of thieves and pirates every bit as nasty as old Port Royal in the Caribbean Sea!

In any case, enjoy the book and learn more about our wonderful Great Lakes maritime history.

Great Lakes MURDER

Damn Near Murder

Whether a death was accidental or murder is not always clear-cut. A good example happened in Marquette in July 1889. As a caboose was backing down the track leading to the ore dock, the conductor and brakeman saw two men fighting behind the station. As the caboose approached the station the two trainmen saw one of the fighters toss the other under the wheels of the caboose and flee. Before the car could stop, it ran over the man's left leg crushing it completely. The wounded man was quickly carried to a nearby boarding house where physicians examined him. They determined he was too weak from loss of blood to survive an operation so he was left in the boarding house for the night. He was identified as Michael Higgins, an ore trimmer. The following morning it was decided to carry him to the hospital but he died before being moved.

Higgins' assailant was August Johnson, another trimmer. Fights between trimmers, especially trimmers from different "gangs" were commonplace, as were fights between sailors and trimmers, sailors and sailors, miners and sailors, well you get the general idea. Fights that ended in death were unusual and the local legal system went into high gear to determine what really happened. The justice assembled a jury, who after carefully examining all witnesses and evidence, returned a verdict of accidental death and no charges were filed against Johnson.[1]

Bodies and More Bodies

Sometime evidence of crime appeared in the oddest ways. On August 22, 1883 in St. Catharines, Ontario a crewman was busy digging coal out of the hold of the burned steamer *Glenfinlas* when he discovered a human skull. The steamer had caught fire from an overheated boiler and burned to a total loss in the Welland Canal the previous week. Authorities immediately investigated but discovered none of the crew were missing and since the steamer did not carry passengers, who the skull belonged to was a mystery. No other parts of the body were found and the mystery remained unsolved.[2]

In the early days of Great Lakes shipping, accidents of every kind were routine. Handling cargoes of lumber, iron, copper or general freight was dangerous work. OSHA (Occupational Safety and Health Administration) was not on every corner and men had to watch out for their own safety. Mix in alcohol and even common activities took on a perilous demeanor.

For example, in the morning of November 1, 1875 a cap was seen floating in Oswego harbor near one of the grain elevators. Old-timers immediately suspected trouble. A quick look around revealed the body of Joseph Laundre, the cook on the steam barge *Ellsworth*. Witnesses remembered he was drunk when he boarded her at about 11:00 a.m. demanding the captain settle his pay. Captain Cole refused, deciding to wait until the cook was sober and ejected him from the galley. It was later surmised the cook lost his balance climbing over the rail and fell into the river, between the hull and dock. There was a large contusion on his face, suggesting he had struck one or the other on the way down.[3]

The Dead Cook

Another case of a dead cook involved the schooner-barge *Harvey Bissell*. Mary Gowman had been cooking aboard for only a short time when she was discovered dead, shot by a bullet to the chest when the vessel was off Sturgeon Bay, Lake Michigan on May 10, 1882. When the *Bissell* reached Sturgeon Bay a day later, the captain reported the death to the police and an official investigation started. Since the coroner was gone, the justice of the peace organized a jury of six citizens including a local doctor. It was a stormy night, certainly an appropriate time to investigate a murder.

The jury questioned the crew including master. After a brief conference, it determined it was suicide, not murder. If everyone thought the episode was finished, they were wrong. A letter soon appeared in the *Chicago Inter-Ocean*, an important shipping newspaper of the time. The writer claimed to be a Sturgeon Bay man with special knowledge of the case. He claimed the cook was a 25-year old woman from Cleveland and was in the process of being divorced by her husband for infidelity. The

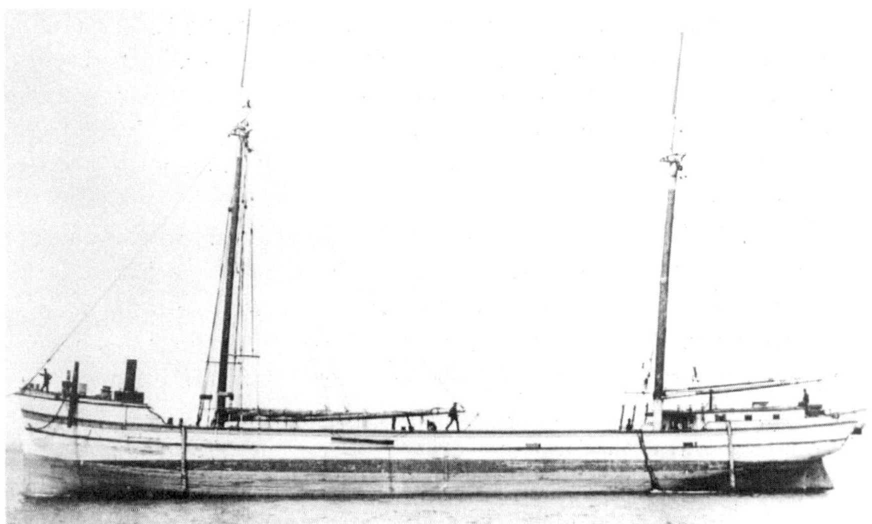

Was the cook murdered or was it suicide? K.E. Thro Collection

writer claimed the doctor had probed for the bullet but could not reach it and that he stated it angled downward from left to right. Clearly the cook could only have fired the gun if she were left-handed. The writer further claimed the entrance wound was too high on the chest for the cook to have self-inflicted it regardless of using either hand. In addition, the letter stated two rings on her hand were badly damaged, one broken in two and the other bent nearly double, implying the body was violently handled after death. However a later story in the *Chicago Inter-Ocean* claimed a friend believed the cook was despondent and had attempted suicide before.[4]

The cook was buried on May 12 at Bayside Cemetery, Sturgeon Bay. The mystery of her death was never solved. Was it suicide or murder by one of the crew? Did the jury reach their verdict honestly or was it a cover-up?

"We Didn't Do It"

It is one thing to be a murderer but quite another for people to think you are one. That's the situation the crew of the steamer *Depere* found themselves in on February 12, 1884.

The *Depere* was a Goodrich vessel running on it's regular winter route on the west shore of Lake Michigan when she became stuck in the ice about five miles off Winnetka, Illinois. Unable to break free, the captain sent a party ashore to secure provisions in the event the ship was trapped for a long period. Second mate Ed Carus headed up the group. When the sailors reached shore they went to the first house they found which turned out to be the summer residence of a wealthy businessman. The caretaker directed the men to the town proper where provisions would be available.

As the small group walked down the streets of Winnetka people either shied away from them or gave them very suspicious looks. When the mate asked a local constable what was going on, the group was arrested and jailed on suspicion of murder.

It turns out that the pervious night one of the local citizens and his wife were brutally murdered in their home. The husband was shot to death and his wife hacked to pieces with a Civil War saber. It was a gruesome affair that had the entire town on edge. Once the sailors were able to prove where they came from they were released and eventually rations were obtained. The murderers were never apprehended.[5]

The propeller Depere. *The crew was mistaken for murderers.*
Stonehouse Collection

"He Threatened the Crew"

Sometimes death did not happen, but it came very close. The following item from the *Oswego Palladium* of August 10, 1881 shows just how near a thing it can be. "Last evening the mate of the schooner *Marcia A. Hall*, which arrived in the afternoon from Toronto, applied for the arrest of Captain Maurice Fitzgerald, master of the vessel, representing that he was insane and had driven off the crew with an axe, threatening their lives. Officers Chauncey and Connolly arrested Fitzgerald and committed him to the county jail, where he will remain for the present.

"The mate says the vessel loaded partly at Toronto, and he took her up to Oakville to finish out, the captain, who had been drinking heavily, remaining at home and telling him to telegraph when he was loaded, but that perhaps he would not join the vessel unless he felt better. He telegraphed and Captain Fitzgerald went up and took command."

"They sailed at 8 A.M. Sunday, and it was soon found that the captain was in a bad way. He was first seen up the fore cross-trees with an axe in his hands, threatening to kill somebody. Off Charlotte he became very violent, chased the men with an axe, and finally catching up, an axe in each hand attacked the mate, swearing he would kill him. He was overcome, disarmed and bound, so as to do no other harm."

"He was full of crazy talk, declaring that he was pursued by the Free Masons who were going to kill him, and that myriads of cats were pursuing him. When they arrived here he was released, but again attacked the crew who dare not stay aboard with him. Captain Fitzgerald owns the schooner. His wife was telegraphed, and the mate will probably take out the vessel, which is loaded for Hamilton."

"There is no doubt of Captain Fitzgerald's insanity. He has had several such tears outside. Last season on a trip from Hamilton to Charlotte he became insane, and putting the vessel's boy in a boat and throwing in an axe, he jumped in, cut her adrift in a big sea and was soon driven out of sight. After several days they were picked up by another vessel. The boy almost perished from fright and exposure, and Captain Fitzgerald himself so prostrated that he became very ill and remained ashore for some time." What ultimately happened to the axe-wielding captain isn't known. Perhaps he met Lizzie Borden and they lived happily ever after.[6]

Running Wild

Running amuck as Captain Fitzgerald did wasn't uncommon. In September 1904 a sailor named Sam Kelly on the steamer *Robert Rhodes* ran wild on the vessel while it was moored in Ashland, threatening the crew with a straight razor. Before he could be subdued he slashed two sailors, badly injuring one with five deep cuts, sending both men to the hospital. Kelly was finally overcome by the crew and turned over to the police. It is claimed he had a criminal record in Saginaw and other ports.[7]

He Did It For the Money

Some captains were successful in murdering their crews. In early December 1879 Captain Andrew McKenzie was arrested for murdering

Thomas Russell, a sailor on the barge *Walton*. The barge was moored at Saginaw when the deed was done. The evidence however was entirely circumstantial. The police knew he did it, but they had no hard evidence.

After being locked up in a cold and dank city jail cell known as the "freezer," McKenzie grew more and more agitated. Although there was nothing to directly tie him to the crime, he felt as if the noose was slowly tightening around his neck. His conscience was eating away at his confidence. The police kept him under constant surveillance, knowing it would not take much to "break" him.

One night detective Dan Morgenstern came up to the cell and started to "jaw" with McKenzie, telling him he was just the night watchman. After a bit of conversation, the detective suggested that he could arrange an escape to Canada if McKenzie desired. The prisoner jumped at the chance and a fee of $40 was agreed to. Getting ready to leave, the detective, now in McKenzie's trust, turned to him and asked, "Of course you murdered the man and I know how bad you want to escape, now what did you murder him for?" McKenzie replied, "Oh yes, I killed him for his money." The detective said he would need the money tonight if an escape was to be arranged quickly. Desperate, McKenzie described where the money was hidden on the barge and the detective left to get it.

After briefing his superior of the situation, the detective and three other policemen went to the ship. By the flickering yellow light from an oil lantern the policemen started their search. It was not a pleasant job. The *Walton* was an old ship and was leaking. The men found themselves standing in ankle deep water in her foul smelling hold. Carefully following McKenzie's directions, they groped along her hull until at the bend of the keelson they found a one and a half inch plank nailed to it, some distance up from the bottom. After prying it loose they discovered the missing money, four $20 bills, six $10 bills and two $5 bills, rolled up in a clump. The $5 bills were covered with blood.

Returning to the jail the police confronted McKenzie with the bloody greenbacks and demanded a confession. Shaking and turning pale, McKenzie confessed, claiming he killed Russell in self-defense. "I went aboard my boat about 2 o'clock on Friday morning and found Thomas Russell in my bed in my cabin. He was asleep. He had been in the habit of sleeping there since we came into port. I went to bed with him, only taking off my overcoat and overshoes, as I entered he said, 'is that you?'"

The two men then spoke about the company the Captain had been keeping as well as the character of some of the crew in the course of which Russell used vile and insulting language in describing McKenzie's daughter. Russell also said he wanted to settle up their debts. McKenzie continued, "I settled with him on Saturday. I am certain of this. I paid him $35.65. I paid him some silver. I gave him one ten dollar bill and I think two five dollar bills and the balance in silver. I told him that I could not conclude a settlement with him until morning." He replied, "Settlement be damned. I will not sleep another hour on this boat." Russell again berated McKenzie's daughter. McKenzie continued, "I then hit him with my fist. We clinched, he threw me. We then entered into a struggle and here we had a pretty hot time, he having the best. I probably hurt him some. We had no light and could not see. I struck him anyway. I had him by the throat for a long time. There was no fighting in the cabin but with fist. After some time I got clear and ran out on deck. He came out after me. He grabbed a handspike that was lying on deck and followed me forward with it. I hallowed to him, "Don't kill me Russell." He said, "Pay me, you damned scoundrel." "I told him I would if he would wait until daylight. He wanted his money then, as he was going to Cleveland on the 6'o'clock train. We walked from the forward aft one on one side and one on the other talking pretty loud. I started to go into the cabin on the port side and he on the starboard side and as I entered he struck at me with the handspike. Then I told him that we wanted to keep still and stop this noise or we would both be arrested. He replied that he did not give a damn whether he was or not. We jawed some time and then clinched again. I took the spike away from him and I think I struck him when I took it. He got it again and came for me and I tried to get it away from him and go over the rail. He was close to me when he said, 'Damn you, I will kill you.' I said, "Will you?" and picked up the gas tongs and struck him. I guess that I hit him on the head. As he fell and did not move any more I realized that I had killed him and did not know what I would do. At first I thought I would go over and give myself up. I did not give myself up because I was too big a coward to tell the truth. That is what I ought to have done. After pondering for a few minutes, I dragged him along and pushed him through the scuppers. I only hit him once with the gas tongs. He went through the scupper hole pretty hard. I put nothing on him to sink. I did not look to see whether he sank. I thought he would sink. I do not know what led me to do this. I took the shirt and pillow both of which were covered with blood and tied a chain around them and threw them into the creek to hide them. I supposed they would sink but they did not. The pillow was on the floor, but it got bloody as we rolled around. My nose was bleeding freely. I did not murder him for his money. I had no such intentions. After I went into the cabin I found the money on the floor. I expected to be arrested on suspicion and I thought if the money was found on me there would be a greater charge on me. So I hid it. The money was on the floor and the cabin floor was pretty bloody. I owed Russell for five days work and also $5 borrowed money. I was afraid of Russell. I suppose we were intimate. I did not count the money. He told me at Saginaw, Michigan that he would have over $100. I did not know how much he had. It fell out of his pocket in the scuffle. I covered it over with a piece of pine. It was about 4 o'clock in the morning when I killed him." What makes this tale most interesting is the clear admission of homosexual activity, something only whispered in dark corners in 1879 America.[8]

The North Light Mystery

There is a real life murder mystery at North Light on the tip of Grand Island, off Munising, Michigan on Lake Superior. What actually happened that terrible day in June 1908 is still open to the wildest speculation.

Although North Light is located on the largest island on Lake Superior's south shore, it can be a dreadfully dreary and lonely place. Grand Island, roughly thirteen by seven miles in size, is only a mile or so

North Light, Grand Island. Was it the scene of a murder?
Stonehouse Collection

off the mainland but is nearly unpopulated. For the lightkeepers at the extreme north end it meant all they had for company was themselves and perhaps a passing trapper.

The first North Light was built in 1856. Located at the brink of a 185-foot sandstone cliff it had a spectacular view of Superior. Poorly constructed, by 1876 it was reported to be in "wretched condition." In spite of the poor circumstance, it was critically needed to help guide ships along the shore from the rich iron and copper mines to the west and new Soo Canal to the east. The old lighthouse was demolished in 1867 and the present one built adjacent to it. The light was based on the typical harbor lighthouse design, a brick structure with a forty-foot tall tower and attached story and a half keepers quarters. It is unchanged to this day. During the same period nearly identical lights were built at Ontonagon, Gull Rock, Huron Island, Granite Island and Marquette among other locations. A fourth order Fresnel lens was mounted in the tower.

Little ever happened at the light. One day ran into another and the weeks and months piled up into years of nothing changing but the weather and even then there was a numbing sameness. The only real interruption was in October 1856 when nine of the survivors from the wreck of the sidewheeler *Superior* showed up at the light looking for shelter. The *Superior* wrecked at Spray Falls on the Pictured Rocks coast with the loss of 36 lives, making it one of the worst shipping disasters on Lake Superior.

The light was automated in 1941 when a special "sun valve" was installed. This unique device operated by using the suns heat to cause a metal valve to contract or expand, in turn regulating the flow of acetylene gas to a lamp. In 1961 the light was relocated from the tower to a steel pole in the yard. In the 1960s the property was declared surplus and sold to Dr. Loren Graham, a professor at the Massachusetts Institute of Technology with deep roots in Grand Island. After a tremendous effort, he renovated the building into a summer cottage.

So much for the background of the light. On June 12, 1908 the battered body of the assistant keeper, 30 year old Edward S. Morrison, was found in one of the station sailboats on the beach near Au Sable Point, 25 miles to the east. At first there was a mystery as to who the victim was since Morrison had only been at the light a short period and was largely unknown. Identification was eventually made, in part because of a tattoo of thirteen stars on his left arm. One witness reported that his head had been "battered almost beyond recognition" and that "the head and shoulders were fearfully crushed, as if battered by a club." This evidence is in sharp contrast to the official finding of a coroner's jury which rendered a verdict of death due to exposure. There was a storm on June 7 and if Morrison was caught in it, perhaps the injuries could be explained away. Although there is no proof of it since a courthouse fire destroyed many of the records, there is a newspaper report that a second jury looked at the evidence and concluded that while the members could not determine the cause of death, there was a strong suspicion of murder!

Edward Morrison had been the assistant keeper for only six weeks before his demise. He joined the Lighthouse Service on May 1, 1908 and immediately was assigned to North Light. He was remembered as having "a bright and sunny disposition" and that he "didn't have an enemy in the world." Born in Techumseh, Michigan, he spent four years in the Navy and later worked at the Imperial Wheel Works in Flint, Michigan before joining the Lighthouse Service. He and his wife Lena had been married only two years. She was waiting in Flint for the right time to move up to Munising to be with her husband and she was reported to be "prostrated with grief" when she learned of his death.

The principal keeper at North Light was George Genery (also spelled Genry). He was an experienced keeper with service as the assistant on Menagerie Island from 1887 until transferring to North Light in 1893. It was later said Genery was a hard man to work for. Certainly the records bear out that between 1900 and 1908 he had nine assistants, some transferred out and others resigned outright. North Light was his first assignment as principal keeper. Perhaps it was a case of a little authority making him into a despot so over bearing his subordinates could not work for him.

Actual facts in the case are sparse but it is known that Genery was in Munising on June 6 to get supplies. Whether Morrison was with him or not is not proven.

When the news of the discovery of the assistant's body spread it was perplexing. Why hadn't Genery reported Morrison missing? And come to think of it, why had the North Light been dark for a week? A delegation from Munising went out to investigate and found more questions than answers. The supplies Genery had brought from town were still stacked on the dock. An empty wheelbarrow stood nearby. His coat still hung from a peg in the boathouse. When the men entered the quarters they found Morrison's vest neatly hanging on a chair with watch and papers still in a pocket. The last journal entry was June 5 and the slate entry for June 6 was in Morrison's hand.

Down at the boathouse only one boat was still present. It was known the light had three. If Morrison had one when he was found and one still at the station, then it stood to reason Genery took the third, maybe. There was no evidence of anything being amiss other than the keepers being gone. Volunteers manned the light until the arrival of acting keeper Joseph Prateo on June 12.

The authorities immediately began to search for Genery but he utterly disappeared. There were reports that he had been seen in Munising at varying times between June 9-12 and that he was drinking heavily. Even his wife, living in Munising with five children, reportedly had no knowledge of his whereabouts.

Eventually several theories developed to explain the death of Morrison and disappearance of Genery. Fishing was a common method for lightkeepers to augment their food supply and income. The men could have gone out to lift nets with Genery falling overboard in the process and drowning. Morrison, unfamiliar with the sailboat then drifted around helplessly until finally perishing from exposure. Morrison's friends disagreed with this theory, stating he was an expert boatman and had previously owned a 32-foot sailboat on the Detroit River. Another friend claimed, "the theory that Morrison came to his death as a result of exposure while drifting about in a sailboat which he was unable to handle is preposterous."

Both men were paid on June 6. They could have been murdered by one or more assailants and robbed, their bodies thrown into sailboats and cut adrift in the hope it would look like an accident. Morrison's sailboat came ashore and Genery's didn't. The robbers simply proceeded on their way. Without witnesses and considering the long period until the body was found, guaranteeing their escape. The nearest neighbor on the island was the Cleveland Cliffs game-keeper who lived seven miles to the south. It was later claimed but not verified that a body was found in Munising's east channel. Whether it was Genery or just a "floater" from a shipwreck was unknown.

The obvious theory is that Genery murdered Morrison. One of the investigators speculated that Morrison had brought the wheelbarrow down to the dock to help haul supplies back to the light. Since Morrison's vest and Genery's coat were hanging up, both keepers were in shirt-sleeves suitable for laboring. Judging from the supplies stacked on the dock they had just finished unloading the boat and were preparing to load the wheel barrow. At this point the men began to argue. Perhaps it was

Genery who started to criticize Morrison for some fault, real or imagined. In a moment of anger, the keeper crushes the assistant's skull with a heavy object, perhaps a shovel or hammer. To hide the crime, he places Morrison in a sailboat and shoves it out into the lake, hoping Superior would swallow all evidence of the crime. After a short interval he could claim Morrison deserted his post, just another case of his being unlucky with assistants. Should the boat wash up on shore then the keeper could claim the assistant had gone on a sail and must have experienced a tragic accident. Perhaps his head was hit by the boom during a jibe. Shaken by the murder, Genery took off for Munising and a good stiff drink or two. This would explain the apparent sightings of the keeper in several Munising saloons. At some point he realized the danger of his scheme and went home where his wife hid him from the authorities until it was safe for him to flee town. Where he ended up is unknown, but there were claims he went to Canada and lived out his days in obscurity.

Morrison may have been surprised by the keepers action in killing him, assuming this is what actually happened, but there is some evidence he had a premonition of his own death. At the least he was very discontented working for Genery. Four days after his body was found at Au Sable Point, his wife received a letter written just before his death. Ominously he wrote, "...don't be surprised if you hear of my body being found dead along the shore of Lake Superior." He further said the keeper was of a "...quarrelsome disposition" and that he feared, "...an accident if he opposed him..." She also related that her husband and Genery quarreled often. Based on the large number of assistants Genery went through, the argument that the keeper was a difficult man to work for would seem valid. The question is did Morrison "oppose" Genery and did Genery respond with murder?

It is interesting that while Genery clearly either deserted his post or was murdered by unknown parties, Lighthouse Service records show him as "resigning" on June 6, 1908. Whether this was an actual action on his part, perhaps a letter submitted to the district superintendent, or just a government clerks way of covering up an embarrassing situation isn't known.

There is some speculation local authorities tried to cover up the murder. The first coroners jury verdict of death by exposure instead of murder is some evidence of this. Why they would cover it up is another question but perhaps it boiled down to the fact that Genery was considered a "local." He had been at the light for fifteen years and his family lived in town. Although he may have had some trouble keeping assistants, that wasn't clearly evident to the locals, or they just didn't care. Everyone knew it was difficult to find good help anyway. When Morrison turned up dead, coupled with the fact that it was not absolutely clear it was murder and the new assistant keeper was an "outsider," it was easier just to brush the whole thing under the rug than to doggedly pursue the justice the crime deserved.

There is an old adage that death always comes in threes and Morrison was part of that deadly triangle. Two years prior his sister was murdered in Toledo. The previous fall a brother was killed when a locomotive he was riding fell through a wooden trestle.

What really happened at lonely North Light will never be known. Certainly the answer could be tangled up in the terrible isolation of the early lightkeepers. The desperately long and monotonous days stringing out into weeks, months and years of sameness, certainly could affect people in different ways. Could it drive a keeper to murder?[9]

Vigilante Justice

Child molestation was handled far more directly in the old days as this short news item from an 1854 *Green Bay Advocate* indicates. "Excitement at Rock Island, Door County–James McGill, an old man, was tarred, feathered, rode on a rail and thrown into the lake three times, at Rock Island, on Saturday last. The cause of this violence was on account of a charge made by a Mrs. Mariah Wellsby that McGill had taken improper liberties with her daughter, a girl of 12 or 14 years. Previous to this Mrs. W. had endeavored to kill McGill, first with a knife and afterwards with a gun. Our informant thinks that when McGill recovers from the injuries received at the hands of his lynchers, he will be able to establish his entire innocence of the charge made against him, which will place some of the Rock Island citizens in no enviable situation."[10]

A Man's Home Is His Castle

Everyone has heard the old saying that "a man's home is his castle." Others may be aware of the warning that a homeowner may use deadly force when defending his "castle." Few however are aware that the legal basis for this action stems from a killing committed in a little fishing village in northern Lake Michigan.

In the 1850s northern Lake Michigan was incredibly rich fishing grounds. Many authorities considered them the most productive in North

Augustus knew he was in deep trouble. Not only had he killed a man, but his victim was very well connected. Blanchard's father, Isaac Blanchard Sr. was Justice of the Peace for Mackinac County. Seul Choix was part of the county, so clearly he would not get a fair trial. Augustus immediately went to his brother Louis who was the local constable and asked to be taken to Beaver Island so he could turn himself in there. This would keep him out of the elder Blanchard's clutches. Augustus and his two hired hands headed for the island in a small rowboat. In hot pursuit was Constable Wilson Newton in a second boat with five men rowing. About seven miles from Beaver Island Newton overhauled Augustus and placed him under arrest for murder.

The trial began on August 30, 1859 at the courthouse on Mackinac Island. Augustus's lawyers argued self defense, that "a man's home is his castle." But plainly he had shot Blanchard and with the political climate on the island, the outcome was preordained. Augustus was found guilty and sentenced to ten years of hard labor at a state prison.

When Augustus' lawyers appealed the case to the Michigan Supreme Court it overturned the verdict, ordering a new trial. The idea of a man's home being his castle was long established in English law and in the decision Justice James Campbell clearly established the principles of self-defense and defense of home that are still used today. "Human life is not to be lightly disregarded and the law will not permit it to be destroyed unless upon urgent occasion." Further that, "A man is not however obligated to retreat if assaulted in his dwelling but may use such means as are absolutely necessary to repel the assailant or prevent forcible entry, even to the taking of life. But he must not take life if he can otherwise arrest or repel the assailant. Where the assault or breaking is felonious, the homicide becomes justifiable and not merely excusable."

Augustus was never retried. Based on Campbell's ringing decision, he was allowed to continue with his life, unaware of the legal implications his case established.[11]

Kitty Leroy's Demise

Lumberjacks considered Kitty the best jug dancer in the entire Saginaw Valley during the rough and tumble 1870s. When she danced at the old Bay City Opera House the jacks packed it to the rafters. They yelled, cheered, slapped their calloused hands on tables and against their knees, anything to keep Kitty dancing. She had, in the term of the times, "an ankle that would turn any man's eye." For men who just spent six months in the woods harvesting timber and too tired at night to even dream about a real flesh and blood girl, her ankle did more than just "turn an eye!"

Kitty was married and the mother of a little boy but such domestic activities did not dampen her enthusiasm for the life of an entertainer, both on and off stage. She was well paid for her skills but she had traveling in her blood and wanted to see the world. When she grew bored with the action in the Saginaw Valley, she moved on, leaving her family behind. She danced (and worked) her way across Michigan to Texas and eventually ending up in San Francisco where she took up with a saloonkeeper. When the action slowed in Frisco, or Kitty grew bored, (more likely she grew bored,) the pair moved on to Deadwood in the Dakota Territory. The gold miners took over where the lumberjacks left off. And they had a lot more money! Kitty entertained them in all the ways she knew how. Sometimes she danced and sometimes took a lucky miner into an upstairs room for a little private amusement.

She also dropped her San Francisco saloonkeeper and latched onto a Faro dealer, named Curley. Soon they were married, making her a bigamist since she still had husband number one in Michigan but that was a long distance away and what's a girl to do?

Faro dealers are moving men. If they stay too long in one saloon the customers pick up on his "habits" so for everyone's sake, it is best to keep moving. Curley departed for Denver. His mistake was leaving Kitty behind. Perhaps she was enjoying herself too much with the gold heavy miners to leave? As soon as Curley left, she started right back with her saloonkeeper.[12]

While dealing (and likely double dealing Faro) at Denver, Curley received a letter from an informant claiming Kitty was two-timing him. Outraged by her infidelity, (what did he expect, Mother Teresa?) he took the first stage back to Deadwood. Rather than come directly into town, he left the coach on the outskirts of town and walked the back alleys to the saloon Kitty was working at. He attempted to trick the saloonkeeper into meeting him in a back alley but smelling a rat, the man refused. Curley then runs into the saloon and directly to Kitty's room where he confronts her. After quick words are exchanged, he hauls out his revolver and at a range estimated at three-feet, plugs her, the powerful slug tearing through her chest between the fifth and sixth ribs. He then put the gun to his mouth and blew his brains out. It was said both thumped to the floor nearly simultaneously and died before any one else could rush to the room.

So ended the entertainment career (and life) of Kitty Leroy, the best jug dancer to ever grace a Michigan saloon. "Done in" by a jealous husband who just didn't understand a wayward woman's wandering ways.

Murder At Sand Point?

The death of lightkeeper Mary Terry at Escanaba, Michigan's Sand Point Lighthouse may have been murder. While the facts are clear, the conclusions are murky.

Mary L. Terry, whose maiden name was Mary L. Thurston, was a native of Dartmouth, Massachusetts. In February 1845 she married Captain John Terry, a native of St. Johns, Canada. John and Mary moved to Escanaba in 1863 where he worked for the Chicago, Northwestern Railroad surveying and building the new line.

The story of Sand Point Lighthouse really began in the mid-1860s when a railroad between Marquette and Escanaba was completed. Mine owners in Marquette discovered it was more efficient to send the ore to the docks in Escanaba than to ship it over sometimes rough and dangerous Lake Superior and then down through the Soo Locks. As a result of the new railroad, Escanaba became more important as a port and the need for a reliable lighthouse more critical. In response to the lobbying by shippers and city, the new Sand Point Light was finished it 1867. It was a very typical harbor light built nearly identical to those at Marquette, Granite Island, Huron Island, Copper Harbor among others. Sand Point did have one distinctive difference however. The contractor built it backwards! Instead of the tower facing the lake as it should have, it faced the shore. As far as the fourth order Fresnel lens

Captain John Terry of Sand Point Light.
Stonehouse Collection

Was Sand Point Light the scene of a terrible accident or murder most foul? Stonehouse Collection

was concerned it made no difference since the light was equally visible. It just looked strange!

As the final touches to the lighthouse were being made, the Lighthouse Service looked around for a reliable man to take the job of lightkeeper. John Terry was appointed to the position. However he died of consumption on April 6, before the light became operational. Mary was appointed in his place and continued to the do the job until 1886.

All continued normally for Mary until about 1:00 a.m. March 4, 1886 when a fire broke out in the lighthouse. By the time the alarm was given the flames had broken through the roof and the entire building was ablaze. Nothing could be done to save the structure or contents. When 69 year old Mary turned up missing, it was realized she had been lost in the fire. A careful search of the burned out building at daylight revealed her charred remains in the oil room.

There was precious little left of Mary; a portion of her skull, a few bones and a small part of the viscera. A coroner's jury duly examined the evidence and determined that her death was from "causes and means unknown."

The evidence in the case was at best incomplete and contradictory. Mary had been the keeper for nearly eighteen years and had demonstrated she was very methodical and careful performing her duties as a lightkeeper. Her cool-headedness was well known. Many residents believed she was the victim of foul play. Surely the fire could not have been accidental. Thieves must have broken into the house, robbed and murdered her and set the fire to cover their dastardly deed.

When officials scrutinized the still smoking lighthouse they found the south exterior door was open and the lock had the bolt shot forward as though it had been forced and not unlocked. Could robbers have broken their way into the house through this door? Mary was known to have accumulated some property in the city and was considered as a woman of some means although by no stretch rich. As an older woman living alone she was certainly a prime target for thieves. It was considered important that she was not found in her bedroom on the north side of the house, but instead in the oil room on the southeast corner. If the fire was accidental and she died by smoke inhalation, then her remains should have been on her bed not on the oil room floor. Did she discover the robbers and confront them, only to in turn be murdered?

Evidence working against the robbery theory was that money, including some gold pieces, were found on the floor where they apparently fell from a cupboard it was known she kept them in. A bundle of badly charred legal papers, including insurance polices and deeds, was also discovered nearby too, helping to argue against robbery as a motive.

Perhaps the robbers (or single robber) broke into the house, was confronted by Mary and desperate to avoid jail, murdered her (or left her injured but alive) and set the fire to destroy the evidence and witnesses. The robber knew nothing of her money stash in the cupboard, thus it was untouched.

Was it an accidental death or something far worse? My guess is breaking and entering, murder and finally arson to cover the crime. Only Mary Terry knows for sure.[13]

Great Lakes MUTINY & BARRATRY

Mutiny

The Naval Terms Dictionary defines mutiny in part as a "rebellion against constituted authority aboard ship." At least in the great tradition of *Mutiny On the Bounty*, Fletcher Christensen and Captain Bligh, no Great Lakes crew abandoned their officers in a yawl and sailed off to an island paradise of warm breezes and bare-breasted, chestnut skinned native girls. But there were incidents that were locally called mutinies.

"We'll Let the Fools Drown"

In one August 1899 example, the deck hands on a steamer decided they had worked enough for the trip and barricaded themselves in the forecastle and refused to return to duty. No threats by any of the officers could entice the men out.

After thinking over the problem for half an hour, the mate suddenly began blowing distress signals and taking a position near the forecastle hatch, called out, "Lower the boats. We'll let the fools drown!" Immediately the deck hands rushed out of the forecastle in a panic to reach the lifeboats. Once within the mate's reach, the men were put back to work![1]

The Matanzas *Incident*

In another instance the crew of the barge *Matanzas* demanded more canvas on the hatch covers. Canvas covers were essential to keep the hatches watertight and the men felt the ones on board were unsafe. The hatches were covered first with fitted boards, which were then covered with tightly stretched canvas tarpaulins. If the canvas was not tightly fitted and secured boarding seas could leak though the hatches or even

The schooner-barge Matanzas. *Stonehouse Collection*

sweep them off. Open hatches in a gale or storm meant certain death. At the time the crew made their demand, the barge was under tow by the steamer *Shenandoah* and had just left Duluth. The captain immediately swung the pair back to port where a representative of the Seaman's Union investigated and upheld the sailor's claim. After new canvas covers were provided, the *Shenandoah* and *Matanzas* continued downbound without incident.[2]

Sail or Jail

A smaller mutiny of sorts happened on the schooner *W.S. Nelson* in Oswego in 1860. It seems a sailor named McPherson signed articles for the schooner, and then refused to board her. In response, Captain Parker had him arrested and jailed until the ship was ready to leave. When the time came, the constable escorted McPherson to the ship but he again refused to board and another sailor named Napier took up his cause. In the resulting scuffle, the two sailors tried to prevent the mate from casting off. The mate apparently "dusted up," both sailors and the constable hauled Napier off to jail. Once the schooner was under tow, the reluctant sailor jumped over board and swam ashore where he was met by the friendly constable who welcomed him appropriately and again hauled him off to jail.[3]

"I'm the Captain"

It wasn't always sailors who caused trouble aboard the vessels. In 1880 the tug *R.K. Hawley* lost part of a valuable raft of oak logs in a storm on Lake Erie. The load was owned by the firm of Sheldon and Thompson of Vermilion, Ohio and they tried to legally attach the *Hawley* in an effort to secure payment for the loss but were not successful in catching her. In April 1883 the tug was in Vermilion to pick up the old wrecking tug *Relief* so the company had another opportunity. Just as the *Hawley* was pulling away from the dock with the *Relief* in tow the local constable jumped aboard and standing on the foredeck, demanded that Captain Bowen return to the dock. Captain Bowen ignored this legal worthy, which irritated the constable greatly. Running into the pilothouse the lawman grabbed the wheel and again demanded the captain put back. Captain Bowen ordered him to let go, that while he was on the water, he was answerable only to federal authorities. When the constable turned the wheel, the captain knocked him back into the cushion seat behind the wheel with a powerful fist. Grabbing the man by the throat the captain told him to leave his pilothouse or he would "treat him with more logic of the same sort." When the captain returned to the wheel the constable again attacked him, wrenching the wheel from the captain and ripping all of the buttons off his coat in the process. Captain Bowen again replied with his fist, knocking the constable to the deck, apparently out cold.

After the tug was safely out on the lake and enroute to Cleveland, Captain Bowen woke up the constable and asked him what the problem was. The man responded that he was only trying to serve papers to impound the tug on direction of Sheldon and Thompson, but that he might have been wrong in his enthusiasm.

The fight between the two men had been visible from shore as the tug pulled away from the docks. When the witnesses told the mayor of Vermilion, he wired to Cleveland and had Captain Bowen arrested on arrival. He was immediately released on bail pending the resolution of the mayor's charge of assault and battery. Vessel men were unanimous in supporting the captain's actions.[4]

Obey the Captain

Sailors were paid to obey a captain's orders, especially in a storm. Sometimes however there was a difference of opinion!

When the schooner *Mears* arrived in Detroit in October 1883, Captain Stephen Langston had sailor George Henderson arrested by the U.S.

deputy marshal, charging him with "willful breach of duty tending to the serious damage of the vessel." A quick examination before the U.S. Commissioner found him guilty and he was bound over for district court with a bail of $500, a large sum for the time. As Henderson was unable to post bail, he was lodged in jail.

Captain Langston claimed that on October 16 the *Mears* and three others were being towed down Lake Huron when they were overtaken by a heavy gale. About 40 miles from Port Huron and a couple of miles off-shore, the tug's engine failed. As a result the towline to the *Mears* was cut which caused her to collide with another schooner, the *O'Neil*. Henderson was at the helm and was given orders to "harden up." Instead he left his station, went forward and let the main sheet and mizzen sail go, which in turn caused the schooner to become unmanageable and fall off into the trough of the sea. She rolled so badly she nearly capsized and the waves sweeping her decks almost caused the loss of several men. He then returned to the helm.

At the examination several of the crew claimed that his actions were correct. Henderson claimed neither captain or mate knew anything about sailing and that if he had not let go the sails, the ship would have been lost. He stated he had sailed for 28 years, both salt and freshwater.[5]

Shanghaied

The term "shanghai," a practice as old as sailing, generally is given to describe the act of kidnapping a sailor while he is drunk or doped up and placing him on an outbound vessel, originally headed for Shanghai, China. Although the expression "shanghaied" is usually thought of only in reference to manning ocean ships, it was on occasion, also used on the Great Lakes. During the hey day of sail, it was often difficult to get a crew to make one last run in the fall when gales and storms made sailing more hazardous. When freight rates were up, owners were anxious to squeeze in a final, very profitable trip before winter lay-up.

To get a crew under such circumstances, vessel owners offered higher pay to compensate for the greater danger. Sometimes this enticement was not enough and the only answer was shanghaiing. An example of how the process worked on the Great Lakes was the case of the 1,000-ton, three masted schooner *C.C. Barnes*. In late December 1888, she was laying in the Chicago River heavily loaded with 38,000 bushels of grain for Buffalo. Although three inches of ice trapped the schooner fast to her

Wabash elevator dock, a tug managed to break her free. Other than for a crew, she was soon ready to sail.

The shipping agent, Big Jack McQuade, took care of the crew problem rather simply. Walking into the Sans Souci Bar on South Clark Street, he cornered the bartender, "Olaf the Swede" and told him he needed a six-man crew. When Olaf protested it was too close to Christmas and men couldn't be had, McQuade threatened to have the saloon's license revoked if Olaf didn't find the men, by "hook of by crook." McQuade set their pay at $50, plus train fare back to Chicago.

The bartender came through, as the shipping agent knew he would. After all, business is business. Just past midnight, a heavily loaded wagon clattered up to the *Barnes*. The Swede and a helper, none too gently, hauled six prostrate men down the foc'sle hatch. Whether the sailors were victim of a quick "billy"or a "Mickey Finn" wasn't known but the results were the same, the schooner had a crew.

Five days later the schooner safely reached Buffalo, earning a fat $3,800 for the trip. Promptly paid off, her shanghaied crew made straight for "Big Nell's" on East Canal Street and proceeded to celebrate their arrival in riotous fashion. There would be no official complaints from them. They may have objected to how they joined the schooner, but $50 is $50 all the same.[6]

As late as the turn of the century shanghaiing was used. Captain Edward C. Baganz, a veteran of 51 years on the Great Lakes and the retired commodore of the U.S. Steel fleet was shanghaied at the start of his career. At the time he was a 14 year old working for a Detroit architect when during a lunch hour he wandered down to the docks to watch the sidewheeler *Owana* moor. Ships always fascinated him and he would be down to the waterfront at every opportunity. When one of the crew came up to him and said, "The captain wants to see you," he was awestruck.

After quickly scampering aboard he started looking for the master but was waylaid by the cook who threw him an apron saying, "glad you are going to help us." Realizing he had been tricked, Baganz went to run off the boat but it was already moving away from the dock and churning it's way upstream. He had no choice but to go to work in the galley! By the time he finally reached Port Huron, 18 stops later, his distraught parents had the police looking for him and were searching the hospitals. Finally able to cage a dime to call home, he notified them of his dilemma and returned the following day.[7]

In Jail

A strange kind of reverse mutiny involved the barque *Malta*. In the 1850's she ran as part of a railroad connection from Collingwood on Georgian Bay to Chicago. An extremely fast vessel, she once made the trip in a mere fifty hours! Before one of the trips the captain discovered he had a major problem, half of her crew were in jail! The problem was easily solved. The mate and a several of the remaining crew simply marched down to the jail and broke the men out! A good knockdown, drag out fight was needed to get the job done, but that was just all in a days work for an old time sailor.[8]

Drunken Crew

Captains sometimes had trouble dealing with drunken crewmen but when everyone was "three sheets to the wind," officers included, the situation did get very interesting as this short item from the *Detroit Free Press* of October 24, 1906 indicates. " Steamboat Inspectors Peck and Mansfield have revoked the license of Captain George W. Starkey of the steamer *Shenandoah*, until its expiration in March 1907. The captain's record will stand against him if he should apply for a renewal of his papers.

"Complaint was made to the inspectors that Captain Starkey and members of his crew were intoxicated while operating the steamer and investigation brought out the fact that the boat had been backed into a wharf at South Chicago and then sent full speed ahead into the opposite wharf. The ship was stove in at both bow and stern.

If it had been loaded, Captain Mansfield declared, the boat would have sunk. In this condition, he further said, the ship was steamed to Chicago, the captain still intoxicated and when moored in Chicago the condition of affairs was discovered. The danger in instances of this nature, Captain Mansfield declared, from collision and chances of beaching are so great that they cannot be estimated."

The *Shenandoah* lost its rudder on Lake Michigan after leaving Chicago and was towed to port by a lighthouse tender.[9]

Too Many Mates

Usually sailors complain about being short-handed, sailing without enough crew. But here is a problem of too many men as related in the *Detroit Post and Tribune* of October 16, 1883. "The schooner *Annie M. Peterson* arrived in port Wednesday says the *Milwaukee Wisconsin* and in

The schooner Annie M. Peterson. *Stonehouse Collection*

the afternoon the captain left the vessel, leaving a full crew on board. The jolly skipper met many friends and formed a number of new acquaintances during the afternoon, including several parties in quest of new employment. Before nightfall he had engaged three mates and two cooks sending each aboard the schooner. The result was that on the return of the commander in the evening the vessel had five mates and three cooks. A conflict of authority followed, which at one time bade fair to terminate seriously. Upon the appearance of the captain the anxious candidates excitedly examined in chorus, "Who is to be mate?" "We are all mates, my lads," replied the skipper, " I couldn't spare any of you." The attention of a policeman was called to the matter and the officer repaired to the scene with the idea that trouble could ensue, but the utmost good nature prevailed. Yesterday the captain paid each of the extra five men one day's wages, $3 and they departed for shore well satisfied with the result of the captain's queer whim."[10]

Persuaded With A Revolver

This 1900 mutiny wasn't an attempt by the crew to take over the ship. Instead it was an effort not to avoid doing their duty. The *Detroit Free*

Press described the problem. "Joseph Recor has laid a complaint against Captain Edward Cummerford, of the schooner *John Miner*, charging him with assault. Commissioner Graves will hear the case this morning. The *Miner* was bringing down a cargo of cedar posts to Detroit and the alleged assault occurred Monday afternoon when the big squall struck the vessel on Lake Huron. Recor claims that the Captain caught him by the throat and choked him, threatened him with a revolver and when prevented by the crew from using this weapon, seized an iron bar and threatened to brain him. When Deputy U.S. Marshall Cash P. Taylor served the papers yesterday, Captain Cummerford told another story. He states that he commissioned an acquaintance to hire some hands for him and Recor was one of those engaged. He says none of the party was a sailor and they knew nothing about handling a vessel. When the squall came up Monday afternoon Recor was at the wheel and the captain ordered him to put the helm to starboard, but Recor put it to port. The captain jumped to the wheel and pushed Recor to one side. The squall frightened the green men, he says, and they went below, refusing to come on deck to shorten sail when ordered to do so. The captain put an experienced sailor at the wheel and then got his revolver and used it as a persuader to bring the men on deck. This the captain says is the extent of the alleged assault."[11]

An Accident is Not Always "Accidental"

There are many examples of businessmen who burned their enterprises during economic downturns to collect the insurance money. Fire inspectors will often claim there are "independent" contractors who can arrange such "accidents" and make them look perfectly natural. When such self-destruction happens to ships it is called "barratry," defined as "the willful casting away of a ship by her master." There are numerous instances of barratry on the high seas as well as the Great Lakes.

Because the act is criminal, we will never know the true extent of barratry on the Great Lakes although we can make some good estimates. Great Lakes maritime historian Dave Swayze suggests at least 40 attempts to destroy vessels by arson alone. The number of vessels, large and small, deliberately sunk could reach into the hundreds.

The loss of the small two-masted schooner *Explorer* is widely considered an act of barratry. Built in Chatham, Ontario in 1866, she was sunk the following year near Bear and Flower Pot Islands near Tobermory in Georgian Bay. The captain was the lone survivor.

When the vessel was recovered in 1882, it was reported a dozen holes were found cut into her centerboard box and she was heavily weighted with rocks. Others claimed such reports were just sensational reporting.

The reconditioned schooner sailed until September 4, 1883 when she wrecked on Greenough Shoal, Lyal Island on Stokes Bay, Bruce Peninsula, Lake Huron. Again the only survivor of the five-man crew was the captain.[12]

A clear case of deliberate sinking was that of the schooner *Hubbard*. She was upbound from Oswego to Chicago with coal when the startled mate and steward found Captain Frederick Themble below decks happily using a large auger to cut holes through her hull. The two men quickly seized their captain and bound him up to prevent further mischief. Themble has a reputation of being a "well known and experienced navigator who had the confidence of all."

When the schooner arrived at Chicago the vessel's owner, onc Captain D.L. McGraw judged Themble insane and fired him. The good captain promptly disappeared. As way of explanation, McGraw stated Themble had been driven mad by his first wife, who he claimed was unfaithful. McGraw's second wife was sailing with him when he tried to sink his ship but the mate put her ashore in Port Huron thus avoiding any embarrassing questions in Chicago.

McGraw also owned another vessel involved in willful sinking, the *Chicago Board Of Trade*. In fact she was almost the "poster child" for the problem. Built in Manitowoc, Wisconsin in 1863 as a three-masted barque, she was 156-feet in length and considered a fine vessel.

On July 29, 1874 the *Chicago Board Of Trade* was booming along on Lake Erie about 25 miles north-northwest of Fairport Harbor when she suddenly developed an unholy appetite for freshwater and settled to the bottom. She was insured for $20,000 and valued at $25,000. Her cargo was 30,000 bushels of corn. The crew escaped in their yawl eventually reaching Fairport Harbor.

During the period the ship was wrecked, a rash of losses was ravaging Great Lakes insurance companies. Too many owners were "selling" their ships to the insurance companies through the vehicle of accidental loss. Freights were depressed and getting a good cargo at profitable price was impossible. In the spring of 1874 ships insured for $18,000 against a value of $25,000 had dropped to a value of $17,000 - $18,000. Clearly if an owner could "arrange" a loss on such a vessel it was to his advantage.

Questioned later, Captain Thomas Fountain claimed the vessel struck bottom while being towed in the Detroit River. At the time he did not think there was any damage so he proceeded on his way when the tug cast off the towline. About 7:30 in the morning on July 28, when off Point au Pelee, it breezed up and the ship started to roll heavily. When the wind

The schooner Chicago Board Of Trade *was a victim of barratry.*
Stonehouse Collection

died later in the day the ship showed no sign of damage. At 4:00 a.m. the following day the captain discovered three feet of water in her hold and the crew went to work on the forward pump. Strangely the aft pump did not work, severely limiting the crew's ability to dewater the ship. The lone pump could not keep up with the flooding and at 8:45 a.m. the crew left her. The schooner sank ten minutes later.

Interviewed later, some of the crew stated, something was, "rotten on the *Chicago Board Of Trade*." The men said the ship didn't hit anything in the Detroit River and that there was no reason for her to suddenly develop such a large leak. More ominously they also said that when the ship began to leak, instead of heading for shore in an effort to save the ship or crew, he headed for the open lake and deep water. Some of the men reasoned that if she had hit something in the river, then why did she wait 27 hours to leak? Water should have started rushing into the hold immediately. Fueled by such comments, as well as a healthy sense of curiosity, the underwriters were very anxious to take a good close look at her. Captain Fountain did have his supporters. The *Chicago Inter-Ocean*, an important shipping newspaper, stated the master, "…is well known on the lakes and here is no man in his capacity in whom greater confidence is placed." Regardless of the backing of the paper, the insurance company smelled a rat and they gave the Coast Wrecking Company $10,000 contract to raise the schooner. There had been a rash of sinkings and since depressed freight rates had decreased vessel value, in some cases below their insurance value, there was a great opportunity for unscrupulous owners to "cash in" at the expense of the underwriters. As typical, the salvage contract was on a "no cure, no pay" basis, meaning if they failed to bring the ship into a safe port within the stipulated time period, they received nothing for their efforts.

The salvagers worked hard and despite numerous troubles and setbacks managed to drag the schooner into shallow water before winter. By early July the following year they had her safe in Buffalo. When the insurance men looked her over, their suspicions were proved correct. They discovered at least six holes cut in the water closet pipe and a special committee of experts concluded they were made solely for the purpose of scuttling the ship. They also found the special tool used to make the holes and that the maker of the holes was clever enough to cover them with a piece of carpet in order to deaden the sound of water flooding in to the ship. The aft pump was not broken, but had been purposely disabled. It was clearly a case of barratry.

The Steamer Lakeland. *Stonehouse Collection*

The *Chicago Board Of Trade* was eventually repaired and sold back into service. On November 21, 1900 she wrecked on Niagara Reef, Lake Erie in a powerful gale. This time there was no suspicion of foul play.[13]

There is also some confusion over the Canadian schooner *Bangalore*. In October 1882 the vessel was in dry dock in Detroit to have routine bottom work done when her captain saw something very strange. When he was checking her hull he noticed a half dozen small auger holes. Apparently they were cut from the inside out and each was carefully plugged such that the caulking would come loose when the schooner was working in a seaway.

The question of who was trying to sink her was unknown. Whether it was the owner, disgruntled crew or just plain vandals, was never determined.[14]

While it was never proved, it was suspected by some marine men that the sinking of the 280-foot steamer *Lakeland* was a deliberate action. Built by the Globe Iron Works in Cleveland and launched in 1887 as the *Cambria*, she was only the second steel ship built on the Great Lakes. The first was the steamer *Western Reserve* in 1892. The steamer was converted to an automobile carrier in 1919 and owned and operated by the Tri-States Steamship Company.

On December 2, 1924, the steamer was working her way from Chicago to Detroit with a load of new automobiles when the captain reported several hull plates buckled in heavy seas and water began to flood into her. Her captain brought her into the Sturgeon Bay Ship Canal to get out

The Lakeland *before she dove for the bottom.* Stonehouse Collection

of the stress of the waves. Since her pumps were able to keep up with the leak and the seas had apparently moderated, she sailed at about 1:00 a.m. on December 3. The storm had not stopped however and within a couple of hours the *Lakeland* was in a sinking condition about nine miles off the Wisconsin shore. At 9:30 a.m. her engines shut down and she was listing to starboard. When the Ann Arbor Railroad carferry No. 6 arrived in response to distress calls, the last of her crew was preparing to abandon her. Minutes after the crew left her, at 11:25 a.m., the steamer plunged stern first for the bottom of the lake, her wooden cabins blowing off as she sank. All 27 of her crew were safely taken aboard the carferry.

Although it seemed initially like a simple case of a vessel sinking as the result of storm stress, the insurance company wasn't so certain. Before the company turned over a check for $116,800 it carefully investigated the disaster. In August 1925 it paid for a crew of five hardhat divers to closely survey the wreck. The divers report was damning enough that the underwriter concluded something was fishy and refused to pay. The case was taken to federal court in October 1925 but a jury was unable to reach a verdict. Another trial in February also resulted in a hung jury so the insurers reluctantly paid off the claim, doubtlessly feeling they were the victims of a scam. There was considerable belief she was sunk to claim the insurance on vessel and cargo.

The *Lakeland* carried some rare (for today) automobiles, including Rollins, Kissels and Nashs. The Rollin was named for Rollin H. White, a member of the family that owned the White Sewing Machine Company in Cleveland. The Rollin Automobile Company started in 1923 as a subsidiary of the Cleveland Tractor Company. Only produced from 1923-1925, the Rollins were considered stylish and efficient. However, they never were popular with Americans, perhaps due to their European look.[15]

Great Lakes RUM RUNNING

Legislating morality is a hopeless cause and prohibition well illustrates the folly. When the U.S. Eighteenth Amendment banning the sale, manufacture or transportation of intoxicating liquors took effect on January 16, 1920 it spawned an atmosphere of general lawlessness the effects of which the U.S. had never experienced. Considering that Prohibition started when the flower of American manhood was overseas fighting the Germans to "make the world safe for democracy," many people considered it a stab in the back to those brave young Americans.

The Volstead Act, the enabling legislation giving legal definition to the term "intoxicating liquors" as stipulated in the amendment and establishing enforcement mechanisms and penalties for violation, was passed by Congress on October 28, 1919. Although vetoed by President Wilson, Congress quickly overrode the veto. (Some suggest this veto was the only worthwhile effort of this useless president.) It was named after the Minnesota congressman who sponsored it (and was subsequently defeated in his attempt at reelection).

How the drys, or proponents of Prohibition, were able to ram the amendment into law is remarkable. It was grass roots politics at its most basic level. The Women's Christian Temperance Union (WCTU) and Anti-Saloon League (ASL) and others, conducted a massive public relations campaign against the evils of ardent drink. By 1916, fully two-thirds of both houses of Congress were elected by "dry" constituents and the politicians knew it and would support Prohibition when necessary. Previously the Prohibition forces had concentrated at local and state levels such that by 1913 half of the U.S. population lived under some sort of dry restrictions. The step to national Prohibition was therefore a comparatively short one.

Campaigning by the Anti-Saloon League and Women's Christian Temperance Union for prohibition was constant. Characters like Carrie Nation and her little axe were an enduring symbol against demon rum. Born in Kansas in 1846, her family background reeked with deep insanity. Her mother thought she was Queen Victoria, to the extent her father eventually built a fancy carriage to keep her happy. The Kansas "Queen" ended her days in a mental hospital, as did other members of the family. As a child Carrie was afflicted with visions. Following the death of her first husband, Carrie married David Nation, a failed preacher, lawyer and journalist. She became an early member of the WCTU and after a conversation with Jesus (with whom she regularly conversed), she started busting up Kansas saloons with an axe in the 1890s. She smashed mirrors, trashed expensive paintings of nude women reclining (a standard of every turn of the century saloon) and slapped drinks from the hands of customers. The newspapers knew a good story when they saw one and the axe wielding temperance tigress received massive publicity. At some of her saloon bustings she passed out miniature hatchets.

Carrie became a national sensation and the darling of the WCTU. However, after president McKinley was murdered in 1901 and she wrote an editorial condoning it, the public and WCTU backed away for her. Her later performances were that of a carnival freak. She died in a mental asylum in 1911 at age 65.[1]

An early temperance campaigner, Carrie Nation specialized in breaking up saloons with her little hatchet. Stonehouse Collection

Once the amendment was law the various proponent groups, Presbyterian, Baptist, Methodist and other evangelicals of their ilk as well as WCTU and ASL celebrated, believing they had struck a blow against the devil. Instead, they accomplished the opposite, opening the door wide to organized crime, a curse still plaguing the nation. A strong case can be made that the actions of these misguided, ill-informed, booze bigots led directly to many of society's ills today. On the premise that the road to hell is paved with good intentions, the zealots believed banning alcoholic beverages would help combat family abuse, alcoholism and violence. During World War I, it was thought prohibition would increase the efficiency of workers and soldiers.

The temperance movement had a long history in the U.S. In 1733 Georgia became the first colony to establish a prohibition decree. The first anti-drinking society was formed in Boston in 1826 as the American Temperance Society and the Anti-Saloon League, founded in Ohio in 1892, was a major player in the eventual passage of Prohibition in 1920.[2]

Temperance forces had been pushing for Prohibition for a long time. In the 1840s and 50s they achieved great success forcing comprehensive laws in Maine, Vermont, Connecticut, Massachusetts, Ohio, Minnesota, Rhode Island, Michigan, Indiana, New Hampshire, Delaware, Illinois, Iowa and New York. They nearly succeeded in New Jersey, Wisconsin and Pennsylvania. The reformers were selling Prohibition as necessary to defeat "demon rum." They pictured drinkers of any moderation as mental deviates, the lowest of society. When the Civil War erupted in 1861 thoughts of national prohibition were pushed off center stage, the issues of preserving the Union, slavery and reconstruction consuming the nation's attention.

Prohibition provided the opportunity for organized crime to prosper as never before and made many otherwise honest people criminals. Law breaking became commonplace. People considered absolute solid citizens made illegal booze at home and frequented the neighborhood "speakeasy." While little good came of Prohibition, much evil did and it all can be laid directly at the feet of those miserable sour faced "holier than tho" zealots who rammed its passage through a spineless Congress.

The manufacture and distribution of illegal booze expanded throughout the prohibition era. The greater the resources thrown against the problem, the more imaginative ways to dodge enforcement were devised. It was a constant game of one up, the bootleggers always managed to win.

If any of the prohibition zealots had the slightest degree of historical perspective, they would have realized the utter futility of their inane cause. In large measure men driven to avoid high imperial taxes by smuggling cargoes of rich French wine and other goods ashore in lonely New England coves founded the United States. Cheating the tax collector was (and remains) an old American tradition. Smuggling was an American custom of great regard. To assume that Americans would ignore their past and meekly follow the dictates of an oppressive government is to ignore history.

For example, Rhode Island was a notorious den of pirates. Almost the entire economy of the colony was based on shipbuilding and rum running. The French West Indies colonies grew sugar, which they shipped to France in exchange for brandy. Some of the sugar was converted into molasses in the islands but never into rum since that would interfere in the established sugar for brandy trade. Rhode Island took the molasses and manufactured rum out of it and shipped it to the other British colonies in fast ships built in the colony. Rhode Island's action was strictly against British policy and the distillers were constantly dodging revenue agents.

Early Americans were very sensitive to government interference with their whisky. In 1791 Congress placed a tax on liquor in an effort to raise revenue. Farmers in western Pennsylvania rebelled against it since they were in the habit of rendering their rye into whisky to ease transportation. It was much easier to move comparatively few whisky barrels to market over rough roads than many huge hay wagons. Angry farmers attacked, tarred and feathered the tax collectors. The "Whisky Rebellion" raged for two years eventually forcing President George Washington to send 15,000 troops into the area to quell the uprising.[3]

For better or worse, whisky has been an fundamental part of American history. It was the preferred beverage of the early pioneers and was prized for its refreshing taste and medicinal value. Doctors recommended it for teething children and rum mixed with milk was thought good for pregnant women. In some parts of the country whisky was used for currency with prices set in pints and quarts. There is also an old Army tale about the regimental colonel warning his officers that, "there is nothing wrong with an eye opener in the morning, a quick pick me up at mid-morning, a shot or two at noon and an afternoon swig, a couple of more with dinner and snort or two at taps, but gentlemen, the heavy drinking has to stop!"

Alcohol was deeply integrated into American society. Most business transactions were "sealed" with a drink, as were weddings, graduations, confirmations and other ceremonies. Ships were always launched and christened by breaking a bottle of champagne or other liquor over their bow. Some public buildings even had a bottle of whisky sealed into the cornerstone. Harvard University had its own brewery on campus.

Early temperance crusaders. Stonehouse Collection

Traveling ministers were often treated to large amounts of alcohol when visiting parishioners. It was said Sam Adams always had a large mug of hard cider every morning before breakfast. Alcohol in many forms was indeed an important part of American culture.

National Prohibition was immediately ignored. Less than an hour after it took effect-armed bandits stole two train cars full of liquor valued at $100,000 from a Chicago rail yard. Another band stole four barrels of grain alcohol from a government bonded warehouse and a third group hijacked a truck full of booze from a rival gang. Chicago was getting in the swing of things![4]

Auto manufacturer Henry Ford was one of the great proponents of Prohibition. He warned his Detroit workers that the possession of alcoholic beverages "on his person or in his home," or even the smell of it on his breath will result in being fired. There would be no excuse or appeal. Henry always was an ornery and self-righteous cuss.[5]

Liquor distilleries were very sensitive to temperance pressure. When Detroit distiller Hiram Walker saw Michigan flirting with an early version of prohibition he relocated his firm in 1856 to a site near Windsor, Ontario. The move was very timely. At the start of the Civil War, U.S. distilleries were declared non-essential industries and closed. Walker's

Canadian distillery ran overtime to supply U.S. demand in a precursor of 1920s prohibition. Everyday fleets of boats crossed the Detroit River to load liquor and bring it to thirsty U.S. customers.[6] When National Prohibition was enacted in 1920, Walker was again in an ideal position to capitalize on the opportunity. So much booze was shipped from the Walker distillery to the U.S., accusations were made that he built a pipeline under the river to expedite delivery! Of course, following Canadian law, everything he did was completely legal. Walker was simply meeting customer demand.

During prohibition, liquor essentially came from three sources. First there was that manufactured in private residences for personal use. The second source was that produced by moon shiners. Thousands of stills in the back country of the U.S. and a fair number in cities produced a prodigious amount of product. Invariably this was the worst rotgut imaginable. Most of the cases of alcohol related deaths could be traced to "poisonous" swill from moon shiners. The third source and by far the best one was liquor smuggled in from outside the border, especially the excellent Canadian whisky. It was still the original high quality product, at least when it left the distillery. There however was a fourth way to get a bottle of good whisky. Medical doctors were authorized to dispense small amounts of liquor for medicinal purposes. It became common practice for a doctor to sign a pad of prescription blanks and leave it with a druggist. The customer paid the druggist $3 or so for the prescription and another $3 for a pint of good whisky.[7]

When booze became illegal, the shared border with Canada became key to slaking the thirst of Americans and the Great Lakes quickly became a key part of the new smuggling network. For both U.S. and Canadian border towns, running booze became a cottage industry. Whether by boat, airplane, automobile or dog sled, the booze flowed to the thirsty citizens of the U.S.

In the Western states, Canadian bootleggers ran liquor into the states over a myriad of roads and pathways crossing the largely mythical border. Unless the police lined up shoulder to shoulder, it was indefensible against the rum runners. False floorboards, second fuel tanks, secret compartments, fake bottom suitcases, all were used to fool the customs agents. A new conduit opened through the Thousand Islands area of New York, small craft ferrying liquor around the maze of islands from Canada to the U.S.

A whisky row ship filled with booze.

On the east coast, enterprising Canadian businessmen loaded booze on old schooners and nondescript tramp steamers, sailed south on the Atlantic to a point safely beyond the U.S. three-mile international boundary, dropped their anchors and waited. An eager flotilla of small craft soon appeared, the occupants carrying handfuls of greenbacks eager to purchase cases of booze and haul it back to thirsty consumers. Some of the boats coming out from shore were not so small, ranging up to 160-feet in length and capable of hauling 15,000 cases of liquor. For a country founded on smuggling, such activity was natural and in the highest traditions of American business.

Profits were immense. Scotch could be purchased in Canada for $8.00 a case and resold for $65.00 a case. Considering that most booze was "cut" three times and rebottled with counterfeit labels, profits were even larger.[8] One Chicago lawyer started with an investment of $8,000 and made more than $3 million in a mere thirteen months.[9]

There were so many Canadian ships and eventually other nation's vessels, the anchorage soon gained the name "rum row." It would operate with some revision, throughout the long sad history of prohibition.

The most famous of the sellers was Captain William S. McCoy. Based on the purity of his product, his goods were soon known as the "real McCoy," a phrase that has since found it's way into American lexicon. Eventually the federal government forced the limit out to twelve miles, the distance a ship could sail in an hour, but the old rum fleet still hung in, transferring booze to a fleet of larger rum runners capable of traveling the greater distance offshore.

The main rum row was off the New York-New Jersey coast. It was after all where the greatest concentration of customers were located and the rum runners were nothing if not consumer focused. Smaller rum rows were off New England, Virginia, Florida and California. Wherever the need was greatest, the black fleet was there.

More booze crossed the U.S.-Mexico border and fleets of boats ferried liquor from the West Indies into the country via the Gulf Coast and southeast Atlantic states. The swamps and bayous became a haven for rum runners.

Although Canada followed the U.S. false lead and enacted a variation of prohibition, it was essentially considered a provincial issue in many regards. The provinces could outlaw consumption but not manufacture for international export. Only the federal government could do that and for most of the Eighteenth Amendment's misbegotten life, the Canadian federal government refused to do so. Monetarily, it was best for the Canadians to take a hands off attitude. After all, America was the largest market for high quality Canadian whiskey and while prohibition may be morally defensible, it would be a financial disaster! After all, business is business.

In Ontario, the Liquor Control Act forbid public or hotel consumption but did allow manufacture and export of liquor. Again, business is business.

Ontario prohibition was double boon to the Canadian rum runners. They didn't know whether it was more lucrative to smuggle the booze to the states or back into Canada!

Many old saloons on the U.S. side of the border immediately reopened, making only minor changes in their operation. As would be expected, most of the federal attention went to the big cities. Small "corner bars" and taverns often slipped under the official radar screen. There simply were not enough federal agents to cover everywhere. A drinking man's favorite brand wasn't always on the shelf and sometimes what was in the bottle didn't match the label, but at least a man could get a good snort when he needed one!

Doctors were allowed to prescribe liquor for medicinal purposes making their prescription books valuable items. *Stonehouse Collection*

As federal interference increased some bars were forced underground. Various names applied to such places, blind pigs, speakeasies, or roadhouses were common terms. In many instances, local law enforcement provided "protection" either for a "retainer" or just in the spirit of public service.

Drinking and eating establishments known as roadhouses opened up in Canadian and U.S. border towns. The Edge-Water Thomas Inn in Windsor, Ontario was considered the best in the area. Patrons came from far and wide to enjoy its hospitality. The food was reported excellent and so was the liquid refreshment. Secret passages led to well-hidden gambling dens and booze storage rooms. In was said during prohibition a single switch caused liquor bottles to disappear only to be replaced with soft drink bottles! Special lookouts kept watch for police raids and service staff were trained to hide the evidence within moments of an alarm. Many of the roadhouse's secrets were revealed during a 1970 fire. Prior to then, the stories were all only rumor.[10]

Some taverns changed their business plans. For example, one bar in the American Soo on the St. Mary's River, turned into an ice cream parlor and made more money than ever before, but never reordered any ice cream beyond the original stock! There were reportedly 400 "soft drink" parlors in Detroit in 1923, all of which dispensed high test "shots" on demand.

Within six months the flood of violations overwhelmed the legal system. In Chicago alone there were 500 violations, clogging court calendars. One authority estimated that in New York City in 1926 if the 400-500 violators arrested in a single month demanded a jury trial, the courts would be tied up for a year. Multiply that by the remaining eleven months and the courts would be jammed for a dozen years! In the first three years the population of federal prisons doubled. Federal prosecutors were spending nearly half their time on Prohibition related offenses. Federal agents also arrested nearly 315,000 people in the first six years. State and local arrests matched the number. Plainly, it was all absurd! Everyone couldn't be arrested and jailed. In spite of all the arrests, it was still estimated less than five percent of all bootleg booze was intercepted.[11]

The cost of enforcement was massive. In 1926 Congress authorized $10 million and that was just for the Prohibition Bureau. It didn't include funds for the Customs, Coast Guard, or various federal attorneys. The Prohibition Commissioner told the Congress in 1929 it would take $300 million for enforcement, an astronomical sum for the time! State and local costs were all in addition to federal costs.[12]

Prohibition agents only intercepted five percent of the smuggled booze. Stonehouse Collection

Initially, enforcement of Prohibition was the responsibility of the Internal Revenue Service, which was to refer cases to the appropriate district attorney for prosecution.[13]

Eventually federal enforcement activity shifted to a newly created Prohibition Bureau. The first year it numbered just over 1,550 agents. It never had more than 3,000.[14]

The agents often responded to the rumors of bootlegging with overwhelming force. They once sent carloads of agents to the little town of Iron

River in Michigan's remote Upper Peninsula to seize nine barrels of homemade wine![15]

The Prohibition Bureau was infamous for crooked agents ready to provide inside information to the bootleggers or look the other way when shipments came in, all for a pile of cold cash. The agents were commonly seen hanging out in speakeasies and usually not just when they were undercover on a case. The figures are at best questionable, but at least 12 percent of the agents were dismissed for cause, including accepting bribes and concealment of criminal records, extortion, conspiracy, robbery, assault, graft and contempt of court. Between 1920-30, nearly 12,000 agents were also separated "without prejudice" meaning the bureau knew they were guilty of a crime but couldn't (or wouldn't since the publicity was bad) prove it in a court. It was easier just to fire the corrupt agents.

Bootleggers regarded a Prohibition Bureau badge as nothing more than a way to make money. One group of brewers reportedly offered agents $300,000 just to "look the other way." Roy A. Haynes, the Prohibition Commissioner claimed, "bootleggers bragged of having top connections to the Department of Justice."

The bureau was exempt from Civil Service rules, which allowed the agents to be hired strictly for political patronage. Criminals of all types, misfits and other lowlifes were often sworn in, handed a gun and told to go out and catch bootleggers. There was no training or instruction. Even good agents were fired when their political patron lost an election.[16] An effort was made after 1925 to make the bureau part of Civil Service but when three-quarters of the agents failed to pass the simple test, it was quickly forgotten.[17]

The Coast Guard became the primary enforcement agency at sea, which was in itself a problem. The Coast Guard's primary job was always search and rescue, saving life from peril on the sea. Although one of the antecedent organizations of the Coast Guard was the old U.S. Revenue Marine Service, an anti-smuggling agency started by Secretary of the Treasury Alexander Hamilton in 1789, it was not a major mission practiced by the Coast Guard in 1920. Other than search and rescue, the agency was committed to the Bering Sea Patrol, International Ice Patrol (remember the *Titanic*), removing derelict vessels from shipping lanes and inshore life saving stations. Prohibition did not bring the responsibility to just catch the odd rum runner or two; it was a case of intercepting a mass of violators daring the authorities to catch them. It was a tall order for the Coast Guard overloaded as it was with other responsibilities. Considering that the coastline of the U.S. including the Great Lakes, was over 6,000 miles long, with innumerable coves, inlets, rivers, etc., each a potential landing spot for smugglers, it was a "mission impossible." This was all before radar, so adding in the cover of night or fog, only made the job more impossible.

Prohibition spawned some incredible rumors that had the Coast Guard chasing wildly about. One printed in a major New York newspaper claimed an entire ocean liner was anchored just beyond the three-mile limit and filled with "booze, broads and gambling tables." Supposedly boatloads of the well heeled ran out nightly to enjoy themselves in its splendor. Although the Coast Guard searched long and hard, they never found the mythical floating sin ship. Another rumor said a surplus World War I German freighter submarine was running liquor directly into New York harbor under cover of night.

At the start of Prohibition the Coast Guard fleet was small and lacked the capability to intercept smugglers. Their big cruising cutters were well designed for offshore duties but generally had a top speed of only 12 knots, too slow to catch a rum runner. The service only had 26 inshore vessels and they were too slow with a design speed of only 18 knots. Again, the fast rum runners could easily out distance a Coast Guard pursuit boat.

Often when the Coast Guard did catch a rum runner sympathetic courts released them with a slap on the wrist or threw the case out on a technicality. The court's action was due to a combination of problems including the overwhelming number of cases necessitating plea bargains and the high quality of defense lawyers. The quality of justice is often based on the quality of the lawyers and it was no different during Prohibition.

All Coast Guardsmen were not supportive of the new mission. Like American society in general, many saw no reason to zealously enforce stupid laws and prohibition certainly fell into that category. It was usually a case of just following orders.

Coast Guardsmen were comparatively poorly paid and when a rum runner offered large sums of money to simply look the other way, it was a tempting offer not always refused, especially at small stations distant from headquarters supervision. A junior officer earned $130 a month and a new recruit $21. So the lure of quick cash was sometimes hard to resist.

Once a rum runner unloaded his cargo directly at the Coast Guard base in New London, Connecticut! The authorities only discovered the transgressor when a "snitch" squealed. After an extensive investigation

A rum runner speeding across the water.

the U.S. Attorney General released information detailing extensive corruption between the Coast Guard, Customs and Border Patrol.[18]

Coast Guard strength was a bare 4,000 men in 1920. Within ten years it increased by 188 percent but there was never enough men or boats to secure the thousands of miles of coastline. Accusations by mariners that the Coast Guard was ignoring its traditional safety at sea mission in favor of chasing harmless rum runners didn't help it's battered image. In at least one instance, when the rum runner *Krazy Kat II* went aground off Long Island, New York during a gale, the Coast Guard managed to save both crew and booze.[19]

Given it's mission, however distasteful and ill conceived, the Coast Guard did it's best to execute it. New techniques for finding, tracking and harassing rum runners were devised with increased success.

Detroit River

The Detroit River was one of the most violent sectors of the border. Gunfire along the Detroit-Windsor sector was common, especially as organized crime gangs fought each other for control of the highly profitable trade.

The river was perfect for rum running. Only a mile wide in some places and 28 miles long, it had hundreds of coves and beaches where small boats could land secretly. The St. Clair River and Lake St. Clair added another 60 miles of hiding places.

One source estimated that in 1920, 1,000 cases of booze crossed the river every day. While bribes were a necessary part of business, hijacking was too. Defending a run with lead was an important skill. Commander N.W. Rasmussen of the U.S. Coast Guard estimated that in July 1929 nearly 5,000 rounds of rifle and machine gun ammo were fired at rum runners on the lower part of the Detroit River and western Lake Erie.[20]

Detroit was also the home of the infamous Purple Gang, a group of some of the worst thugs and killers to ever curse the earth. During the late 1920s the gang "owned" Detroit. Savage beyond belief, with over 500 murders to its credit, it was common for the gang to hijack a load of booze and kill everyone connected with it. The gang practiced the old truism "dead men tell no tales." The Purple Gang was often at war with other Detroit gangs so bullets flew with abandon, hitting mobsters and innocents alike. The river was unsafe for everyone including fishermen, rum runners, police, Coast Guard, and just plain people. The Purple Gang finally self-destructed in the 1930s only to be replaced by the Mafia.[21]

The Purple Gang controlled most of Michigan as far west as U.S. Highway 31 running through Grand Rapids south to Indiana. Capone owned everything west of U.S. 31. Big Al certainly wanted Detroit too, but thought it was better to work with the Purple Gang than tangle with them. Discretion was the better part of valor.

The Purple Gang kept a tight control over underworld rackets in Detroit but between the city's north limits and Mount Clemens, the River Gang controlled smuggling. The gang charged a flat 25 percent tax to haul the booze and assumed no liability. If it had to be dumped because of close Coast Guard pursuit, it was the customer's loss, not the gangs. Anyone trying to smuggle his or her own booze was quickly and ruthlessly dealt with and by the late 1920s the River Gang had driven all competition out of business.

Mob on mob violence was common. In one instance a competing gambling operator was tied up and taken to a hole cut in an iced over Lake St. Clair and repeatedly dunked until he agreed to "mend his ways."[22]

The Coast Guard wasn't the only enforcement fleet on the river. The U.S. Customs and the Border Patrol agencies provided another sixty machine gun equipped speedy patrol boats. Running the river could be a difficult proposition, unless appropriate financial arrangements were made. This was easily the worst part of the entire war. Because of the huge amount of money involved there was an equally huge potential for corruption. The temptation for government men, especially the poorly paid Coast Guardsmen, to take the money and just look the other way for a few hours or let the runner know when the patrol boats would be where was often irresistible. Add in a few old-fashioned "death to family member" threats by organized crime and the river became increasingly porous. An investigation toward the end of prohibition claimed $2 million a year was paid out in bribes to smooth the rough water of the Detroit River. Supposedly the money went into trust type fund that was used to pay the various personnel. The system was sophisticated enough that a fixed tariff was established of $1.87 per case of whisky and $.29 for beer. As an added incentive, occasional "free nights" were allowed. It was a lucrative business, with some border patrol agents receiving $1,000 to $5000 a month.[23] To assure the honesty of all involved, off duty agents went to Windsor to the docks to check the amount of liquor actually being smuggled. The government periodically tried to "crack down" on the corrupt customs agents. One year in a force of 129 inspectors, 175 were dismissed, giving an annual turnover of 135 percent![24]

Even when the government tried to enforce the law, it discovered it was it's own worst enemy. In the case of Detroit the duties of the Customs Service, Prohibition Bureau and state and local police often overlapped making coordinated action difficult. Add in petty interdepartmental jealousies at the federal, state and local levels and effective coordination became nearly impossible.[25]

The Windsor side of the river was lined with warehouses and docks loaded with legal export booze. The booze went from the distillery by rail or truck under the protection of the government B-13 customs document which listed it as consigned to companies in Mexico, Cuba or Bermuda. The Canadian government didn't care where it went; only that it went somewhere other than Canada. Under cover of night or fog, a fleet of fast small boats tore across from Wyandotte or Ecorse, quickly loaded the high proof cargo and shot back across to their home base. The next night they would be back again for another load bound, according to their customs document for the Caribbean!

In a July 1925 treaty between the U.S. and Canada both countries agreed to share information on cargoes that could be smuggled into either nation to avoid payment of duty. Liquor fell into this category. Canada also agreed to prohibit the clearance of liquor vessels for countries it was plain it was unreasonable for them to reach. Twenty-one foot speedboats

A boot legger watches for patrol boats on the Detroit River.

could no longer be cleared from Windsor to Cuba. However, the treaty did not prohibit clearing vessels of any size for U.S. ports![26]

Sometimes the Coast Guard pursued them. Other times it was rival gangs trying to capture the hooch. Obviously when fog shrouded the river, the "running" was better but if the runners were able to make a deal with the appropriate law enforcement agency, an official "fog" could be arranged to settle over the water. If the "fog" settled in, transporting liquor was easy. One writer at the time claimed, "To go to Canada and bring back a large cargo of liquor or beer in a slow, scow-like boat was not much more difficult than going out into the backyard of a farm yard and pumping a pail of water to be carried back into the kitchen."[27]

If enforcement tightened up on the river, the large craft were sent south to Lakes Erie or Ontario or north to Huron and Superior. In their place the rum runners used small flat-bottom craft called "scooters" powered by outboard motors. They had the advantage of being very fast and needing very little water. Not only could they outrun the law, they could "scoot" over shoal water the official boats couldn't navigate. When throttled back they were very quiet, perfect for sneaking into a lonely dock on a dark night. If the U.S. agents were laying in wait with speed boats, the rum runners often sent ten or more scooters at a time with perhaps only a couple actually carrying liquor. The tactic drove the agents wild![28]

When the Coast Guard claimed in 1925 that they had destroyed the Atlantic Rum Row, the Detroit River gained in importance as an entry to the U.S. for liquor. The Coast Guard claim was perhaps somewhat suspicious since the following year a New York newspaper announced eight loaded ships were at the row waiting to unload and seven others had just departed after disposing of their cargo.[29] Regardless of the continued operation of Rum Row, one authority claimed 75 percent of all Canadian whiskey going to the U.S. floated across the Detroit River. Eventually an estimated 27 percent of the total U.S. enforcement budget was obligated to Michigan and most of the money was directed to Detroit. That rum running was a major industry isn't questioned. In 1929 illegal booze was the second biggest business in Detroit, surpassed only by the auto industry! The bootleggers were not impressed when a massive effort in 1929 resulted in the assignment of 27 more patrol craft to the Detroit River and Lake Erie, including ten seventy-five foot fast boats carrying powerful guns.[30] To some observers it seemed the only real effect of the increased patrol craft was greater harassment of legitimate river users such as yachtsmen and fishermen. There were constant complaints from both groups of illegal search and seizure. The government took the attitude that the vessel operator had to prove he wasn't a rum runner, not that the officials had to prove he was. It was a total turnaround of the "innocent until proven guilty" theory.

An estimated 50,000 people worked in the Detroit bootlegging trade in 1929 and the number of drinking establishments was staggering. One agent claimed the same year the city had 25,000 blind pigs. When the Michigan State Police raided one of them they hauled off the mayor, a Michigan congressman and the county sheriff! It seemed like everyone was in the business. Even high school students sometimes took a day off from school to load or unload liquor at a fat fee of a dollar a day. "When Dizzy Einstein, who called himself "Prohibition Agent Number One" hit Detroit he disguised himself as a longshoreman. Before anyone realized he was in their midst, the rotund agent made fifty arrests. As typical, all were working class men, never the "big shots."[31]

Before Prohibition the small village of Petit Cote, six miles or so west of Windsor was a subdued settlement of French extraction. It didn't take long before the inhabitants realized that a quick row across the river with a case of whisky doubled their investment. The case became a rowboat load, which became a motor launch, which meant several trips a night instead of only one. There was money to be made![32]

Winter ice provided other opportunities. Runners in Amherstburg, Ontario equipped an old car with tire chains, loaded it up with booze and ran it across Lake Erie. Planks were carried in case weak ice or cracks were encountered. Not all cars made it. Many fell through weak ice to land on the bottom of the lake. Sometimes the booze was recovered. Often it wasn't.

The same trick was used to cross the Detroit River, but the ice was usually less safe than on the open lake. In 1928 alone 28 bodies were fished out of the river, many the victims of weak ice but others certainly were the result of mob "rub outs."[33]

U.S. officials excused their lack of success intercepting the Detroit River runners by claiming spy ships from Canadian distilleries kept watch on the river for enforcement vessels. If they saw a patrol, they signaled the rum runner to lay low until the danger passed.

The Windsor side of the river was filled with illegally operating saloons known as blind pigs. The Windsor Hotel at the corner of Pitt Street and Windsor Avenue was a popular watering hold for people from both sides of the border. As on the U.S. side, a few well-placed bribes assured a degree of official blindness. By 1927 however, pressure from the drys increased to the point that police harassment closed many of the

Crossing the Detroit River with a cargo consigned to Cuba.
Stonehouse Collection

more flagrant saloons down. The Canadian government also began to pressure the liquor warehouses on the river. Many had built up huge stocks of booze, waiting until the right moment to "export" it. When the government felt a warehouse had too much on hand, it moved in and seized it. Eventually government action would force the closure of all but ten of the warehouses, greatly simplifying police surveillance.

Sometimes liquor was smuggled across the Canadian border in empty egg shells. *Stonehouse Collection*

While booze came across the Detroit River by the boatload, individual consumers soon developed novel ways to "beat the system" on their own. One enterprising woman brought it across in eggs, literally draining the yoke and white out of the shell, refilling the shells with booze and carefully resealing them. The eggs were cautiously placed in a large basket and thus carried across the border. The scheme only came to light when she was hit by a car at the Detroit ferry dock, knocking the egg basket to the ground and breaking some of the eggshells. Thereafter customs inspectors were told to closely checked all incoming eggs.

Women had special belts strapped under their dresses to hold a couple of bottles thus avoiding an agent's scrutiny. Every once in a while a bottle slipped out of a holder, to the embarrassment of smuggler and agent.

Another smuggler used a boat with a large scuttle plug. When spotted by customs agents or Coast Guard, he pulled the plug, sinking the boat (and evidence) quickly. Hopefully he remembered where he sank it so he could return later for recovery.[34]

Other enterprising citizens fitted cars with special compartments alongside the drive shaft holding up to 30 or 40 gallons of liquor. One father took the rear seat out of his sedan and replaced it with cases of booze. He then placed his children on the liquor as if they were on the seat. To a casual observer it looked like a father and his kids out for a drive.

Some Detroit smugglers, as well as those elsewhere, dressed as priests and thus immune from customs examination carried car loads of booze across the border. Only when a faux priest did an unpriestly thing (like swearing at a flat tire) were such plots exposed.

A clever way to smuggle a drink. NARA

Corruption of the Detroit customs and prohibition agents was often transparent. In 1929 member of the Canadian Cabinet testified to the House of Commons responding to complaints that Canada was not doing enough to help the U.S., "It has been stated that these boats go across at night. That is not entirely true. I took the trouble last fall to go down to Windsor. I was offered a safe conduct by a liquor exporter and I went out on a launch on the Detroit River. I could see the United States Customs Office on the other shore and I could also see that it was not difficult to detect any boats that left the Canadian shore to go to the American side. While in Windsor I got into conversation with a man engaged in the business of exporting liquor. I asked him, 'do

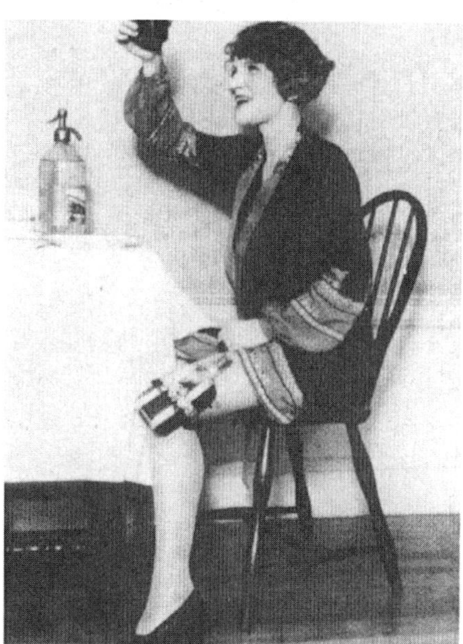

Prohibition made lawbreakers out of many ordinary people. Stonehouse Collection

Many innovative methods were developed to smuggle booze.
Stonehouse Collection

you cross in daytime?' He answered, 'Yes; quite often.' I said, 'How is it they do not get you?' He replied with a smile, 'It just happens that they are not there when we go across.'

"Our inspector went to Windsor not so very long ago. He did not select any special day. While there, on January 14, he observed the following vessels cross the river to Detroit in daylight with cargoes of liquor:

> *Ben*, J. King, master; 10 quarter barrels beer, 11 cases whisky.
>
> *Rat*, J. Sales, master; 24 cases whisky, 4 cases wine, 1 case brandy.
>
> *Bat*, A. Jacks, master; 19 cases whisky, 1 case wine.
>
> *Rabbi*, I. Straight, master; 5 half barrels beer, 8 cases whisky.
>
> *Bird*, J. Bloom, master; 18 cases whisky, 8 cases bourbon, 3 cases scotch whisky.
>
> *Bar*, J. Peters, master; 13 cases whisky, 4 cases bourbon, 3 cases brandy.

That was in a single day.[35]

If the heat was on and the authorities weren't looking the other way, runners crossing the river hid the booze in many innovative ways. Liquor was towed in special containers underwater behind the boats. Sunken houseboats disguised underwater cable delivery devices. A special pipeline actually carried booze under the river (not from the Hiram Walker distillery as once claimed) and an electrically controlled cable hauled metal cylinders holding fifty gallons of liquor from Canada to the U.S. There was even a rumor of a tunnel under the river.

Although small speedboats were the norm, economy of scale was an important consideration to large operators. A Canadian bootlegger named Harry Low used two sizeable vessels, the tug *Geronimo* and trawler *Vedas*

A customs agent inspects a spool of wire used to haul liquor across the Detroit River. Stonehouse Collection

to run booze in large quantities. The 184-foot *Vedas* was built as the British minesweeper *Shearwater* in Scotland in 1901. In 1925 she was declared surplus, joining Low's rum running fleet. The *Vedas* often carried booze from Montreal to Windsor and sometimes, when the coast was clear, slipped into U.S. ports along the river to deliver cargo. She also performed duty on the Atlantic rum row, transferring booze to the many small craft that met her offshore. At one point the *Geronimo* was seized by U.S. authorities and moored on the American side of the river. When a sudden squall parted her hawsers she drifted back to the Canadian side where Low's men recovered her. There was always some doubt whether the squall was natural or man-made.[36]

Detroit was also the city where Prohibition agents stumbled across an entire underground distillery! The product was delivered by an extensive pipeline system to various remote locations so the telltale line up of trucks was avoided.

The city of Hamtramck, Michigan, a suburb of Detroit was so corrupt that in 1923 the Governor used emergency powers to take over the city. Hamtramck had 400 soft drink shops as well as, candy stores and restaurants all selling booze as well as 150 brothels running around the clock. Gambling halls were everywhere. As a result of the takeover, the mayor and 29 other officials were convicted of various crimes and packed off to the federal pen.[37]

Beer being unloaded in Detroit. Stonehouse Collection

Booze wasn't the only commodity to be smuggled across the river. Then as now, narcotics, aliens and other contraband regularly made the trip. Sometimes they all mixed together in the same load.

When all was said and done, the effort to close the Detroit River was abject failure. Whether by subterfuge, graft or speed, the liquor inevitably made it to Detroit. In 1928 for example, after massive increases in interdiction resources, the government estimated they intercepted a mere 3-1/2 percent of all beer and a miniscule 1.2 percent of all hard liquor. These numbers are based on the volume Canadian authorities told the U.S. was cleared for export. The amount of booze coming from other sources was unknown but considerable, thus the amount intercepted was even lower than the official figures.[38]

Lake Erie

Port Colborne, Ontario was a hot bed of rum running. Locals claimed 100 men were involved running booze to the U.S., usually to Erie or Cleveland. The runners paid the officials on both sides of the border to be "less watchful." Today the citizens of Port Colborne look back on the old bootlegging days with some nostalgia. When they built a new golf course recently, they named it Whiskey Run![39]

Middle Island is the southernmost point of Canada, just a bare half a mile or so north of the international border. Four miles to the north is

Pelee Island, a major bootlegger's haven during Prohibition. The nearest U.S. land is South Bass Island, four miles to the southwest. As the saying goes, "It doesn't take a rocket scientist" to figure out the bootleggers staged their product from the mainland to Pelee Island to Middle Island, waited for dark and foggy nights and dashed it to hiding places on South Bass Island. When the opportunity presented, customers either picked it up at South Bass or it waited for delivery to the mainland. If the shipment was large enough it could be run directly into Detroit. In some instances customers ran over to Middle Island and made their purchases. Middle Island was the home of the infamous Middle Island Clubhouse, a relatively small but exclusive establishment featuring gambling, prostitution and alcoholic beverages, all the sins denied to Americans at home. The major population center on South Bass was the village of Put-in-Bay. It was estimated between 15 and 20 bootleggers ran from the island but most were small timers, men who were simply trying to take care of their families.[40]

There is an old prayer recited by towns along the sea coast that goes something like this: "Lord, it's a terrible stormy night and we pray all mariners will complete their voyages safely, but should there be a shipwreck, we pray it will be here." When the steamer *City Of Dresden* sank off Long Point, Ontario it was an answer to the landsman's prayer.

The *City Of Dresden* was an old wooden steamer loaded to the gunwales with booze. Built in Walkersville, Ontario in 1872, she was plainly far past her prime. The hold of the small 93-foot vessel was jammed with cases of the stuff and some was even piled on her open deck. On November 17, 1922 she was plowing west from the Welland Canal into a strong Lake Erie gale. Her clearance papers said she was headed for Mexico, where she would really deliver her cargo was unknown, at least publicly, although Captain John Sylvester certainly must have known.

With the gale increasing the captain decided to anchor in Gravelly Bay, at Long Point, Ontario for shelter from the fierce west wind. When the blasts swung around to the northeast, the steamer was threatened with going onto Bluff Bar. Concerned with saving his ship, the captain ordered the crew to jettison part of the deck cargo. After weighing anchor, the steamer began to work her way around the tip of Long Point.

Meanwhile a lonely Canadian Life-Saving Service patrolman was fighting his way up the windswept beach. He kept a watchful eye on the old steamer but she seemed to be ok. Glancing to the surf he spots an object rolling around in the waves. Waiting for a bit for the waves to push it ashore, he is elated to discover it is a whisky cask. And it is filled! Over the rest of the day forty more casks and cases of whisky came ashore under his scrutiny. To safe guard them from possible damage or theft; he carefully buried each one in the dunes. (Yea, sure, if you believe this I have a bridge to sell you!)

Finally reaching the south side of Long Point the steamer dropped her anchor to ride out the gale. However the anchors failed to bite into the bottom and the steamer was dragging for the beach and deadly breakers. He certainly did not want to draw attention to himself but faced with a life or death situation, the captain blew distress signals on his whistle. Soon a large crowd gathered on the beach to watch the drama unfold. Driven by the relentless wind and wave the steamer smashed into the sandbar off shore and started to breakup. Doubtless the local citizens knew her cargo. The first lifeboat the panic stricken crew launched was blown away by the wind. They all tumbled into the second one but it capsized drowning the captain's son. Eventually the boat drifted with the current a half-mile down the coast where local men waded out into the surf and dragged it to the beach. After assuring the crew were safe and hustling them off to warm houses to recover, the local citizens began to salvage the steamer's liquid cargo. The once lonely beach was filled with booze, by the cask, case and bottle. Brave and noble citizens made certain none would be lost to the lake. All night long and throughout the following day, they worked tirelessly to salvage the cargo. Obviously concerned that unscrupulous people could steal it, much of it was taken away to more "secure" locations like under haystacks, in holes hastily dug in their backyards, etc. Some was buried on the beach but there was fear that neighbors would note the location and return "when the coast was clear." Nearly all of it was in some fashion hidden.

When the local revenue inspector heard about the wreck and it's precious cargo, he hightailed it for the beach but by the time he arrived the area was pretty well clear of booty. He impounded what he could find and threatened the citizens to return whatever they had recovered but with little result. When people were forced to testify in court they simply claimed ignorance or poor memory. "Wreck, what wreck?" Some were given fines but perhaps the judge was caught up in the "spirit" of the moment since the amounts were very low. Once everything returned to normal at lonely Long Point, the bottles and casks appeared as needed to while away the long and dismal winters. Occasionally some of the bottles are still found in the sand or forgotten hiding places at home. There was such a deluge of booze and so little time, especially if a little sampling clouded the mind, that some people simply forgot where they hid the goods.[41]

The small community of Ohio Bay was a favorite drop off spot for area rum runners. Legend claims underground tunnels running from the waterfront to nearby basements facilitated delivery.[42]

The little Lake Erie steamer *Nautilus* was a victim of rum running. During Prohibition she was caught by the Coast Guard, run aground and wrecked. Earlier she was used by the Willard Asylum to run excursions on Seneca Lake in upstate New York.[43]

Cleveland was a major center for bootleggers and mobster Moe Dalitz was a key player. A contemporary of gangsters like Meyer Lansky and "Bugsy" Siegel, Dalitz ran booze and gambling parlors from Cleveland south to Kentucky. His specialty was running truckloads of booze across Lake Erie on barges! Why worry about handling it by the case when for just a little more effort entire truckloads could be shipped? Dalitz also operated gambling joints such as the Mound Club, Pettibone Club, Jungle Inn, Beverly Hills and Lookout House, all places local politicians, judges and police frequented. Unlike many Prohibition era crooks, Dalitz managed to turn legitimate eventually relocating to Las Vegas and investing profitably in casinos.

When a local boater saw the Canadian steamer *Tranquillo* anchor in the Rocky River lagoon in Lakewood, just to the west of Cleveland, he smelled a rat and notified the city police. He should have smelled more than one rat! It was the summer of 1921 and booze by the boatload was coming across the lake. The boater was sure the *Tranquillo* was a rum runner.

It was dark when two policemen arrived but they went out to the suspicious steamer and finding no one around, gave it a good look over but found no liquor. From her size they judged there could be over 2,000 quarts hidden aboard. Returning to shore they saw three men in the shadows. Calling out to them resulted in gunshots, followed by a flurry of feet as the men disappeared into the night.

The cops watched the steamer for a while to see if any of the crew would return. When none did, the police again went aboard and searched again, this time finding thousands of bottles of scotch. It was a bonanza of booze! The policemen, deciding not to turn their backs on Dame Fortune, divided up the scotch and when another officer arrived later, used his car to haul part of it away. Some ended up in their homes and quite by chance, a load actually went to the police station!

Good news travels fast and soon other Lakewood policemen and firemen were shopping at the *Tranquillo*. Unfortunately word of their good fortune traveled to nearby Cleveland and a newspaper, published an expose. The paper claimed there was "...a wild orgy of drunkenness" and a "...riot of boozing. Drunken firemen were seen falling into the river and drunken policemen were guzzling the booze and passing out on the boat." Back at the station some officers tasted the scotch (to check the quality of the evidence surely). One cop passed out cold from his work and was hauled off to the back garage to recover. The newspaper reported that for two weeks after the looting of the steamer, the police were selling booze to anyone with the necessary cash. There was plenty for all. Surely adding to the Policeman's Ball Fund was a worthy use of it? With the cat out of the bag, the federal Prohibition Bureau moved in and the steamer was towed over to the Cleveland Coast Guard Station dock but if anyone thought this provided better security, they were sadly mistaken. The Coast Guard Officer-In-Charge reported civilians were slipping aboard and searching for scotch the authorities missed.

The local Prohibition Bureau agent took charge of the confiscated booze, whatever was left anyway. Under his close supervision, 47 cases of good Canadian scotch was dumped into the Lakewood sewer! As sad as this waste was, it was still only approximately a quarter of the cargo!

While public attention was focused on the tribulations of the Lakewood Police and *Tranquillo*, bootleggers were still bringing liquor into Cleveland. On August 18, the Coast Guard reported watching a mysterious vessel waiting off port for night to fall when she doused her running lights and ran into the Great Lakes Dredge and Dock Company pier on Whiskey Island (aptly named). Where a truck was waiting on the dock to haul off the goods. A quick call to the police resulted in a hastily organized raid on the operation. The vessel, later identified as the *Venice*, tried to escape but police leaped aboard and made the arrest. The captain turned out to be an experienced rum runner who claimed to have brought the *Tranquillo* across the lake several times but denied making the last run to Lakewood. Perhaps most interesting was when the cops searched the captain they found a "little black book" listing not only Cleveland area customers, but more fascinating, a number of local women from very fashionable addresses with whom it was surmised he had "amorous" relationships! A sailor does need a girl in every port, or more!

Meanwhile, while the authorities were busy with the *Venice* it was claimed another rum runner was just offshore, perhaps waiting for a signal it was safe to land. Each time the police began to close in on her, she faded back into the dark night. The Prohibition Bureau agent claimed a lake freighter was running booze down from Montreal. The big ship drifted just out of sight of land and small craft ran out at night and loaded liquor just like Rum Row in the Atlantic. He claimed he had searched the freighter but never found anything.

Fueled by the Cleveland papers, the scandal got bigger and bigger. Eventually it came to a head when the police chief, city street commissioner and two officers were fined between $300-$500. Other participants received fines and or prison terms.[44]

Corruption was also prevalent in Buffalo but judging from the city's shady past, it was only to be expected. Canadian officials claimed there were a dozen boats regularly running booze across the Niagara River, each carrying 800-1,000 cases. The officials stated the Canadians always informed U.S. Customs an hour before the boats left Canada but none were ever caught, in spite of unloading at a dock next to the customs agents. In some instances the agents helped unload![45]

The Minister of National Revenue submitted a report to the Canadian Parliament that clearly illustrated the corruption in Buffalo. "There are about 12 boats plying between here (Bridgeport, Ontario) and Buffalo, New York, the river at this point being about half a mile wide. Some days we only have two or three boats out and on other days the whole fleet will make a trip.

"The liquor and ale are brought from the distillery and brewery by truck, arriving here about two o'clock in the afternoon. The boats are all loaded and clearance granted about five P.M. and they are compelled to leave by six P.M. Some of these boats carry from eight hundred to one thousand cases and on their arrival on the American side, it takes from two to three hours to unload them. No effort is made, as far as we can see, by United States authorities to seize any of these boats, as the United States Customs are always notified by us an hour or two before the boats leave and occasionally we notify them as the boats are leaving, giving them the names of the boats and the quantity of liquor or ale on board. We have had high customs officials from Buffalo, special agents and officers connected with the Coast Guard come over to the Canadian side, watch these boats load and pull out. It is a well known fact that some of these boats land within a few hundred yards of the United States Customs office at the foot of Ferry Street and unload without being disturbed.'

'Our officers who check these boats out were informed by one of the rum runners that they had no trouble in landing their cargo, as they were assisted by the officers of the dry squad on the American side and it would appear that such must be the case, when seven or eight boats will leave here and land their cargoes without any casualties.'

'These boats are loaded directly opposite from the United States Customs office at Block Rock. You can stand by the window in that office and look across and see every case that is loaded on the Canadian side. I know that if conditions were reversed, we would have all those boats tied up in less than a week and if the officers on the American side wished to put a stop to this business they could do it in about the same length of time."[46]

Lake Ontario

Lake Ontario was an especially lucrative area for the trade. The Canadian side of the lake was blessed with breweries at Kingston, Belleville, Toronto, and Hamilton, so the runners had a choice of fine products to offer their customers. The run across the lake was as short as sixty miles, depending on where the cargo was delivered. Sackets Harbor and Oswego were popular destinations. Canada's Main Duck Island was a regular spot to hide both boats and cargo from the Coast Guard and revenue agents until the coast was clear.

In the early days of Prohibition liquor could be smuggled on the Great Lakes by schooners. *Stonehouse Collection*

A great deal of the running was done by young men or small-timers just trying to earn some easy money, especially during the early days of Prohibition before the gangs took over much of the business. Typically the small operators only carried ten cases or so while larger operators often carried cargos of 1,000 cases of beer or whisky at a time. Lake Ontario bootleggers also used a special trick to recover any cargo they may have been forced to jettison. Several bottles were packed in burlap sacks with enough salt to assure the bundle would sink if dropped overboard. After a few days, the salt melted and the bottle bundles floated merrily to the surface ready to be neatly picked up. It was a slick trick, as long as the rum runner remembers where he dumped the cargo.[47]

Erie was a great jumping off place for rum runners too. The city was notorious for all manner of illicit activities including gambling, prostitution as well as bootlegging. The waterfront offered good facilities and the authorities were usually business driven, meaning they were open to a "negotiation." One wag commented, "The only dry thing in Erie was the inside of a light bulb." The Erie Yacht club, the center of activity for the society class, didn't center all of its events on "water."[48]

Lake Huron

Bootlegging also happened on Lake Huron and it wasn't always from Canada to the U.S. A small beach near Algoma Mills, Ontario is a case in point. Known as Bootlegger's Bay it got its name back in 1920 when Algoma Mills was a booming port for bootlegging vessel running through the North Channel. The old tales claimed that it was in this little bay the black ships unloaded cases of whisky intended for Canadian consumption. Remember, Canada allowed the export but not consumption of liquor so smuggling booze within the country was important. There were times when the Canadian rum runners were unsure whether the better market was in the U.S. or Ontario!

One creative Lake Huron smuggler stripped labels off the bottles and froze them in blocks of ice. When everything was ready, he shipped the ice by ship to Michigan. How long the ploy worked isn't known but the jig was finally up when the weather turned uncommonly warm. The ice melted on the trip across the lake and the loose bottles started rolling around in the hold, an easy catch for even a sleepy customs agent.

Lake Michigan

Milwaukee, Wisconsin was another wide open city. Before Prohibition it was the beer capital of the U.S. In 1918 it's nine breweries employed about 6,500 people and produced 2,217,000 barrels valued at $35 million. People working in the city's 1,900 saloons were in addition to these figures. Based on the loss of the brewery industry alone, Prohibition had a devastating impact on the city. While illegal brewing went on and bootleggers worked overtime to supply demand, the decline of the great breweries was an economic disaster.

Milwaukeeans did keep a strong sense of humor. On the day Prohibition became official, a group of twenty-odd sad faced people assembled in a room overlooking the Milwaukee River where a specially made coffin rested forlornly on a makeshift bier. Burning candles stuck in empty whisky bottles scattered about the dark chamber provided an eerie, flickering light. After due ceremony lamenting his passing, the coffin holding the earthly remains of "John Barleycorn" was carried to the edge of the water and pitched in. Empty bottles followed in a series of irregular splashes.[49]

Some people adjusted to the restrictions of Prohibition by moving to home brew or dealing with the local bootlegger, who practiced the fine art of spiking near-beer to bring up the alcohol content. The big breweries however had a tremendous challenge. How to stay in business as manufacturers of something that used essentially the same equipment, factories, marketing and distribution as beer but was legal? The Miller Brewery made a cereal beverage under the "High Life" label but it was not well received. All of the breweries turned out millions of pounds of malt syrup yearly which was a legitimate product but also one easily used by home brewers. Betting on the future, Pabst and Miller maintained all of their equipment in full working order, ready for the day it could be put back into it's intended use. Schlitz manufactured a milk chocolate bar and managed to lose an estimated $17 million on the venture. Ultimately the company survived Prohibition by good land investments, banking operations, an aluminum venture and selling its interest in the American Tobacco Company. [50]

Given its geography, little booze was run into Lake Michigan from Canada in small craft but larger vessels did their fair share. It was usually concealed with or in other cargo to avoid easy detection by federal agents. For example, carrying cases of liquor under coal in cargo holds or under grain for ships running down from Thunder Bay, Ontario were both used to get the contraband into Lake Michigan ports. In some cases small commercial steamers loaded in Canada and hauled it as if it were legal cargo without any particular effort to hide it. Usually this was only done if a payoff assured clear sailing. And sometimes things went wrong.

to secretly report the situation to his supervisor by radio but the captain previously disabled it. As the tug approached Chicago, the agent used the searchlight to alert the Coast Guard of their approach and when the vessel stood into the pier to dock, the Coast Guard intercepted her. The agent's light signal had been seen. Revenue agents also nabbed the bootlegging crew waiting ashore. The captains of the Chicago vessel and *Chief Pontiac* each received sentences of ten years and the crews two.[54]

Lake Superior

Smugglers running out of Thunder Bay, Ontario slipped down the Minnesota Lake Superior coast and dropped the goods in a host of small harbors and community docks. Ghosting silently to the dock the boxes and bags were hastily unloaded and the boat gliding back into the dark and shielding night.

Inbound coal boats helped bring the booze into Marquette, Michigan as well as other ports. Old timers remember the boats coming into the coal dock with cases buried in the cargo. When the local authorities were distracted the booze was unloaded and hustled off to customers.

Isle Royale, forty miles or so off Michigan's Keweenaw Peninsula, also on Lake Superior and only twenty miles from Canada's Fort William and Port Arthur (today's Thunder Bay) was a popular staging point for the rum runners. The island is huge, roughly forty-five miles long, seven miles across and surrounded by over 200 islands and very sparsely populated. While there were some private summer cottages, the largest group was the commercial fishermen who worked the dangerous waters off shore. Fishermen were a hardy group and eminently practical. If the opportunity presented itself to make a little extra cash, always a short

A lonely cove at Isle Royale as a center for bootlegging. Stonehouse Collection

commodity, who were they to turn it down? Canadian runners regularly used the island as a stopping point for smuggling booze into the U.S. or to transfer cargo to other ships or even store it until the right moment. As a scuba diver I can remember exploring the waters off what was called an "old bootlegger's cabin" and finding the entire bottom littered with old whisky bottles. Their necks stuck up from the sand like soldiers in formation. Why they ended up on the bottom is unknown. Resting upright in a small bay on the island's north shore is a small-unidentified tug. Running booze from Thunder Bay to Isle Royale didn't require speedboats. A reliable tug was all that was needed. How she ended up on the bottom is pure speculation but certainly it is likely she was part of the old rum running trade.

The story of the tug *Arbutus* is illustrative of how liquor was run on Lake Superior as well as how the machinery of enforcement could frustrate the enterprise. The tug left Port Arthur on November 17, 1920 bound for Houghton, Michigan at the foot of the Keweenaw Peninsula. Although her customs declaration claimed she was running empty, in reality she carried 70 cases of booze hidden under her bunker coal. Her master was George Stitt, mate M. McEacheron, engineer James Dampier and crewman John Dowd. The run over was uneventful other than the captain and mate seemed to be drunk and navigating without close regard for proper compass headings. When the tug "found" the Keweenaw, they entered the first port they came across, in this case Copper Harbor. Realizing his error, the captain quickly turned back into the lake and headed south. However his unusual action attracted the attention of the Copper Harbor Lighthouse keeper who apparently was a busybody willing to stick his nose where it didn't belong. Concerned the tug was a rum runner, he telegraphed the customs officer at Houghton of his suspicion. The customs officer in turn notified the Prohibition Bureau at La Crosse, Wisconsin.

Meanwhile the intrepid tug captain proceeded along the Keweenaw coast until he discovered Eagle Harbor. Deciding it must be Houghton he entered. Realizing his mistake he anchored in the middle of the harbor intending to continue to search for the elusive Houghton in the morning. Since the tug had done a fair amount of extra running the bunker coal pile had been considerably reduced which exposed the hidden cases of whisky. This was a problem for several reasons. The obvious one was that the tug was facing a coal shortage. There wasn't enough to reach Houghton. The second problem was the engineer was apparently not "in"

The Canadian tug Arbutus *was a notorious rum runner. Kurt Fosburg Collection*

on the smuggling. He later claimed to be shocked by the illicit booze. Most important of all however was that as a Canadian vessel she could not just dock and fuel for fear of being arrested with the illegal booze.

On November 22 the Prohibition Bureau arrived with a swarm of agents. Intimidated by the agents, the engineer surrendered the tug. But it was a hollow victory. The captain and mate disappeared during the night, apparently rowing to shore. They eventually reached Canada safely. Even worse, the tug was empty of booze! Suspecting it may have been dumped over board at night, the agents had a diver search the bottom without success.

What happened of course was clear. When the local residents realized the opportunity the tug offered for a town full of thirsty Yoopers they took advantage of the situation. All night long a procession of small craft rowed out to the tug, purchased booze and retreated to the shore. Under the direction of the Prohibition agent the town was searched and much of the missing booze found. Purchasers included the assistant lighthouse keeper, members of the local Coast Guard crew, county road commission engineer and timber men. It was a "whos' who" of Eagle Harbor society.

Under pressure from the Prohibition agents, the engineer turned states evidence agreeing to tell the whole sorry tale in court. Eventually the case was turned over to the Federal District court in Marquette, which meant the *Arbutus* had to be fueled and taken to court too! When the trial got underway in January 1921 the buyers were all charged with conspiracy against the government, smuggling, importing and the possession of bottled in bond whisky. The engineer's 23-page confession greatly aided the government case especially in charging two prominent Houghton businessmen, Thomas H. McCormick and Michael J. Carroll with being the intended receivers of the cargo.

The engineer was acquitted of any charges based on his prosecution testimony. All charges against most of the Eagle Harbor buyers were dropped except possession and a fine of $500 levied. When the judge at the Marquette court became ill the case was transferred to Grand Rapids where the charges against the two Houghton men were also dropped.

The original plan was to burn the *Arbutus* as was commonly done with captured rum runners. However since she was a Canadian vessel and a Canadian bank held her mortgage, she was released back to the bank. During her delivery to the Canadian Soo, she sank in a storm off Deer Park.[55]

Ashland, Wisconsin at the foot of the Apostle Islands, was a popular destination for bootleggers. A persistent tale involving the tug *Butterfield* and barge *Ontario* well illustrates how the liquor was often smuggled to the city.

On October 12, 1927 the tug and barge were bound from Port Arthur, Ontario to Ashland. Aboard the 297-foot steel barge was 1,100 tons of pulpwood. Built in 1890 and originally used as a car ferry between Windsor and Detroit, she started in the pulpwood trade several years before.

In mid lake the pair encountered a strong northwest gale and the waves started to wash the barge's deckload overboard. Slowly the *Ontario* filled with water. Early on the morning of October 13 when the pair were east of Outer Island, the crew signaled the *Butterfield* she was ready to sink and the tug quickly ran along side the barge and plucked the crew off minutes before the *Ontario* dove for the bottom. The *Butterfield* continued to Ashland to report the disaster. The barge was a reported loss of $25,000 and cargo $30,000.

The barge Ontario *in her days as a Detroit River ferry.* Stonehouse Collection

The tug Butterfield. *Did she run liquor into Ashland? Stonehouse Collection*

Later rumors circulated the *Ontario* carried another cargo carefully concealed beneath the wood, scotch whisky! Sailors claimed at least ten cases were hidden away intended for delivery in Ashland. There certainly could have been much more! Hundreds if not thousands of cases could have been buried under the wood. Who would have suspected a lowly pulpwood barge of such a rich cargo?

The *Butterfield* could have played a different role in the drama than simple barge puller. She also could have carried liquor and with the excitement over the loss of the *Ontario* delivered a booze cargo without special attention.[56]

Guarding the Coasts

In the early days of Prohibition on the lakes, virtually every kind of boat was used to run liquor, from various sized fishing boats, to cabin cruisers. Even large commercial vessels carried a share of the cargo. It was a race to deliver cargo and depending on the conditions, whatever floated did the job. The rush overwhelmed the Coast Guard.

Seeing the vast amount of booze being run into the country, Congress voted a massive increase in funds to allow the Coast Guard to build a fleet of interdiction craft.

Under increasing pressure to improve the Coast Guard offshore presence, in 1924 Congress authorized transfer of twenty reconditioned World War I Navy destroyers. Eventually eleven more would follow. Built in the 1910-16 period, the old "four-stackers" could steam at 25-36

To break up "Rum Row" Congress transferred mothballed Navy destroyers to the Coast Guard. USCG

knots, fast enough to overhaul all but the speediest of the rum runners and with their three and four inch cannon, put a healthy dose of fear into those they couldn't catch.

Congressional largess allowed the construction of over 200 seventy-five foot cutters often called "six-bitters" and more than a hundred picket boats. Approximately twenty-five were built on the Great Lakes. The larger boats could stay out for over a week at a time, carried a crew of eight and a one-pound cannon. Although not fast at fifteen or so knots, the one-pounder covered up any loss in speed. The cannon wasn't particularly accurate, especially when fired from the bow of a racing and wave tossed boat, but it scared the hell out of people, Coast Guard and rum runners alike. The smaller picket boats, in thirty-five, thirty-six and

Coast Guard 75-foot patrol boat. USCG

A Coast Guard 125-foot cutter. They were good vessels for off shore work. USCG

thirty-eight, foot models were capable of twenty-four knots, carried a crew of three and were intended for day runs only. Based on the outstanding Sea Bright dory of New Jersey fame, a design famous in the Coast Guard as the basis for the legendary surfboat, they were remarkably effective for inshore operations. A thirty-caliber machine gun provided a "persuading" influence on fleeing bootleggers. When both cutters and picket boats arrived on the Great Lakes they radically changed the game. No longer could rum runners easily run away from the forces of law and order.

The Coast Guard claimed the infamous "Rum Row" off the east coast of the U.S. was largely destroyed by 1925 and this allowed the reallocation of enforcement resources to the Great Lakes. Whether Rum Row was destroyed or just badly damaged is debatable, but it no longer was able to operate with the previous impunity. The addition of Coast Guard aircraft in 1924 doubtless provided a critical surveillance "edge." The Coast Guard pressure had increased to such a degree that individual boats were assigned to picket and harass each rum rowboat.

Five of the new picket boats were sent to the Lakes in early 1925. Sault St. Marie, Michigan received two and one each went to Buffalo and Oswego, New York and Niagara, Pennsylvania. The boat operating

The Coast Guard 38-foot patrol boats were fast and seaworthy. USCG

from Oswego under the command of Merle McCune, one of three brothers in the Coast Guard commanding such boats was especially effective. He soon gained the reputation of being the best booze boat catcher on the Lakes.

The Coast Guard continued to ramp up their forces on the Great Lakes to deal with increased rum running. By 1929 the Coast Guard had 223 craft on the Lakes ranging from the 188-foot *Seminole* armed with four guns to rowing surfboats with small arms. It was a massive force just to plug a leaky border. Key elements of the fleet were the twenty-nine fast picket boats and their 30 caliber machine guns. As the war between the government and rum runners ebbed and flowed, both sides reallocated their forces constantly probing for weak spots. For example in 1928 the Coast Guard stationed forty patrol

Gun fire was common in the battle between rum runners and Prohibition agents.

boats to Buffalo in an attempt to overwhelm the opposition. While the Buffalo spigot was plugged, the others opened wider.

Captures were not always gentlemanly affairs of the "you caught me fair and square" variety. As the Coast Guard craft stalked the smugglers the black night was often streaked with the flash of gunfire. As the war between Coast Guard and smugglers went on, violence became more common. Many rum runners were only apprehended after their boats were riddled with machine gun fire.

As enforcement improved and the Coast Guard obtained faster craft, the rum runners favorite craft became the mahogany speedboats of the style manufactured by Chris Craft. Reputedly one of the first Chris Craft dealers in the United States was a boat yard in the Les Cheanuux Islands in northern Lake Michigan. The small speedy craft were perfect for delivering liquor to the many small resorts in the area.

Canadian Prohibition

To a point, Canada mirrored the U.S. experiment with national prohibition. Forces opposed to "demon rum" wrecked havoc with the laws of an honest land and on September 16, 1916 the Ontario Temperance Act slithered into existence ending the sale of legitimate nine percent beer and allowing only "near beer" in it's place. The retailing of real booze, whiskey etc., was outlawed. No longer could a hard working Canadian stop by a neighborhood pub for a simple shot and a beer. Now he had to break the law for a drink–just like his brethren to the south. Under increasing pressure from the anti booze army, in the spring of 1918, the federal government cut off the manufacture, sale and export of alcoholic beverage for a period of one year after the end of the First World War. Somehow robbing a citizen of a stiff belt now and then was supposed to drive the hated Hun from the field! The convoluted logic of the drys was at best, questionable but the weak knee politicians where as spineless as their U.S. brethren. A year after the war's end the spigots opened and Ontario politicians, reeling from the constant assault of dry forces led by the "Salvation Army" and Protestant churches, eventually enacted legislation that made the province a desert as dry as the Sahara. The good and loyal citizens could no longer have alcoholic drinks in any form. Provincial distilleries could still make and export liquor since the federal government was blessed with some adult leadership, but Ontario citizens were forced to the local bootlegger to slake their thirst. Of such foolishness are empires corrupted. Canadian bootleggers were faced with the difficult (although certainly pleasing) decision of whether to smuggle the booze to the U.S. or to their fellow Canadians. In some instances if a rum runner was unable to safely deliver the liquor to the U.S., he slipped it back into Ontario where it was readily sold.[57]

The despised Ontario Temperance Act ended on June 1, 1927 and under new legislation Canadians "of good character" were allowed to purchase liquor at government stores but only after obtaining a special permit. Public imbibing was not allowed, but at least a person could drink in private. As with the original OTA, it was a ludicrous effort to regulate morality.

The new law allowed special permits to be issued for tourists who were supposed to spend twenty-four hours in Ontario. This resulted in a massive increase in tourism for border towns and subsequent "smuggling" of liquor back into the U.S.. Canadian politicians were quite willing to rob their own citizens of their rights, but where tourism is concerned, business is business. For a while it was very popular for U.S. groups to hold meetings and conferences in Ontario, especially when it was important the proceedings be "lubricated."

This new cross border tourism caused one poet to scribble:

Four and twenty Yankees
Feeling mighty dry,
Took a trip to Canada
And bought a case of rye.
When the case was opened
The Yanks began to sing–
"To hell with the President!
God save the King!"[58]

The Canadian government was always somewhat unclear on the concept of prohibition. While it worked to restrain domestic drinking, it permitted the manufacture of booze and it's export. Where it went and how it got there was not usually closely examined. The classic examples were twenty-two foot open fishing boats leaving distillery docks on Lake Ontario or Windsor loaded with whiskey with clearance papers stating the destination was Cuba. When the boat returned the following day for another load obvious questions were never asked. It just came down to the idea that business is business. In June 1924 Canada finally succumbed to U.S. pressure and agreed to take steps to limit such activity. Although the carriage of booze on such small craft to distant ports was prohibited, Canada refused to halt ships carrying booze to openly stated U.S. ports.

This was legal under Canadian law and Canada would not change its law to suit U.S. politicians regardless of pressure. From the rum runner's viewpoint the worst part of the agreement encouraged cooperation between the two governments concerning illegal operations. As a result, Canadian authorities often notified their U.S. counterparts when shipments left for American destinations, making it infinitely easier for the Coast Guard to intercept them. The rum runners adapted in a variety of ways including changing ports and laying in at some out of the way location until the authorities grew bored or concluded the cargo had somehow slipped through and went on to other missions.

Tricks of the Trade

One of the old rum runner's tricks when the pursuit became too hot was to dump the cargo in the water instead of landing it ashore. As long as they knew the exact location so they could return when the "heat" was off and if the water wasn't too deep, it was a technique that worked well. A depth of six to twenty feet was preferred but circumstances often dictated otherwise. One night off Amherstburg, nearly 3,000 cases were jettisoned and later recovered. There was a loss factor however. Never was the entire cargo recovered and invariably local fishermen and beachcombers would enjoy a small gift from the lake in the ensuing weeks and months. Once a smuggler dropped his cargo several hundred yards offshore only to be the victim of a seiche the following day. The strong wind literally blew the water to the other end of the lake, exposing the bottles for all to see. Local fishermen claimed "fishing" was never so good. If the drop was a planned one, as opposed to one necessitated by hot pursuit, then the bottles were carefully prepared. Usually this involved tying them together with light rope at regular intervals, perhaps ten or fifteen feet. The bottles lines would deploy overboard such that the salvager could easily hook the line and thus recover the majority of the cargo. Cases of booze were never dropped intact since recovery was too difficult.

Another technique was to send a very fast rum runner ahead of the smuggling fleet in the hope that the Coast Guard would chase the rabbit allowing the real rum runners to slip by undetected. There were also instances of false distress calls to decoy the Coast Guard away from illicit activity. Once on the Detroit River bystanders were shocked to see a Ford sedan go flying off a pier and splash into the water. In the ensuing confusion of "rescuing" the "victims" and finding their bodies, the bootleggers dashed a large shipment of liquor across the river.[59]

Specially constructed rum runners were not only fast but sometimes armored. USCG

The order of the day was always faster and faster boats for both runners and Coast Guard. One thirty-three foot Lake Erie runner was powered by a twelve cylinder Liberty engine giving it a full throttle speed of thirty-five miles per hour. Liberty engines were originally used in World War I combat aircraft and later proved highly adaptable for a variety of purposes. Designed and built by the Packard Motor Company and Hall-Scott Motor Company, various models of the engine produced up to 400-horse power. Eventually 22,000 were manufactured. Following the war, the government sold surplus engines for $100 each, many times less than their true value. The brawny engines were a boon to rum runners. It didn't take great skill for a good backyard mechanic to adopt one or more for marine use. Some of the big east coast runners had four of the powerful engines, providing claimed speeds of 45 miles per hour and hauling 400 cases of booze.

Between June 27, 1927 and September 8, 1932 the Coast Guard on the Great Lakes captured 37 rum runners. Some of the boats were absorbed into the Coast Guard fleet increasing both numbers of patrol boats and speed. Others were auctioned off at prices ranging between $52.00 and $5.50. Many bootleggers were able to buy their own boats back at a fraction of the value. The rest were turned over to other federal agencies or destroyed. Of the 37 captured during this roughly five-year period, 13 were taken into the Coast Guard, three to the Prohibition Bureau, two to the Army Corps of Engineers and two to the Customs Agents. The remaining boats were burned.[60]

These specially built boats were not luxurious or yachts by any stretch of the imagination. They were strictly utilitarian, made to carry the most cargo at the greatest speed possible. Essentially they were virtually bare hulls, although some were armor plated around the engine and crew compartments. It was not unusual for a boatyard to be constructing boats simultaneously for the Coast Guard and rum runners. As a way of a gentlemen's agreement, the yards tried to keep knowledge of construction details secret from each customer. The specialty built boats were expensive but there was so much money to be made, a couple of good runs could pay for the boat.

Speed was not the only technique used to get the product ashore. Subterfuge was equally important. One Coast Guard team searched a fast runner for several hours before finally discovering a false bottom filled with booze. In another case a fishing boat used fake inner gunwales to hide the liquid cargo.

By their very occupation, bootleggers were not the most honest men. If they could fool a one-time customer, they certainly would. One trick involved soldering a narrow tube inside a five-gallon can from the screw cap opening to the bottom. The tube contained whisky and the rest of the can water![61]

Aircraft were used to haul liquor from Canada into the U.S., especially in the Great Lakes. Accidents were also common. NARA

Commercial fishing was an excellent cover for rum running. By the nature of the business, the boats were always out on the water and coming and going at odd and unusual hours. In addition, they were roomy with plenty of cargo space and their captains had encyclopedic knowledge of the local coast. If anyone could successfully slip cargoes of booze ashore, it was fishermen. But there were accidents. Small boats moving at high speed along a dark and rocky coast suffered casualties. How many were lost in such manner isn't known.

Rum runners used every available means to get the product to market. In the Minnesota North Country private planes flew it across the border and delivered it on a host of small fields. Some used airfields while seaplanes crabbed into every available lake, and Minnesota has a lot of lakes!

A fleet of aircraft ran from Ontario to Michigan, landing on established airfields as well as lonely farmer's pastures. As the authorities increased patrolling, the intrepid pilots slipped into forlorn fields at night illuminated only by dim automobile headlights. Pilots normally received $5 a case and up to 40 cases a trip was an average cargo. At one time, Al Capone's brother owned a fleet of booze planes including a three-engine model. The imagination of the pilots was remarkable. It seems at least one Canadian-American team used in flight transfer of liquor. The Canadian aircraft rendezvoused with the American plane and used a trailing hose to pass the liquor. Under Canadian law the flights were entirely legal. Remember, Ontario allowed the production and export of liquor, just not the consumption.[62]

Bribing the authorities was of course the preferred method for the large operators. One prohibition supervisor had a large empty flower bowl in his office and bootleggers just stopped by and dropped an envelope stuffed with cash into it. Not a word was exchanged but the deal was made as surely as if a written contract executed. Border inspectors could be "distracted" with a bottle or two. In one instance the bootlegger arranged for a woman to take the inspector "behind the shed" for the time necessary.[63]

An enterprising bootlegger arranged to use a hearse to carry his product past the inspectors. Since a couple of nuns accompanied the hearse with the coffin, the customs men thought nothing of it until one fateful trip. This time the hearse arrived with a flat tire. One the nuns climbed out of the hearse and explained in a deep voice, " Ain't this a hell of a place to have a flat tire." Their suspicions finally aroused, the customs men discovered the casket was filled with liquor and the nuns were not ordained by any heavenly order.[64]

A Bounty of Booze

Sometimes things went askew and sailors enjoyed an unintended bonus of booze. One old sailor remembered, "During prohibition I sailed on a private yacht belonging to a Chicago manufacturer. He was considered a tight proposition so when he announced one day soon after we had left Detroit that he was throwing open his liquor closet to the crew and for everyone to help himself, we could not believe our ears. We thought he had gone crazy. Just the same we didn't argue, but made a rush for the closet and cleaned out the stock in a hurry, so that not so much as a half a pint of whiskey was left in the place. He was particular about this. "Take everything, boys! Don't leave a thing–not even a smell of liquor!" We never obeyed an order with more joy. The liquor, which consisted of whiskey, rum, brandy, gin and everything else, which was scarce in those days, went into the bunks of the sailors–all except a case of good whiskey, which was seized by one Andy Mac Nab, a Scotch A.B. He tucked the bottles into a partially reefed topsail and then reefed her tight. Bunks, he said were not safe places. Everybody got as drunk as possible, although the officer insisted that enough men remain sober to operate the ship. When we got to Chicago the whole crew was pinched for violation of the liquor laws. You see, somebody had sent a wireless tip to the owner and that old fox, knowing that his liquor would be seized anyhow as soon as we reached Chicago, figured that he could dodge trouble with the authorities and at the same time be a good fellow to the crew of his ship for once in his life. We were all held for a couple of hours while the yacht was searched. They found the booze in the bunks of course and decided that it was just a case of a bunch of sailors with too much money being reckless with Canadian liquor. The fact that we were all more or less drunk was in our favor, since it indicated that we wanted the stuff for our own purposes and not to sell. When they questioned the owner he played innocent and said that sailors would be sailors. Everything turned out well, although some of the crew actually shed tears over the liquor that was confiscated by the feds. In the bunk of Andy Mac Nab of course, nothing was found, which the feds would have thought strange if they had known Andy like we did. When we were out of sight of land once more willing hands helped Andy to unreef the top-sail and the unconfiscated case of whiskey brought cheer to all hands."[65]

Prohibition Death

While Prohibition was certainly a rough and ready era with bathtub gin, flappers, speakeasies and mobsters, all adding color to a unique period in

American history, there was certainly a major downside to it all. Not only did Prohibition open the door to organized crime becoming the major force it has, but also the number of people poisoned by adulterated booze was staggering. While a definite figure is impossible to determine, in 1927 alone there were 11,700 deaths attributed to bad booze. The problem was especially severe in areas distant from good outside sources of supply and where moon shining and home brewing were common. Government chemists found bootleg liquor containing wood alcohol, phenol, iodine and sulfuric acid among many other poisonous ingredients.[66]

Accidental killings were also common, especially as the Prohibition wars heated up in the middle and late 1920s. In 1928 an innocent member of a Niagara Falls, New York, Elk lodge was shot to death by two out of uniform Coast Guardsmen. They were certain the man was smuggling booze and when he failed to stop his car on their command, they open fire. The victim claimed since the Coast Guardsmen were not in uniform he thought they were highwaymen out to rob him. No liquor was found in the car and both Coast Guardsmen were indicted, tried and acquitted by a Federal court. A year later in Minnesota a man with his wife and two small children was killed in a volley of 26 shots when he didn't immediately stop his auto when ordered to do so by federal agents. No liquor was found in the car and the agents were not punished. In 1929 Prohibition agents clubbed a suspected bootlegger unconscious, then shot his unarmed wife when she went to his aid. A particularly nasty incident occurred in the Detroit River in 1929. It seems a suspected bootlegger was on the river in his speedboat with his eleven year old daughter when their boat was run over and sunk by a Prohibition Bureau patrol boat. Both drowned. The Prohibition agent was immediately fired and tried in Federal Court for manslaughter. The trial ended in a hung jury and the agent "walked." Over zealous Prohibition agents even managed to shoot a U.S. senator in the head while exchanging gunshots with bootleggers in Washington, DC. The Senator had been innocently walking with his wife. Such incidents of flagrant abuse of power were all too common and further eroded public support of Prohibition.

Certainly many local law enforcement agencies were also trigger-happy. For example a county sheriff in the upper Midwest frequently established roadblocks using two 50-caliber machine guns! Fifty yards ahead of the guns he had a sign warning, "Stop, Sheriff Roadblock Ahead." Failure to stop had consequences.[67]

Another shooting incident occurred in the Apostle Islands, Wisconsin, on Lake Superior. It seems the authorities had determined the islands were being used as drop-off point for booze being run in from Canada. Two agents were sent in to investigate. After renting a small motorboat in Ashland, the two men started to search the islands looking for clues to the bootleggers. Neither agent had ever been in the area nor even on the Great Lakes before and they were clearly overwhelmed by many islands and numerous hidden bays and beaches. The second night out they spotted a large 48-foot tug running without lights. When they began to run up on her port side someone on the tug started firing on them with a high-powered rifle. One bullet went through the stern of their boat and struck the rear of the inboard motor. Another shot broke the windshield. A third struck the top of the 120-gallon gas tank. The agents rammed the tug and one leaped aboard with his 45 caliber automatic blazing.

When things calmed down they discovered about 300 cases of booze and a dead female laying on deck as well two alien men. Both had paid $300 to be smuggled into the U.S. All three were from the Mediterranean area. Holding the crew at gunpoint, the agents brought the tug into Ashland. When they arrived at the dock, it was apparent the dock master as well as the two waiting sheriff deputies were expecting the tug and it's cargo, but not under Federal arrest! One deputy tried to arrest the agents when the tug crew alleged they were hijackers. Only the timely arrival of the agent's supervisor and sheriff prevented a very ugly scene, as neither agent was willing to be "arrested" by the deputies.

Prohibition agents celebrate seizure.
Stonehouse Collection

The deputy eventually lost his job and bootlegger received ten years in the Federal Pen.[68]

There is another version to the story. In it the agents spotted the tug and as they approached a single rifle shot was fired at them. Increasing speed, the agents ran up to the vessel and blasted away with a 45 caliber Thompson machine gun. After running through a few drums of bullets they moved close enough to toss a couple of hand grenades into the tug. Once they exploded, the agents climbed aboard the stricken vessel to find a scene of bloody carnage. Which version is true is unknown. Both were related by one of the agents involved at different times.

The federal government tried to keep such shootings secret, admitting to only 171! A U.S. senator however "discovered" 51 more. A New York newspaper counted 1,550 killed, including those involved in local and state shootings. On the government side of the ledger, 55 agents and 15 customs inspectors and Coast Guardsmen were killed.[69] Of the 55 agents however it must be remembered that a significant number were likely executed by gangs for failing to deliver on corrupt promises. In effect the mob "rubbed" the corrupt agents out. It was in the governments interest to portray all the deaths as in the line of duty when the reality could be very different. Regardless, it was a terrible period in U.S. history.[70]

The Great Lakes and their connecting waterways were a key highway for the transportation of liquor into the U.S. It remained so until the passage of the twenty-first Amendment ending Prohibition on December 5, 1933.

The End Game

Throughout Prohibition groups worked for repeal. The Association Against the Prohibition Amendment (AAPA) was an organization of industrialists who thought Prohibition was sheer lunacy. It was a victory of stupidity and ignorance over civil liberty. They also feared the additional powers the federal government had usurped to enforce the amendment. After the 1929 stock market crash, AAPA argued repeal would increase the number of men working, something desperately needed. Plus selling liquor would vastly increase government tax revenue. The organization received considerable support from the Women's Organization for National Prohibition Reform. Both groups campaigned hard for congressmen willing to vote for appeal.

The AAPA estimated in 1930 consumers were spending nearly $3 billion on bootleg booze, making it one of the largest businesses in the country. Considering the majority of the money was going to illegal operators of various sorts, it was an incredible boost to organized crime.[71]

Fiorella H. LaGuardia, a prominent New York City politician who served several terms in the House before becoming mayor was an outspoken critic of Prohibition. His testimony before the Committee on the Judiciary in 1926, is telling in its' candor.

"It is impossible to tell whether prohibition is a good thing or a bad thing. It has never been enforced in the country. There may not be as much liquor in quantity consumed today as there was before Prohibition, but there is just as much alcohol. At least one million quarts of liquor is consumed each day in the United States. In my opinion such an enormous traffic in liquor could not be carried on without the knowledge, if not enforcement of the law. I believe that the percentage of whisky drinkers in the United States is now greater than in any other country of the world. Prohibition is responsible for that. At least one million dollars a year is lost to the National Government and the several states and counties in excise taxes. The liquor traffic is going on just the same. This amount goes into the pockets of public officials in the shape of graft. I have heard of $2,000 a year prohibition agents who run their own cars with liveried chauffeurs."[72]

Make no mistake; there was some immediate good to Prohibition. Drinking fell to the lowest levels in history (likely under a gallon per capita annually from 2.4 gallons prior to Prohibition). Alcohol related traffic accidents, industrial injuries and health problems of all kinds declined. There were also fewer cases of drinking related family problems. Drinking however did not disappear. A sizeable minority continued to drink and alcohol consumption gradually climbed toward pre-prohibition levels. The increasing illegal market kept bootleggers in business and certainly gave a major boost to organized crime.[73]

Under the relentless pressure of both groups as well as leaders like Congressman LaGuardia, Congress for the first time since the Constitution had been ratified, called for ratifying conventions in each state with delegates elected in 1933 for the specific purpose of saying yes or no to the Twenty-first Amendment. The Congressional call was heeded by the states and two-thirds of the conventions voted yes. On December 5, 1933 national Prohibition died. The states were again in control of their own liquor legislation.[74]

Great Lakes PIRACY

The Great Lakes never were a freshwater version of the wild Caribbean, but none-the-less there were episodes of piracy. Many incidents were more fiction than fact but all are worthy of retelling.

Pirates on the River

The *Detroit Post and Tribune* of November 15, 1877 reported that, "The gang of pirates that have been committing depredations the whole length of the Detroit and St. Clair Rivers have got a check put on their operations for a while. A black sloop scow, about 40 feet long by 12 feet wide, with a covered cabin 10 feet wide by 16 feet long and 5 feet high had been seen lying along the shores at different times, was suspicioned (sic) and a watch was set over her doings. Last night she was captured, together with one able bodied seaman, and had there been less haste, the balance of the gang, together with their boats might have been captured. The man captured was lodged in jail and when the officer went to carry him a warm breakfast, behold; the lockup had no doors on it. But the boat, which was a very nice new scow with a perfect outfit, is in charge where moths and rust will not injure or thieves yank her away."

"The boat, on the 3rd of October at night, stole 100 bushels of barley from Henry Rankin, three miles above here and about the 4th of November, 150 bushels of barley from Henry Caswell and between the time stole 60 bushels of oats from Harsen's Island. The boat has a good supply of bags to do business with. Six of the bags are marked "R" in black paint, two with a blue cross and one with "WLL." The boat has no name."[1]

There were also a number of "nickel and dime" pirates. A case in point is that of the Alpena scow schooner *Trader*. In August 1885 she was seized in Wyandotte, Michigan on the Detroit River on a charge of piracy. It was charged she had been quietly appropriating loose gear from the various ports along the river. When authorities searched her they discovered a topsail stolen from an Amherstburg, Ontario yacht, as well as a mountain of material stolen from other vessels including paint, fishing nets, vessel hardware as well as a complete camping outfit taken from a party of anglers camped at the mouth of the River Rouge. Her captain, a man named Williams, was promptly arrested and locked up in the Detroit jail.[2]

The Pirate Dan Seavey

Perhaps the nearest the Great Lakes ever came to a real "pirate" in the tradition of the Caribbean was Captain Dan Seavey. Some called him "roaring" Dan, others "the lone pirate of Lake Michigan." The exploits attributed to him are many and separating fact from fiction at this date is impossible. In the early part of the 20th Century, Dan Seavey tales were common in all the Lake Michigan ports, especially in Manistee, Charlevoix, Naubinway, Sturgeon Bay, St. Joseph, St. James, Milwaukee and Green Bay, all places without much of a genteel veneer.

Seavey was supposedly born in Portland, Maine in 1865 and got his taste for the sailing life on the broad Atlantic when he shipped out at the tender age of 13. After a stint in Uncle Sam's Navy he came west to the Great Lakes and started a fishing outfit in Milwaukee. Bored with the hard work and looking to get rich quick he went to Alaska to find gold. Returning nugget-less, he established a small freight service in Escanaba, Michigan. It seems he never really transported any freight on his small schooner *Wanderer*, at least not any that was considered by normal folk as legitimate. The claim was made that Seavey and his small picked crew of roughnecks and reprobates would spend their time sneaking into small ports and stealing anything they could get their hands on, including ship's gear, freight, livestock and one source even claimed the occasional woman or two. Before light the *Wanderer* slithered out of port to disappear into the wide expanse of Lake Michigan. Seavey either returned to Escanaba and sold the cargo dockside to residents eager for a good bargain, or sailed to Chicago and disposed of it there. Then as now, Chicago had the reputation of being a fine place to cut "shady" deals. If indeed Seavey made off with the odd woman or two, the white slave market was far better in Chicago than Escanaba.

It was also claimed that Seavey used the *Wanderer* to transport entire flocks of "soiled doves," working girls trying to earn a living in the oldest profession. It was common to ship the women from town to town to continually rotate the product among the consumers. The *Wanderer* was perfect for the work. Sometimes the girls even worked from the ship, not even bothering to come ashore. The customers just rowed out and made their "arrangements."

He also occasionally poached venison from the northern islands and small Upper Peninsula ports, reselling it in Chicago too. Summer Island was his favorite "farm." There is a tale that the Booth Fisheries, a major Great Lakes fishing company attempted to drive him out of the illegal venison trade so they could take it over. Although Booth was momentarily successful, Seavey later caught up with the Booth boat and sank it with a small cannon! Reportedly there were no survivors and as a result, Booth left the trade to Seavey.

Not content to survive by dockside thievery alone, some detractors said he also practiced "moon cussing," the fine art of setting false lights to lure ships to their doom. Once the ship was wrecked, the mooncussers attacked, killing the crew and passengers and stealing the cargo. If Seavey happened on a wreck still unsalvaged, he helped himself to whatever could be carried away regardless of ownership.

Above all, Seavey was a fighter, one of the rare men who loved a good brawl above all else! He fought just as he lived, bare fisted, with no quarter asked or given. He didn't fight over women, money or even insults but for the pure joy of it. Sometimes in the midst of a knock down, drag out, eye gouging, ear biting fracas he and his opponent would take a break for a couple of belts of "red eye." Thus refreshed, the men started swinging again. Saloon after saloon suffered a tornado of broken glass, smashed chairs and tables and bloodied floors as Seavey and his adversary waltzed away. Invariably the bars gained in reputation after a Seavey fight. Everyone wanted to socialize were "roaring Dan" did.

Seavey is famous for hijacking the small schooner *Nellie Johnson* from Charlevoix. It seems Seavey appeared at the ship with a small keg of hooch and asked the crew to join him in a drink or two. Never men to turn down a free dram, the crew eagerly did their best to drain the keg. Seavey also participated but was careful not to imbibe too much. When the crew fell into a drunken stupor, Seavey hauled them to the dock, hoisted canvas and sailed off for Chicago where he sold the cargo. Here the tale gets murkier. Eventually the law, in the form of the U.S. Revenue-Cutter *Tuscarora* gives chase although it is not clear if Seavey is in the *Nellie Johnson* or another small sailing vessel. In any case, as the chase nears

Point Betsie on the Michigan shore and night is falling, Seavey shoots out a buoy light with his trusty revolver and replaces it with an old lantern set on an empty beer barrel. Taking Seavey's buoy as the real thing, the *Tuscarora* runs aground. Just as the pirate captain is about to make his escape the combination of the cutter's bow gun and a sudden wind shift proved his undoing. Taken to Federal court in Chicago, Seavey is made to stand trial for the hijacking of the *Nellie Johnson*. Strangely however the owner of the schooner couldn't be found to press charges, leading some observers to think Seavey may have simply covered his bases very well and very permanently. Without conflicting testimony, the pirate spins a yarn about the owner giving him the schooner in payment of past debts and since they were old friends, a bill of ownership was not needed. With little choice, the judge released Seavey. Now the tale becomes very bizarre. On the theory that it takes a crook to catch a crook, Seavey is appointed a U.S. Marshal and ordered to close down the illegal whisky, venison and smuggling on Lake Michigan. The old pirate took to his new job with a passion, chasing miscreants and outlaws wherever he could find them. It is said he killed an illegal whisky peddler during a hellacious bar brawl in Naubinway with his powerful fists. No charges were ever filed. While Seavey died penniless in Peshtigo, Wisconsin in 1949 he left behind a legacy of sea-going tales.[3]

Beaver Island Pirates

The Beaver Island area of Lake Michigan was considered by many mariners a center of pirate activity during the "reign" of the infamous King James Jesse Strange. His story is an extraordinary one and to understand the charges of piracy the reader must comprehend the background of this amazing individual.

Born in the State of New York, he had tried careers as a teacher, lawyer, temperance lecturer, newspaper editor and postmaster before finding his true calling as Mormon prophet. In the confusion following the death the founder of the Mormon movement, Joseph Smith, in a gunfight, Brigham Young and Strang dueled for leadership of the group. Although Strang had been a Mormon for a mere five months he claimed to have a letter from Smith designating him as the leader should death take Smith. Whether Smith gave Strang a letter or not, the Mormon leader did think enough of the young convert, that he made Strang an Elder, in spite of his relative inexperience. Doubtless this rankled the always status conscious and egotistical Young. Eventually the council of elders selected

James Jesse Strang, the leader of the reputed Beaver Island pirates. Stonehouse Collection

Young as the new leader and refusing to be led by what he regarded as a false prophet, Strang split away with a small following. Today the mainstream Mormon Church does not recognize Strang as an early leader of Mormonism.

In 1848, Strang took his group to the Beaver Islands with the goal of establishing a colony in the isolation offered by the remote location. The main island of the group, Beaver Island, is about 13 miles long and six wide and is roughly 24 miles off the Michigan mainland. A number of smaller islands, Garden, High, Trout, Hog, Gull and Little Beaver comprise the entire group. Only Beaver Island had significant habitation.

This was a wild and wooly time on the Great Lakes. The vast deposits of iron and copper were just beginning to be explored on Lake Superior and the huge tracts of white pine were largely still unharvested on the western lakes. Rich stocks of whitefish and lake trout were caught and marketed without the interference of government agents. Timber pirates cruised Lake Michigan and set up portable sawmills on the beaches, cut what they thought they could get away with and moved on. Unscrupulous traders bartered illegal whiskey to the Indians for rich furs. In short it was a land of tremendous opportunity for a charismatic leader willing to take risks to carve out his own kingdom.

When Strang and his flock arrived only traders and fishermen occupied Beaver Island. His reception on the island was mostly negative. The inhabitants were well aware that the history of the Mormon movement was filled with conflict and bloodshed. In addition, having such a group on their island who thought themselves to be God's chosen people and everyone else was not, which by implication meant all others were damned to hell, was not good public relations. To make matters worse, Strang referred to his people as "Saints" and all others as "Gentiles."

Friction on the island over land, fishing and trade was constant. The beliefs of the Mormons that conflicted with the non-believers only added tension. Key among these contentious viewpoints was polygamy, which was deeply offensive to Christian values. Strang alone had four wives (two were sisters) and 14 children.

Did the Mormons pirates seize small vessels, plunder the cargo and murder the crews?
Stonehouse Collection

At first the Mormons were an annoying minority to the islanders. Over time more and more arrived and by 1850, seventy-four percent of the inhabitants were Mormon. In the spring election they gained the majority of public offices giving Strang political control of the area. Eventually more than 2,000 Mormons would inhabit the islands.

Inspired by divine revelation (what religious leader is not), on July 8, 1850 Strang had himself crowned "king" of Beaver Island. Although short of physical statue, he was not short of ego. His coronation was high theater, in more ways than one. One of his disciples was a former touring stage actor who arrived at the island with all of the costumes and sets needed to perform King Lear. Strang adopted them for the performance, appearing in a flowing robe complete with tin crown and glass jewels against a set depicting an English castle.

Strange also claimed it was revealed to him from heaven "God gave the islands of the Great Lakes to the Saints." This divine intervention neatly solved any minor legal hassles with deeds, plots and real property registry as well as making him a pirate of the first rank in terms of property theft! Unsure of how to best handle the growing problem on Beaver Island the authorities did nothing to "reign" in the Mormons. There were lots of accusations, but very little real proof! Never a modest person, Strang renamed the harbor "Saint James."

Under increasing Mormon pressure the remaining Gentiles on the island fled. Strang had given them ten days to convert to Mormonism or leave. Carrying what little they could, most settled in the Charlevoix, Michigan area. The *Green Bay Spectator* wrote that families were "...driven from Beaver Island in a state of destitution and misery by the so called "Latter Day Saints" because they refused to affiliate with Mormonism and refused to be participators in the crimes and enormities which have signalized the course of the followers of James J. Strang and shocked the moral sense of the entire country." The newspaper further claimed the Mormons were plundering local fishermen of their catch and equipment. It was reported there where three "ships" in the Mormon pirate navy, the *Dolphin*, *Emmlin* and *Seaman*.

A Buffalo newspaper stated that the Mormons had "driven off all of the fishermen from the island, stolen most of their property and made a business of appropriating whatever they can lay their hands on belonging to boats which call there."

It was during his period that Strang and his Mormons gained a reputation for thievery and piracy. Gentiles referred to them as a, "band of forty thieves" or "Society of the Illuminati," who sailed boats ready to assault any lakeside town should they discover the men gone and families left unprotected. At one point a group of Mormons was driven off by gunfire when settlers felt they were attempting to raid a settlement at Pine River on the mainland of Michigan.

When some Gentile fisherman were forced ashore by a gale on Beaver Island, a group of Mormon fishermen suggested killing them outright.

After considerable arguing amongst themselves, they merely robbed the fishermen and set them adrift.

On the plus side, Strang did lobby for lighthouse construction and was able to have the one at St. James Harbor on Beaver Island built. He wanted the light to make the harbor and island attractive to steamboats so he could sell them cordwood for fuel as well as general trade purposes. By virtue of his election to the Michigan Legislature, Strang was also able to have one of his men appointed as keeper of the Aux Galets Lighthouse (Skillagalee), on a small island east of the Beavers. As soon as the Mormon keeper took charge, lake captains started complaining he would extinguish the light and display false signals in an effort to lure ships on to the rocks so the Mormons could plunder them.

Strang was instrumental in having a light placed at St. James Harbor. Stonehouse Collection

Old-time sailors also told tales of ships disappearing with all hands near the Beaver Islands in the middle of summer. They simply "sailed into a crack in the lake." In the fall, storms could account for such losses, but in mid-summer it could only be the Mormon pirates. The old-timers said the Mormons boarded the ships, murdered the crews, stole the cargos and then burned the vessels so all evidence of the crime was hidden forever. Dead men would give no testimony in any earthly court.

C.R. Baker of Cleveland, a sailing captain from the period after the demise of Strang, remembered stories of Mormon pirates. "They would lure passing vessels on nearby shoals with fake lights, surprise the crews and take what they wanted of the cargo, then wreck the vessel."[4] One common technique to entice a ship into foul water was to tie a lit pine knot to a cow's horn to replicate the motion and light of a vessel safely at anchor. When the incoming ship discovered the trick, it was too late.

Cassier's Magazine of April 1899 carried the story of the brig *Robert Willis*. Bound from Chicago to Buffalo with a cargo of flour in the fall of 1850 she is said to have disappeared near the Beaver Islands. No trace of her was ever found and it was commonly thought she was the victim of Mormon pirates.[5] This vessel does not show up in common lists of Lake Michigan shipping losses however.

An article in the *Oswego Palladium* of December 30, 1876, reportedly by an old lake captain, sheds more light on the Beaver Island buccaneers. "The lakes have had their pirates in their day," remarked a weather beaten old hulk, and he rolled his quid to starboard as he cast a sidelong glance at three or four incredulous young fellows who were seated with him around a ship-chandler's store, spitting on the hearth."[6]

"You youngsters must not think because you can put two ends of a rope together and steer a vessel within four points of her course on a bright starlight night with the north star to look at, that you're sailors and know all about the lakes and schooners that have sailed them. When Bill Hayes, the Pacific pirate, sailed on the lakes he was not the only one who could steal a vessel or lure one on a rock bound coast. On the east shore of Lake Michigan were fellows who pretended to follow fishing for a living; but who, if the truth be known, made more by luring vessels on to the beach by false lights and robbing vessels and crews than they did by their nets and hooks."

"For several years the followers of Joe Smith, the Mormon, lived on Beaver Island, Lake Michigan and several vessels disappeared in that vicinity in mid-summer and neither they nor their crews were ever heard from. It was said the Mormons boarded becalmed vessels, murdered the crews, discharged the cargoes on the island and burned or scuttled the craft. Iron of a platter that could only have been of use on board vessels–travelers and such like, pork and beef barrel-heads of a brand that Mormons never bought–were found on the island by sailors and although an effort was made to ferret out the crime nothing ever came of it."

"In the fall of 1849 I was fore-the-mast on a little brig belonging to Buffalo. She was a trim little thing–she would serve as a yawl for the big hulks of today–clean and smart, but wet as a muskrat in spring time. As we neared the Beavers on our passage to Buffalo from Chicago, we caught it stiff and hard from the north and although the old man thought he could breast out the breeze, he found when we worked abreast of the island that the seas were too lumpy for our duck, as she was making dives that would do credit to a loon. It was late in the afternoon, well on towards the edge of nightfall and as the sky threatened snow, if the wind held, the old man concluded to go under the Beavers and let go our mud hooks until the storm had spent its fury."

"We made our lee, luffed the brig up into the eye of the wind, let go both anchors, paid out chain and soon the little brig was brought to a halt. After the canvas was furled, anchor watches were appointed and the rest of the crew turned in. About eight bells, midnight, Jack Stevens, who was on watch, shouted so loud that had we been mummies instead of men he must have awaken us. We did not scramble out very lively until the mate came to the scuttle and shouted, 'Tumble up here, you beef eating, lazy dogs,' for we thought that Jack had fallen asleep and tumbled off the forecastle deck and was frightened. When we heard the mate, a big brawny fellow, with a fist like a sledge- hammer, we turned out mighty smart."

"On reaching the deck we could see by the lights in the Mormon's houses that the brig was drifting fast toward the beach. A couple of smart fellows (modesty forbids that I should name one of them and not to be partial I'll say nothing more about the other) ran nimbly up the fore rigging and quicker than thought, cast the gaskets off the topsail and as the buntlines and clew lines had been let go on deck, rode down the topsail halyards till the yard was high as the double reef, which had been tied outside, would permit the yard to go."

"The jib was hoisted, as also was the peak of the mainsail and when the canvas filled, the brig picked up her feet and clawed off the shore like a green turtle after a sunning digs back to the water. The cause of the brig's dragging was plain to be seen as soon as the matter was investigated. Both chains from the windlass to the hawser pipes were, instead of being taut as they should have been had the anchors been at the ends, lying on the deck. When we pulled inboard the ends of the chain we found that both chains had been cut not far from the bow with steel saw–cut as clean as though the links had been held in a vise."

" It was evident that the Mormons had been at work and that had it not been for the timely discovery of Jack Stevens we would have been washed ashore and murdered. We stood off and on until morning and then the old man hove the brig to, lowered the yawl and went ashore to try to pry about and find the anchor if possible. He said nothing; he saw by the faces of the "Latter Day Saints" that they were disappointed at the turn things had taken on the brig."

"The brig never recovered the anchors and soon after the old man returned aboard we sailed away. The next season while on a schooner hailing from Ashtabula (I did not want to go on an Ashtabula vessel, for you could always tell an Ashtabula sailor by canvas patches on his trousers, but had to or skip for salt water). I saw the same two anchors the brig lost the season before at the Beavers. I spoke to the old man about it and he told me that he bought the anchors off the Mormons that spring. How did I know the anchors? Why I knew them by marks Tom Jones, a shipmate made while sitting on them spinning yards. Tom was a bouncing big fellow and he sat on the anchors so much that he marked them with hearts–canvas hearts he had sewed on the seat of this trousers." While the last part of this old sailor's rambling is a bit "tall," the basics of it, piracy at the Beavers does match similar tales."

Another old sailor told a story of murder and kidnap. "Old Strang was a bad one. One time there was a fine schooner anchored down here in Sand Bay to wait out a blow. She was a fine new schooner and when it came dark them Mormons came done on her and murdered the whole crew except the two daughters of the captain who were making the trip with him. Strang sees them and has them put in his boat and struck for the harbor with them but on the way one of the girls jumps overboard and they think she was drowned and went on but she swam back to the schooner and got a hold of the bob stays and there she was a' hanging when two Irishmen seeing the schooner and thinking she might be in trouble, rowed out and found the girl almost exhausted. Well, she told them her story and they took her back with them. One of the men was married and his wife took care of her and the fellow who wasn't married went to the nearest Mormon house and with two loaded pistols, stole a horse and rode as fast as it could run right up Strang's big palace and went in and made them all put up their hands except the girl who he told to go out and get on the horse and as soon as she did he backed out still keeping their hands up. There was old Strang and his five wives and some others and he got out and on the horse and rode with the girl. He later married her."[7]

Strang, in his newspaper *The Northern Islander*, always editorialized that such charges were all slanderous and politically motivated broadsides by his enemies. There simply was no truth to any of them. But then again there is the old saying, "where there is smoke, there is fire" and there was a lot of smoke over the Beavers.

As time passed, Strang seemed to be come more tyrannical and more and more of his followers became dissatisfied. He established a ten percent income tax for Saints and Gentiles. Saints bore it with some ill feeling, especially if they suspected any of the proceeds were being used more for Strang's good than theirs. Gentiles took a sharper view, feeling they owed him nothing. Failure to pay however often meant a public flogging. Strang also used a special group of "enforcers," men dedicated enough to impose Strang's law as needed. Sometimes it meant a fine, or whipping. And sometimes the objector just disappeared. The final straw apparently was when he issued a dress code for women requiring the wearing of a sort of bloomer costume; many resented it and refused to follow it. When one woman openly defied Strang he had her husband whipped. Revenge was carefully plotted and two men lured Strang from his house to the boat dock where they ambushed him, unleashing a fusillade of bullets at the Mormon leader. After lingering for a while, Strang died on July 8, 1856, six years to the day he had himself crowned "king."

When the Gentiles learned that Strang was dying, retribution against the oppressive Mormons was swift and bloody. A band of 50-60 well-armed Gentiles arrived at Beaver Island July 5-6 fueled by the fire of retribution. The Mormons were driven onto ships waiting in the harbor and transported to Detroit or Chicago, losing virtually all their possessions, similar to the situation when Strang drove the original settlers off the island. The Mormon era on Beaver Island was dead as were any accusations of piracy and murder.

There is a story told that when the original inhabitants returned to the island. One later recorded that, "...when people came back to the island there was still a great quantity of goods left stored away in some houses ...about a mile distant from the harbor. There were several boxes of shoes, crates of (china?) partly full, screens, cupboards, furniture, chairs and tables. One small house was almost full of stores. All these goods were new and did not appear to have been damaged. The people who came had helped themselves to all they wanted and wondered where all the goods came from. This helped make the rumor truer that vessels had been plundered and crews killed. One of our lake captains had told me he had a brother who was last seen at Beaver Harbor. The vessel and crew were never heard from again and no one knew their fate."[8]

Whether Strang and his Mormons were guilty of the charges of piracy and murder their enemies leveled at them or not is unknown. In today's more politically correct climate, the feeling is that the charges were trumped up by their enemies, who were jealous at the success of the "Saints." As usual, the truth is likely somewhere between the two extremes.

There is a persistent rumor of treasure on Beaver Island. As the old tale goes it is part of King Strang's ill-gotten gains and is "buried" in Fox Lake in a large chest. Over the years people have searched for it without result, but of course if someone did find it, is it wise to announce it to the world or just keep mum?

Pirate Ship Over the Falls

The term "piracy" was also sometimes grossly misused. Mansfield's History of the Great Lakes reports "in 1827 the schooner *Michigan*, having been condemned as unseaworthy, was announced in sensational handbills, which proclaimed "the pirate ship, *Michigan*, with a cargo of furious animals, will pass over the Falls of Niagara on the 8th of September, 1827." Entertainment was promised for all who might visit the Falls on that occasion, which would "for its novelty and the remarkable spectacle which it will present, be unequaled in the annals of infernal navigation." The *Michigan* was 136 ton burden. The event was witnessed by several thousand people."[9]

There was an attempt to send the barque *Detroit*, one of the British warships opposing Commodore Perry's Fleet at the Battle of Lake Erie in 1813 over the Falls too. The *Detroit* was sunk during the battle and raised in 1835-36. After a refit, she was used as a commercial trading vessel. When she became too rotten for further use, it was decided to send her over the Falls and the big day would be September 10, 1841. For reasons that are unclear, the second spectacle was never carried off.[10]

A fascination with sending vessels over Niagara Falls remained. The September 26, 1848 Schenectady (New York) Cabinet carried the following piece. "It is announced today in the *Niagara Falls Iris* by Mr. W. Conklin that he will send two vessels over the falls on the 29th of September. At 12 o'clock P.M., the "*Pirate*," a vessel of 100 feet in length, with several wild and tame animals on board as passengers, with appropriate flags and streamers, will be started from her moorings two miles above the falls. It is intended to have this craft so well secured, hatched down and all tight, that she will make the awful leap entire, with spars and rigging all standing. At 9 o'clock in the evening of the same day a fire ship loaded with all manner of combustibles, will be ready to slip her cables, showing a ship on fire, until after floating two miles through the rapids, she will make her fearful plunge in a blaze, forming one of the grandest scenes ever beheld at Niagara Falls."[11]

Confederate Pirates On the Lakes

Whether ships operating in support of the traitorous Confederate States of America are truly "pirate" ships or not is open to interpretation. In my view they certainly are. For an officer of the United States to forsake a scared oath to "support and defend the constitution of the United States against all enemies, foreign and domestic" let alone fight for slavery, are actions that place him beyond the bounds of the rule of law and clearly into piracy.

During the Civil War the Great Lakes represented a tremendous opportunity for the rebels to cause mischief for the United States. The Great Lakes were the industrial heartland of America and ominously, were virtually unguarded. Secretary of War Stanton recognized the peril and warned the area's governors of possible ship borne raids by rebels based in Canada. There was a special concern that the raiders could use a ship to free the thousands of Confederate prisoners at Johnson's Island, Lake Erie.

In early 1863 a Confederate officer concocted a desperate plan involving seizing the gunboat *USS Michigan*, which would then be used to free the prisoners. The *Michigan* was the only armed U.S. vessel on the Great Lakes and therefore exerted tremendous power. The scheme was so far developed that the crew from the burned

The USS Michigan, *the key Union vessel on the Great Lakes.* *Stonehouse Collection*

The small steamer Island Queen *was part of the Confederate plot.*
Stonehouse Collection

Confederate steamer *Virginia*, defeated in the famous duel with the *Monitor*, were designated to form the bulk of the Confederate force. Before the plot was set into motion, Confederate President Jefferson Davis vetoed it.

Months later the plan was resurrected and a crew of 22 rebels traveled to Nova Scotia aboard a blockade-runner. Eventually 32 more men were recruited from escaped Confederate prisoners living in Canada. A secret message was smuggled to the prisoners at Johnson's Island warning them of the attempt. The reckless enterprise reached the point of the rebels buying passage on a steamer to Chicago, which they planned to seize and use to capture the *Michigan*. Before the men left Montreal however, Canadian authorities warned the United States government of the plot. Apparently Canada did not want its neutrality compromised by a bunch of wild-eyed slavers. Disheartened, the pirates returned to the Southern states.

Not to be discouraged by failure, the Confederates again resurrected the scheme the following year, although with a new wrinkle. A rebel officer named John Cole, operating in the guise of a Yankee businessman was to ingratiate himself with the *Michigan's* officers while the ship was moored off Johnson's Island. At the designated time he would either get them drunk or drug them such that they would be unable to take action. A steamer earlier seized by a Confederate crew under the command of John Beall would then come along side and take over the gunboat. Once in command of the *Michigan*, the confederate crew would use her powerful guns to force the release of the Johnson's Island prisoners. A quick run to nearby Sandusky, Ohio would allow the gunboat to capture enough steamers to transport the prisoners to Cleveland. Thousands of rebels suddenly appearing in this bastion of the Union would spread panic throughout the North. Eventually the prisoners could seize trains and reach West Virginia, Virginia and finally back to Southern lines.

The plan was set into motion. Cole soon became friendly with the *Michigan* officers. Failing to get the men drunk, he attempted to bribe them with $2,000 each. They refused his offer, their loyalty being too strong for such temptation.

The propeller Philo Parsons. *She was key to the plot.* Stonehouse Collection

Beall's part of the plot continued on track, for a time anyway. He and his men seized the steamer *Philo Parsons* and proceeded to Kelly's Island, five miles distant from Johnson's Island, where they waited for Cole's signal. The *Philo Parsons* was short of fuel so Beall ran her to nearby Bass Island to load cordwood. Unfamiliar with the area or fueling routine however, Beall was startled when the small steamer *Island Queen* lay along side. Seeing Union soldiers aboard the small ship, he panicked and opened fire, easily overwhelming them. The soldiers were simply troops on leave and had the misfortune to be in the wrong place at the wrong time. Since he didn't have men enough to guard prisoners, he abandoned them on Bass Island.

When Beall failed to receive a signal from Cole indicating the *Michigan* officers were out of action, he knew the plot failed and ran the *Philo Parsons* up the Detroit River to Sandwich, Ontario near Windsor. Before abandoning the steamer the rebels looted and burned her. Most of the Confederates escaped before Canadian authorities arrived.

It was well Beall had not attacked the *Michigan* since the details of the plan had been revealed by an unidentified Canadian to Union officers. Rather than acting immediately however, the *Michigan's* commander merely arrested Cole and waited patiently for the attack when he could capture the entire nest of rebels. When he realized the assault was off, he tried to catch the steamer at sea, but she escaped to Canadian waters two hours before the *Michigan* arrived.

In early November 1864 the captain of the *Michigan* was warned of another desperate Confederate design. It was claimed Confederate agents purchased the 130-foot Canadian package and freight steamer *Georgian* and armed her, intending to attack U.S. cities and capture or destroy American flag vessels. Others claimed she too would attempt to free Confederate prisoners at Johnson's Island. The general paranoia over the ship was fueled by her builders, who were strong Confederate sympathizers who had earlier sold a vessel for use as a blockade-runner along the Confederate coast. Authorities in Buffalo were so concerned they mounted cannon on two small tugs intending to defend the port against the *Georgian*. There were other scares about raids by rebel sympathizers from Windsor across the Detroit River into Detroit and from Sarnia to Port Huron. The uncertainly over the *Georgian* only fanned the flames of hysteria. However the Union managed to infiltrate a crewman aboard the *Georgian* who loyally kept the *Michigan* informed of the ships intentions. When the *Michigan* eventually ran the *Georgian* down on the open lake and searched her, no arms were found. None-the-less, the *Michigan* still kept her under observation, especially through the onboard spy.

When the *Georgian* was reportedly fitted with a ram during winter lay-up at Collingwood, Ontario, U.S. authorities strongly protested to Canada. In response the Canadians seized the *Georgian* and turned her over to the U.S. The *Georgian* incident ended the scare of Confederate pirates on the Great Lakes after the war ended. The *Georgian* went into commerce and eventually was lost in Georgian Bay in 1888.[12]

Captain Bully Hayes

Bully Hayes was one of those figures it is impossible to completely define. Some sources claim he was the reincarnation of a true buccaneer from the golden age of piracy in the rolling and rugged Spanish Main. Others allege he was a trustworthy sailor who was the victim of circumstance and was as honest as the day is long. As a writer I can only base my conclusions on the available sources and the weight of history seems to be toward the pirate instead of the preacher.

The Great Lakes proved a fine training ground for perhaps the greatest pirate ever to sail the wide expanse of the Pacific Ocean, including the magnificent Francis Drake! His name was William Henry Hayes and he was a native son of the Sweetwater Seas. As with most characters larger than life, his formative years are open to speculation. It is believed he was born in 1822 (one source says 1829) in Cleveland, Ohio. His father Henry Hayes ran a saloon on the banks of the Cuyahoga River. Fur traders, Indians, land lookers, lumberjacks and sailing captains all passed through the portals of the saloon. Hayes received little formal schooling but was able to read and write and do simple math.

Captain Bully Hayes, the terror of the South Seas. Stonehouse Collection

The young man soaked up tales of adventure, mystery, theft and murder like a dry sponge takes water. But of all the characters that he ran across, it was the sea captains that most impressed him. With the freedom of the open seas, all matter of exploits were possible. He also witnessed fights of epic proportions as his father's customers settled differences of opinion with fists, knives, axes or guns. It was strictly no holds barred frontier style brawling, no quarter asked or given.

One writer claimed his reputation was such that, "They would never have got Hayes stumbling down the stone steps of the Pirate's stairs at Wapping before being slung in chains at Blackwall Point no, nor would he have sat biting his nails at Newgate like that plucked crow, Captain Kidd, waiting and waiting in vain for the King's pardon which never came. Bully Hayes would have fooled his gaoler; taken tea with the Governor of the prison; asked the chaplain to pray for him, emptied the prison safe and then vamoosed with the Governor's daughter–and what's more, he'd have dropped a donation into the poor-box before leaving."[13]

By age 20, Hayes was the captain of his own vessel sailing the lakes. Observers said he was a handsome young man, a blonde and blue-eyed giant rippling with muscles. His jovial and easy-going nature allowed him to easily "bilk" those unaware of his true motives. He was a "sharp" operator and his trips always returned a handsome profit. Sometimes his dealings were on the "shady" side and there were accusations of outright piracy, but the times were too wild for law and order to restrain his ambition.

Hayes was also a gambler, brawler and womanizer. Like many sailors the world over, he had a "squeeze" in every port. Sailing from Cleveland, he helped establish its reputation as one of the great hell-raising ports on the Great Lakes.

Eventually Hayes found a wife in Cleveland but if anyone thought a wife would slow him down, they were wrong. A short while later he was reportedly involved in a horse stealing scheme that drew a little too much attention from the authorities and he was forced to flee ending up in San Francisco with a second woman who would also become his wife. Another source claims he went first to New York City where he learned his deepwater sailing skills as a bucko mate on a down-easter voyaging round Cape Horn to San Francisco with a load of gold seeking 49ers.[14]

Hayes found San Francisco to be an exhilarating city. The gold rush was in full swing and the streets were awash with money and adventure. Abandoned ship's hulls served as hotels and canvas "buildings" were everywhere. Miners, desperadoes, Mexican cowboys and sailors "flying free" were thick as flies. And most important, law and order was sadly lacking. To the west spread the broad Pacific Ocean, a canvas on which he would paint a fantastic series of adventures.

Before departing however, he left part of himself in the city, his right ear! It seems he was involved in a high stakes poker game in the cuddy of one of the deserted ships with miscreants as slippery as himself. As he slowly turned up his cards after being called on a bet, tension weighed heavy at the table. Still somewhat wet behind the ears, he was caught using marked cards. Quick as lightning a razor sharp Bowie knife stabbed into his right hand, pinning it and the card to the table. Blood oozed silently on to the varnished wood. With cobra like speed, Hayes' left arm shot out and his hand grabbed the knife wielder's neck with a powerful clench. As his fingers tightened, the man's eyes bulged from their sockets. When it was clear Hayes intended to choke the man to death, the other players tore him free. Grabbing the knife, he threw it across the room where it buried itself deep into the opposite wall. Another player drew his six-gun and kept Hayes under it's threatening barrel as the others tied him up with some rope they found in the cabin. When the fuming men threatened to lynch him from the ship's yard as a lesson to other card cheats, Hayes just laughed in their faces! Yelling with rage, a player yanked the knife out of the wall and in nearly the same motion, neatly sliced off Hayes' right ear. Howling in rage and pain, Hayes rose up and burst his bonds, then swung a mighty right arm, knocking his attacker out cold with a single sledgehammer like punch. The other players ran for their lives, with a wild Hayes fast on their heels. Ever after, Hayes took special care to keep his hair long enough to hide the missing ear.[15]

Illustration for a book cover on the adventures of Captain Bully Hayes of Cleveland. Stonehouse Collection

In what would be a scheme Hayes repeated again and again, he made a deal with a San Francisco merchant to sail his ship to the Orient on a trading voyage. However when he reached Singapore he promptly sold ship and cargo pocketed the money and never looked back. It is claimed he repeated the swindle of selling ships and cargos he didn't own 15 times throughout his career.

He soon became known as Captain Bully Hayes and his reputation as a pirate was recognized far and wide across the Pacific. He was an extraordinary navigator and very skillful sailor. When working his way through coral reefs he usually conned his ship from the masthead, shouting directions to the wheelsman below.

Hayes was reportedly involved in a galaxy of illegal activities, including forging early Hawaiian postage stamps. He was regularly engaged in "black birding" kidnapping South Seas islanders to work on farms, ranches and mines in Australia, New Zealand, Fiji and South America. In theory the islanders would be paid for their labor and returned to their homes but in practice this rarely happened. It was said he cleaned out entire islands of natives, carrying them to their eventual deaths. He often relied on guile rather than brute force. On occasion he baited his ship with pretty island girls and anchored in a quiet lagoon. When the men swam out to the ship to "socialize" he captured them. Working closely with Chinese pirates he sometimes hauled cargos of coolies to unknown but illegal destinations. When the market was high, he filled his ship with shrunken heads and even ran guns and ammunition to revolting Maoris when the price was right.

Women of the South Seas. Stonehouse Collection

Kidnapping was also in his bag of tricks. He held tribal chiefs for a ransom of copra (oil bearing coconut husks) when things were otherwise slow. Sometimes he swept down on the pearl fisheries, appropriating both pearls and the girls. At sea he sometimes repainted his ship to fool authorities. They never knew when or where he would strike next.

On occasion he stole ships right out of port, loaded to the gunwales with goods he obtained from local merchants on credit. Of course the merchants were never paid. In today's parlance, he left "bad paper" across the entire Pacific.

It was claimed Hayes married three times, never bothering to obtain a divorce, and had several children, not counting any native wives or off spring. He must have been a Mormon in the tradition of Brigham Young!

A former U.S. consul for the Pacific later wrote, "...this pirate could when he liked, assume a courteous behavior and address positively fascinating and calculated to deceive even the greatest skeptic. Although self-educated, he could converse fluently and cleverly on all ordinary topics and if he were judged from the his handsome and gentlemanly personal appearance, the lie direct would be given to the multitudinous reports of his lawless habits.

"To see in the year 1876 an elderly well-dressed man, in missionary black frock-coat and tall hat, with a flowing gray beard sweeping his expansive chest, above which smiled a handsome and benevolent countenance fit for a bishop and be told that the entire person was that of

Island schooners of the type Bully Hayes mastered. Stonehouse Collection

an undoubted pirate who was far from being free from suspicion of having committed murder, would astonish any man in his sober senses: yet such was "Bully Hayes" in his best rig on shore in the Colonies."

Hayes was killed on March 31, 1877 while sailing aboard the yacht *Lotus* bound for Samoa. A storm was roaring in from the northwest and a tremendous sea running. Hayes and a cook called the Dutchman were on watch. When the Dutchman failed to obey an order Hayes gave him, he moved as if to strike the cook. The night was black as sin, with loud claps of thunder booming overhead. Only the occasional flash of lightning provided any illumination at all. As Hayes charged, the Dutchman pulled a revolver and repeatedly fired at Hayes. How many times the old pirate was hit isn't known. Although it did stagger him some, he kept coming at the cook who finally smashed him over the head with the tiller bar, crushing his skull. Hayes fell overboard and disappeared in to the thundering seas. He died as hard as he had lived.

Hayes has been the subject of at least a couple of films. The last was "Nate and Hayes" made in 1983 starring Tommy Lee Jones, Michael O'Keefe and Jenny Seagrave. It is described as "A swash-buckling adventure, which takes place in the mid-1800s on the south Pacific islands where bloody raids and battles were once the rule of the day. A notorious buccaneer and a young reverend team up against the villainous rule of a cut-throat gang." It seems like Hollywood has made Hayes into a goody-two shoes–the old pirate must be spinning in the deep! From the waters of Great Lakes to the broad Pacific, Bully Hayes was a pirate's pirate![16]

Flying the Jolly Roger

There was one Great Lakes vessel that became an authentic Caribbean carrier of the skull and crossbones. The ship in question is the *C.H. Hackley*, built in Milwaukee in 1868. After a productive career sailing the Inland Seas, she went salt water in 1916. World War I was raging in Europe and the demand for shipping, any shipping was extreme. During this period a number of Great Lakes ships went salt water and many were lost there. The *Hackley* soon became a normal part of the lumber trade in the Caribbean Sea. By the 1920s time had passed the old wind wagon by and she spent most of her time laid up. It was during this period however she served as the pirate ship in the annual recreation of the capture of Tampa, Florida by the infamous pirate Jose Gaspar. So for a time, she was a real pirate ship. By 1935 she was too far-gone for even this light duty and was taken out and sunk, a noble end for a fine Great Lakes vessel.[17]

The Fish Pirates

Fish were a major part of the Great Lakes scene. They were an extremely valuable commodity and the source of a great deal of conflict, especially between U.S. and Canadian interests.

In the 1830s Detroit was the largest market for salted fish on the lakes. Rapid methods of transporting fresh fish were still a long way in the future and the best way of preserving the catch was still salting. Concurrently, Toronto was developing into a major Canadian market for fish. Both governments tried to manage commercial fishing in their national waters, but American fishermen were very aggressive and constantly poached in Canadian territory causing constant friction between the two governments. Much of the pound net fishing in Canada's Lake Ontario water was done by Americans and U.S. companies controlled the fishing in eastern Lake Superior, including that in Canadian waters. In the 1880s the poaching became more difficult when Canada started forceful fisheries patrols. If caught, the poacher could lose his entire outfit, boat included. To circumvent such direct action American companies sometimes sent their collection vessels across the border and purchased the catch of local fishermen at a higher rate than their own Canadian buyers would pay. This action worked to bind the fishermen to U.S. interests at the expense of the Canadian ones.[18]

American companies also trespassed on Federal waters banned to commercial fishing. In 1892, the A. Booth Packing Company, the major U.S. fishing operator on the Great Lakes established an outfit at Whitefish Point in eastern Lake Superior. Not only did they work the grounds at Caribou and Michipicoten Islands, both in Canadian waters, they also made a deal with the lightkeeper at Whitefish Point to set nets in the

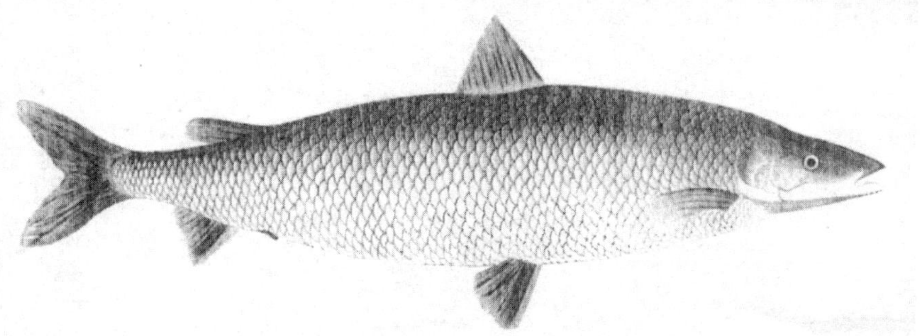

A whitefish, the "gold standard" of the Great Lakes commercial fishery. Stonehouse

Early Great Lakes sail powered fishing vessels.
Stonehouse Collection

lighthouse reservation waters. Previously the lightkeeper maintained the sole right to fish there, to the extend of having a U.S. lighthouse tender drive off a competing company trying to infringe on his domain. In his agreement with Booth the company's men used the keeper's nets and boats, splitting the catch with him.[19]

Canadian fishing regulations were typically tighter than American ones. This caused resentment among the Canadian fishermen. It was common on Lake Ontario for the Canadians to watch American tugs hauling in rich catches on their side of the line while they were prevented from fishing by restrictive regulation. It was even worse when U.S. boats wandered over the line and pulled catches out of Canadian waters. As angry as they were about the poaching, they were powerless to stop them. Government enforcement vessels had to catch the perpetrators red-handed and that rarely happened.

Another American threat to the Canadian fishermen was the huge log rafts towed through the fishing grounds. Some rafts were a half-mile across and usually moved at a bare mile an hour. Typical raft tows ran from Georgian Bay across Lake Huron to Michigan sawmills. Behind they left a mass of torn nets. Compensation was unheard of and the fishermen took the loss.

Detroit garbage scows regularly dumped their filthy loads in Canadian waters off Amherstburg, Ontario and much of the refuse eventually drifted ashore fouling the lakeshore. The dumpsite was also perilously close to the city water intake adding the potential of introducing typhoid and other fevers to the populace. An Amherstburg customs agent attempted to energize the government in Ottawa to take action but received no response. Taking another tack, he worked out a deal with the local constable, health officer, a rich American yacht owner and most important, the captain of the government fisheries cruiser *Petrel*. When the garbage scow, which was owned by the Detroit Sanitary Company, arrived in Canadian waters, the *Petrel* promptly steamed out and intercepted her. A quick shot across the bow with the one-pounder halted the scow and she was arrested and her crew jailed for breaking bulk without clearing customs and dumping garbage without a permit. Eventually the men were released after a stiff fine of $450.

Taking heart from the Amherstburg success, the Canadians arrested an American crew and seized the vessel for dumping garbage from Buffalo in waters just off Fort Erie, Ontario. Again heavy fines were levied.[20]

Canadian authorities worked aggressively to enforce fishing regulations and exercise national sovereignty. While the cruiser *Petrel* was armed with a one-pounder cannon, she also had rifles, pistols and even cutlasses, surely sufficient firepower to apprehend illegal fishermen. In the spring of 1894 the *Petrel* arrived in Lake Erie and went immediately to work, seizing four tugs operating illegally and 127 nets. A major incident developed when the cruiser seized several sportsman's yachts off Pelee Island. The boats were filled with wealthy sport fishermen from Chicago, Boston, New York and Cincinnati. None of the men had a Canadian license. Fishermen and yachts were taken to Amherstburg where fines were levied. The episode caused quite a stir with the image of a heavily armed warship bravely capturing helpless fishermen brandishing bamboo fishing poles, causing both laughter and anger. *The Detroit News* ran a cartoon titled "the Battle of Lake Erie" lampooning the entire affair.[21]

The busy *Petrel* also had time to run up to Lake Superior and seize skiff caught fishing in Canadian waters. The Canadians enlisted the aid of lighthouse keepers to report on violators and these extra eyes were important in several seizures.

The "fish war" heated up at the turn of the century, especially on Lake Erie. More and more American boats crossed the line to set nets in Canadian waters. Fish prices were up and demand high, making the enterprise well worth the slight risk of apprehension. Most of the boats were running out of Buffalo, Cleveland, Sandusky, Erie and Ashtabula. In

The United States Revenue Marine Service cutter Tuscarora *likely patrolled the American side of the Great Lakes during the fish wars.* USCG

defense of the American poachers, there was no clearly marked black line floating on the water. Nor were electronic navigation aids like GPS, Loran or radar available to assure an accurate location. In addition, if the fish could cross the border, why not the fisherman?

In 1898, the *Petrel* seized hundreds of gill nets and two years later the American tug *Kate Wilson*. American boats were aggressive with entire fleets crossing the line by a mile or more at the same time. When the *Petrel* appeared, the tugs warned each other by whistle and as they were usually faster than the cruiser, easily escaped the government boat. Canadians also believed the Americans had a paid agent to warn them of the *Petrel's* movements.

In 1903 the Canadians captured three tugs and recovered over 1000 nets. Some fishermen responded to the aggressive tactics by arming themselves with rifles. In spite of the increasing hostilities, there were no casualties until 1904 when the Canadian government cruiser *Vigilant*, a faster ship then *Petrel*, ran down the American boat *Grace M.* while she was attempting to escape. Two of the boat's crew drown in the incident. While all involved realized it was an accident, they also recognized the obvious potential for further death. Eventually the U.S. sent a revenue cutter, likely the *Tuscarora*, to assist with enforcement.

The poaching problem was never really solved until the Great Lakes fish population crashed and such activities were no longer economical.

The Fox Gang

Timber pirates were not always large operators plundering hundreds of acres at a single cutting. Sometimes they were small operators who were just as vicious in their approach and as intimidating to the forces of the law.

In 1849 Two Rivers, Wisconsin was a small village on the west shore of Lake Michigan. While it later would become an important commercial fishing center, in the early days its fame rested on lumbering. It was on the edge of the forest containing white pine, hemlock, oak, maple, beech and birch. The lumberjacks and early fishermen were one and the same. In the summer they fished and when the fall gales came calling, they went into the woods to "make wood" as the old expression went.

Normally the men made shingles or fish barrels. Both were hand made. Shingles were split one at a time from a block of pine called a bolt and then trimmed into final shape with a hatchet and drawknife. The bolts were cut from the very best timber with straight grain and unblemished. Well-made shingles or staves were more valuable than cut timber so were a preferred market product. The bolts were cut in the woods during the winter then rafted down river to the village where they were made into shingles or staves. Bolts were invariably cut from government timber by the river pirates who ranged a mile or so out from the banks looking for choice timber. When the bolts were cut, they were stacked along the river until spring.

The Two River pirates were a wild bunch. Old timers remembered as long as they had money they terrorized the town. The men were usually drunk on "forty-rod" whisky and out for trouble. The gang had been "working" the area for several years and the townspeople were getting mighty tired of them.

The worst of the pirates was a man named Fox. Once he and his gang brought a raft to town and had coins jingling in their pockets, it was "party time." He and the roughly dozen men accompanying him frightened the entire town, sending honest citizens into hiding. Wild with drink, they sometimes attacked innocent people and damaged hard won property. When the money ran out, Fox led his crew back into the woods and in a couple of weeks they returned with another raft of stolen bolts and the cycle repeated itself. The gang didn't limit itself to stealing government timber. If they found a loose log, they promptly stole it too, regardless of whose mark was on it. Once the marked end was cut off, no one was the wiser and if there was a protest, the gang just whaled the tar out of the complainer or tossed him into the river.

In the spring of 1949 the town decided the Fox gang had to go. When election time came a man named McCollum was elected constable and given orders to solve the problem. He was told to either make the gang behave or get rid of them! The new constable bided his time.

The gang soon brought another raft to town and headed off for their typical spree. After staggering around for a while they passed the little brewery owned by Edward Mueller. A small flagpole was in front with a flag flying from the top. One of the revelers bet Fox a keg of beer he couldn't climb the pole. Fox took the bet and half way up the pole toppled over, dropping him squarely into a mud puddle causing the gang to break into gales of laughter. Just then a flock of geese waddled by attracted by the noise and began to gabble loudly. Claiming the geese were laughing at him, Fox grabbed a club and started killing the birds just as the brewer, who owned the birds arrived on the scene. He rushed to stop the slaughter but was struck senseless by Fox's club. The gang promptly fled, fading into parts unknown.

When he recovered from his attack, the brewer went to the justice of the peace and swore out a warrant for Fox's arrest. Warrant in hand, Constable McCollum rounded up a posse and went looking for Fox, eventually locating him hiding in a small shanty along the river. Entering alone, the constable found Fox sitting on a stool nearly stupefied with booze. Shaking Fox's shoulder, the constable told him he was under arrest and to come along quietly. Fox stood up slowly, as if to follow the constable, then lashed out with a knife. The constable was ready for the attack and jumped aside, but the blade still gave him a bad wound. Running out the door, Fox encountered one of the posse members, a giant German mill worker named Linstedt, who told him, "drop the knife, or I will kill you." Fox dropped his knife and was lead away to court. While in court Fox was very quiet and submissive, apparently remorseful of his actions. When he asked to go to the privy he was allowed to do so, but only under guard. The night was so dark however, that once outside he slipped away from his guard and disappeared. Neither he nor his gang was seen again.[22]

Timber Pirates

The greatest piracy on the Great Lakes didn't involve gold, silver or jewels but instead wood, white pine to be exact. It wasn't just hijacking a cargo or two of it either. It was a theft unprecedented in scale or value and some of the most prominent names in the lumber industry were involved.

It began simply enough. When the eastern forests were cutoff, the lumbermen moved west to the massive pine forests of the Great Lakes. Settlers were coming west too and they viewed the forests both as an impediment to settlement, seeing the pressing need to clear off the woods so the land could be used for agriculture and as an inexhaustible supply of wood for construction of homes and fences. The lumbermen viewed the forests also as an inexhaustible supply of wood but for resale not personal use. They knew there was a ready market in the western prairies as well as the burgeoning Midwest.

The problem was neither settler nor lumberman generally owned the land. Usually it was still part of the Federal domain. However both harvested the forests without a second thought.

Stealing timber was an old American tradition. In colonial days the British government basically claimed all non-privately owned land. The Royal Navy was always in desperate need for quality timber for building and repairing ships, especially replacing the critical masts. The great forests of the Old World were long gone and New World forests were expected to provide the vital timber. The Surveyor General of His Majesty's Woods in North America would inspect the forests and mark a "broad arrow" on all trees suitable for masts. The official used a hatchet to chop three marks in the rough shape the arrowhead and maintained an inventory of their location. If colonists stole a marked tree, he was to prosecute.

The colonists saw the situation differently. They wanted the timber to build their communities and they would take it regardless of the king's wishes. Everywhere, from the forests of Maine, Massachusetts, New York, Maryland, Pennsylvania, Carolina and Georgia colonists stole royal timber. When the king's agents tried to prevent it, they were treated harshly. After the American Revolution the federal government assumed ownership of all unassigned land, including the timber rights. It made little difference. The public saw the forests as inexhaustible and the timber theirs for the taking, whether for private use or company profit.

The favorite technique the timber pirates used was known as a "round forty" or "rubber forty." The company would obtain the legal right to cut a forty-acre section of timber in a publicly unassigned forest. The right to do so could be acquired in a variety of ways including outright purchase, homesteading, or declaring their intention to purchase (but never doing so). The company then cut the timber from their forty plus all those around it and those around them etc. If challenged they argued that the survey lines were poorly marked or untrue. In this way crews from Chicago tanneries harvested hemlock bark in western Michigan. Timber men cut round forties in the white pine in western Michigan, along the Chippewa, Red Cedar and Wisconsin Rivers and on Green Bay in Wisconsin and later on the St. Croix River in Minnesota. One company made off with two million board feet on Thunder Bay on Lake Huron and others stole similar amounts from the Menominee River in the Upper Peninsula of Michigan. Canadian companies also profited from the unprotected forests, crossing the St. Marys River to cut Michigan timber and hauling huge rafts of timber from eastern Michigan across Lake Huron.[23]

The government had essentially four possible courses of action. First it could send an army in to protect the forests but this was plainly impossible. There was too much forest and too few soldiers. It could create a strong forest department in the government to manage the timber. It could also ignore the entire problem and just let anyone, farmer or lumberman, take what they wanted. Finally it could establish an inadequate system of management that would not seriously hamper the larceny of the forests. The last course was what the government did. One historian referred to the result as the "Era of Magnificent Plundering."[24]

Knowledge of the forest thievery was not a secret but the public was more focused on the great issues of the day including the increasing stress

Timber for the American Navy was a vital concern for the new nation.
Stonehouse Collection

between northern and southern states, slavery, temperance and women's rights. Cutting a few too many trees wasn't seen as a pressing problem.

Shortly after the birth of the new nation Congress recognized the need to assure a steady supply of quality wood for the Navy and established live oak preserves in South Carolina and Georgia. Live oak was incredibly tough and vital for warship ribs and knees among other uses. Later preserves were added in Florida, Alabama and Louisiana. All were plundered. Finally in 1831 on the urging of the Secretary of the Navy, Congress passed legislation providing for "the punishment of offenses committed in cutting, destroying, or removing live-oak" and any other trees on either naval reservations or any other lands of thc United States.[25] This became the basis for subsequent government legal actions to protect timber. While the initial thrust of the law was the preservation of live oak, a later court case extended it to include white pine, which was the primary target of the Great Lakes timber pirates.

The Interior Department was created in 1849 partly to manage the western expansion and the General Land Office transferred from Treasury

Much of the forest of the Great Lakes was plundered by the timber barons. Stonehouse Collection

to the new department. Under the Treasury Department little effective action had been taken to prevent timber plunder. The new Land Commissioner was more of an activist and in 1851 on his own authority, sent agents into logging areas to find trespassers, provide information to U.S. attorneys and Marshals to promulgate arrest, seize the stolen timber and follow the subsequent legal proceedings. There were few agents and they were poorly paid, but the results were impressive. Soon 40 cases were pending in Michigan, seven in Minnesota and an equal number in Wisconsin.[26]

Although the agents had only scratched the surface of the plundering, the howl the lumbermen and their interests put up echoed all the way to Washington! Midwest newspapers screamed about, "Unmitigated oppression." Catching "real thieves" was fine, but certainly not respectable lumber companies. The timber interest bootlicker ward heelers like Senator Dodge of Iowa and Congressmen Eastman of Wisconsin and Sibley of Minnesota among other lake states politicians railed against the heavy-handed outrages against their "honest and law obeying" constituents. To obscure the wholesale thieving of the lumber barons, they purposely spoke about the need of settlers to harvest the forest to build homes etc., giving the impression the government agents were going after the "little guy."

In Michigan, Agent Isaac Willard stirred up a nest of hornets. To better understand the scope of the problem he used a small boat to run the coast from the Wisconsin border at Menominee, Michigan to the Grand and Muskegon Rivers in the Lower Peninsula. Enroute he investigated all rivers and bays and gathered evidence of the widespread plundering. After covering the roughly 600 miles of coastline, he prepared the warrants of the arrest of the violators. He found virtually no one in the area would support his efforts. The more he tried to enforce the law, the greater the resistance.

The timber interests were prepared to defend their businesses with deadly force. Willard's life was threatened by lumbermen and one deputy land agent murdered. Three others died under suspicious circumstances. Tough as nails, he refused to bend. In 1853 Willard, never a man to back down from a difficult job, went directly into the viper's den. Manistee, Michigan, on the east shore of Lake Michigan was the home of the worst of the thieves. Refusing several bribes, he demanded the companies quit stealing the timber and surrender that illegally cut. They refused. When he seized the cut lumber it was stolen back by armed mobs or burned. If he tried to sell it, there were no bidders. The political heat increased when the *Chicago Tribune* advocated resistance by force. Mass meetings were held and threats and violence demanded in opposition to the government. This was nothing short of armed rebellion against the government. Willard was not intimidated. Several of the timber thieves were arrested but promptly freed from jail by mobs of angry lumberjacks and mill workers. When the thieves were placed on vessels, the sailors released them.[27] Considering that many sailors worked in the lumber trade during the winter when the lakes were frozen, this isn't surprising.

At one point Willard auctioned the timber he had seized in Grand Haven but could only get half the value with the sale contingent on the government delivering the timber to Chicago. When he arrived at Grand Haven with several vessels to load the timber, lumbermen armed with clubs and guns drove him off. Back in Chicago he obtained warrants for the arrest of those lumbermen he could identify. On return to Grand Haven he and his marshals arrested the men who commanded lumber boats in the harbor. One, Captain Higgie, said he would willing go to jail if given a couple of hours to arrange for the safety of his boat, *Whirlwind*. Once aboard however he started loading the seized timber. Higgie was arrested again and placed with Captain Hammond of the schooner *Barnum* on one of Willard's charter vessels but the crew allowed both to escape. Captain Clark of the *Irwin*, also released to arrange for the safety of his vessel, took on a load of timber and fled to his friends in Chicago. Willard had him arrested there but the judge released him claiming timber stealing was not an offense warranting jail. When all was finished Willard was able to deliver less than a sixth of the seized timber to Chicago. The lumbermen burned the remainder.[28]

Chicago played a major role in the lumber trade with Milwaukee a close second. When the sandbar blocking the entrance to the Chicago River was dredged in 1835 and canal to the Illinois River opened, the city became the major gateway for lumber. The destruction of much of the city in the 1871 fire vastly increased the local market.

Not to be outmaneuvered, Willard called on the assistance of the U.S. Navy in the form of the gunboat *U.S.S. Michigan*. The iron-hulled vessel, the first iron vessel built for the U.S. Navy, began its career in 1844. Home ported in Erie, the well-armed craft normally cruised from there to Lakes Michigan and Huron showing the flag and rending assistance to vessels in distress. Still one of, if not the, fastest vessel on the Great Lakes she would be critical in fighting the timber pirates. Virtually all of the stolen timber, either in the form of milled lumber or logs, had to be transported by water. Powerful tugs towed huge log booms over the open lakes to the mills and steamers and schooners carried the milled lumber to market. Often a single steamer towed several schooners, increasing the speed and efficiency of delivery.

The U.S. Navy gunboat Michigan. *Stonehouse Collection*

A second government vessel, the U.S. Revenue Cutter Service *Ingham*, was also available for support. However she was a 115-foot topsail schooner with little firepower and considering the nature of the resistance, more of a hindrance than asset. The *Ingham* was apparently not very unsuccessful even as a Revenue Cutter. Built in Erie in 1849, she was sold in Detroit in 1856, a very short working career.[29]

The *Michigan* was the only way the government could project power on the lakes. The lumber interests knew this and there is evidence they attempted to neutralize it by direct attack.

At 2:15 A.M. on May 6, 1853 the *Michigan* was steaming upbound off Point aux Barques on Lake Huron in perfect weather conditions. The seas were calm and visibility was crystal clear with bright moonlight. The navigation lights of a second steamer running downbound were visible a dozen miles ahead. Less than half an hour later the steamer, now identified as a large propeller, was close to the *Michigan* and heading directly for her. The *Michigan* turned east to allow more passing room. The other steamer did the same in effect negating the *Michigan's* move and by 3:00 A.M. they were perhaps a couple of hundred yards distant although they would pass clear of each other. Suddenly the unknown steamer turned hard at the *Michigan*. The deck officer on the gunboat shouted warning to the unknown steamer but received no answer. The *Michigan* tried to turn away but the unknown steamer crashed into her port quarter abreast of the mizzenmast. Although the quarterdeck was destroyed, lifeboat smashed and side dented in, she suffered no major damage. The unknown steamer did not stop or identify herself but swung around to a southeast course at full speed. The *Michigan* turned and chased her using her superior speed to come close enough to identify her as the *Buffalo*, the largest propeller on the Great Lakes.

The *Michigan* continued on her original course to Chicago stopping at Mackinac Island to file a "protest" against the *Buffalo* and her owner, a Mr. Walbridge, for the collision. On arrival in Chicago the gunboat went into the shipyard for a month for repairs. In spite of the captain's efforts, no action was ever taken against the *Buffalo* or did she ever pay for the *Michigan* repairs.[30]

In retrospect there is considerable speculation that the *Buffalo* intended to sink the *Michigan*. The *Buffalo* was downbound from Chicago, a major center of the lumber interests thus well aware of the current political climate. The *Michigan*, upbound from Erie, was likely unaware of the true state of affairs, or the potential for danger. The movements of the gunboat were not secret as no danger was recognized. If the *Michigan* were taken off the board, the government would have no effective way of projecting force against the lumber pirates. The *Buffalo* simply ran south looking for the *Michigan*. If she was successful in sinking her, or if she wasn't, political interests could protect her. "Collisions happened all the time. This was just an accident etc."

On October 1, 1853 the *Michigan* arrived off Manistee and sent her boat ashore. A short time later it returned with Willard, two deputy marshals and five prisoners, all major lumbermen. Two weeks later the *Michigan* arrived off Black River (Grand Haven), Michigan and sent her boat ashore. When it returned another unhappy prisoner was aboard. A quick run to Muskegon yielded another eight prisoners. Trips were also made to Chicago, Milwaukee and Green Bay among other locations to seize prisoners.[31] All were taken to New Buffalo at the foot of Lake Michigan where the Michigan Central Railroad delivered them to Detroit.[32]

The following summer the prisoners were tried in federal court in Detroit. As expected, the defense attorneys were the best money could buy and pulled out all the stops to achieve acquittals. The timber lawyers were able to corrupt a deputy marshal thereby invalidating his testimony. One witness was apparently enticed into a hotel room (though unstated in the court document, it likely was through a paid "dove") with the idea

Loading timber for a trip to the sawmill. Stonehouse Collection

of convincing him to make false statements at the trial. It only failed when the witness noticed the feet of a timberman sticking out from under the bed! Most however were convicted with small fines and jail sentences ranging from a day to a year. One year was the maximum penalty allowed under the 1821 law. It was a small price to pay for the massive plundering they were doing and since the arrests were only a drop in the bucket against the flood of plunder, at best a small victory for the timber agents.[33]

With the Detroit trials, the screams of the politicians reached a crescendo of pitch. Presidents normally respond to he who yells the loudest and Democrat Franklin Pierce was no different. He had to take action to satisfy the lake states. He removed John Wilson the Commissioner of the Land Office. Wilson was a Whig (the wrong party) and could be safely jettisoned without penalty. Willard worked for Wilson and it can be surmised was working with his tacit approval. After due course Pierce appointed Thomas A. Hendricks of Indiana, a good safe lackey, as Commissioner of the Land Office. In due course the Secretary of the Interior changed the system of protecting the timber by specially appointed agents and made it a collateral responsibility (among many) of normal local land office agents. The result of course was that Pierce, a good and loyal Democrat, opened the great forests for plunder.[34]

For the next quarter century the forests were essentially unregulated. As a result the public got cheap lumber, the lumber barons grew very rich and the government received virtually nothing. The Land Office developed a method of assessing "stumpage fees" as a way of selling timber.[35] Usually the fees, fifty cents or so per thousand broad feet, were assessed only if the lumber company was caught with stolen timber. Corruption was rampant and some agents allowed cutting after an appropriate bribe. The system was so bad that in 22 years the Land Office spent roughly $150,000 to collect less than $250,000.[36]

Even when the lumbermen actually purchased land, they managed to do it at the government's expense. Prior to an auction they arranged to have a "friendly" agent appraise the land at far below true value. When the auction was actually held, a confederate bid as high as necessary to win the bid. But after the sale was finished he disappeared causing the bid to be forfeit and the lumberman purchased the land at the low appraised value.

Effective government reform waited until 1877 when Republican President Hayes appointed Carl Schurz Secretary of the Treasury. Schurz energetically prosecuted the waste of the public forests. He removed corrupt officials as he found them and directed his agents to strongly enforce the law. He ended the charade of stumpage fees and compromising with the lumber barons. He was also successful in having Congress increase funding for enforcement. However by this time the damage to the forests of the Great Lakes was severe and the greatest benefit went to the developing forests operations in the Pacific Northwest.[37]

Great Lakes SAILORS ASHORE

The Tenderloins

In the early days of Great Lakes sailing, the crews were no different than those of the rest of the world–once ashore they wanted booze, excitement and women, and not necessarily in that order. Their chosen profession was dangerous. Shipwreck and accident were commonplace. There was no guarantee that the next trip would not be their last–forever!

Waterfront saloons and brothels were plentiful and grew in direct proportion to the growth in ships and sailors. The "law" such as it was, was not closely applied in the districts and "decent" folk knew how to stay out of the line of fire.

Tenderloin districts are as old as America. Every major city had them (some still do) and they were always tolerated within varying cycles of reform. Around election time candidates often ran on a reform platform, which affected the district to a greater or lesser degree depending on the situation. But the district always survived. The appropriate payoffs to authorities assured an acceptable degree of operational openness and business went on pretty much as usual.

The phrase "red light district" is often used to mean such areas. One explanation for the term comes from Dodge City, Kansas where railroad men developed the habit of hanging a red lantern from the door of their lady of the evening indicating she was occupied and other callers need not apply. Another claimed it originated at the "Red Light" bordello also in Dodge City. The establishment received the name from the blood-red glass in the front door.[1] Regardless of it's history, the term has become universal.

Each port city had it's own popular area of sailor hangouts, always bordering the harbor or river. Besides saloons and bordellos, there were

"Decent" folk wanted to stay clear of sailors! Stonehouse Collection

tattoo shops, warehouses, fortunetellers and ship chandlers. During the season these areas were beehives of activity.

The docks and train stations were also alive with various bunco men pitching all kinds of crooked schemes. These sharks swam anywhere they could find fresh "fish" to hook, play and finally reel in. Three-card Monte was one of the most popular cons just as it is in many big cities today. It was run just like a shell game in that the operator hid an object under one of three identical cups, rapidly switching them around to confuse the player, then having the player pick the one with the object. If he selected the correct one, the player won the bet. If not, he lost. In theory the player had one chance in three of winning. To start, the operator made certain the player could win every time by moving the cups in clumsy fashion. The operator kept increasing the bet and the player kept on winning. He was now hooked and was being reeled in whether he knew it or not. Finally when a high bet was placed the operator made sure through sleight of hand, that the player lost. Three-Card Monte was played the same way except the operator used three playing cards, usually a queen and two aces. After the bet was placed the operator shuffled the cards and dealt them face down. The player has a single chance to select the queen and win the bet. Again the operator made certain the player won the early rounds but when the bet was increased, he "palmed" the queen, substituting another ace, assuring a player loss. In a variation of the game, an accomplice of the operator "helped" the player notice that the queen had a small mark on the card apparently unnoticed by the operator. He would secretly whisper to the player to keep betting on the "marked" card. He couldn't lose! Of course for the big bet the operator palmed the marked queen substituting an unmarked (or marked) ace thus assuring the players loss. In testimony of P.T. Barnum's famous proclamation, "There is a sucker born every minute" and three card monte proved it.

Saloons

There were also saloons that were social clubs for honest workingmen, especially in areas with large factories or ports. They were usually very ethnic, reflecting the make up of the neighborhood. Men often stopped by in the morning for an eye opener on the way to work and at mid-day youngsters would run in to get a pail of beer for their father's noon meal. In the evening it was a place to relax, perhaps read a home language newspaper or catch up on the local gossip. Such saloons were also neighborhood employment agencies. They knew what firms were hiring and who to see about a job. The bartender also functioned as an ad hoc pharmacist. "Have an upset stomach?" "A glass of stale beer will straighten you right out!" Sometimes the saloons served as a post office for immigrants with no steady address. When you moved out of the workingman's neighborhood and into the districts the function of the saloon changed.

Mates often recruited crews from the various sailor hangouts. He or the bartender "sang out" for either vessel men or steamboat men, giving the name of the ship hiring. Sailors who wanted a berth came up to the mate and followed him to the ship. Once the vessel finished the trip, the men went to another hangout to drink, eat and wait for another trip. Good sailors always managed to get a berth. The ones with a poor reputation usually didn't find one.

Shovel men for the grain elevators were also hired from the dockside saloons. Generally they were a poor lot consisting of old men, tramps, saloon loafers and occasionally a sailor needing a day's work while waiting for a boat. Gradually the practice developed into a saloon boss system of control over the grain handlers. Each elevator operator established a relationship with a particular saloon for a steady source of workers. The saloon boss assumed the responsibility of supplying the men at an agreed price. The saloonkeeper also served as the unofficial paymaster for the elevator operators.[2]

After a trip, a group of sailors would gather and head for a favorite saloon and have a drink on each man. Soon someone would call for a song and after that each man had to sing, dance, tell a good story or buy another round of drinks as a penalty. Many of the songs were strictly "ad lib" and never recorded. These quick dittys are part of lost Great Lakes lore.

Most tenderloin district saloons or dens had a common layout. The larger ones had side or back rooms for dancing and "free and easy" shows. The shows were free in the sense there was no admission charge. Many had professional entertainment, including dramatic skits and lively dancers. Others made do with a single "piano walloper." All the entertainers catered to sailors. Often a small stage was available and the men were always encouraged to "take the floor" with a good song. Women were plentiful and would dance with any of the men. But as American Vietnam veterans experienced with bar girls and "Saigon Tea" the women soon wanted drinks and before a man left he was flat broke. The bar girls worked on commission and it was their job to separate a sailor from his money as soon as possible. The term, "skirt factory" was often given to such places. Beer was a nickel a glass and whiskey a dime. Some bars offered both the beer and a sandwich for a nickel. If a sailor wanted another sandwich, he had to buy another drink.[3]

Sailors weren't always the passive victims of saloon skullduggery. Once an Irish sailor named, "Con" Shay became drunk in a Chicago bar and fell asleep. When he woke, he discovered he had been robbed. After his protests brought no satisfaction from the owner, Con broke a leg off a table and proceeded to wreck the saloon. Since Con was said to have been as big as a gorilla and just as strong, there is no doubt the bar got its just deserts.[4]

Hookers at work. Stonehouse Collection

The "Pretty Waiter Girls"

The men had a variety of names for the gals: hookers, trollops, tramps, punks, madams, fire ships, jilts, doxies, wagtails, smuts, cracks, does, punchable nuns, molls, doves, soiled doves, mother midnights, blowzes, buttered buns, squirrels, nymphs of the night, mackerels, ladybirds, bawdy belles, fairy belles, nymphs, shady ladies, strumpets, harlots, sporting girls, daughters of joy, painted ladies, sporting girls, gay gypsies, girls of the line, filles de joie, nymphs du pave, street nymphs, demimondaines, ladies of the half-world, fallen women, inmates, daughters of Eve, pretty waiter girls, fallen women and chippies among many others.[5] Many used assumed names ending with "ie;" Mamie, Annie, Fannie, Jennie, Janie, Nettie, Lizzie, Cassie etc. being common. As this chapter shows, there also were a variety of colorful names given to particular women.

Union Army general "Fighting Joe" Hooker gave his name to an entire profession. Stonehouse Collection

Likely the most common term was "hooker" which is still in use today. Its' origin is somewhat murky but probably stems from Union General Joseph Hooker. During the Civil War he was camped with his division on the outskirts of Washington, DC and his troops found endless trouble in the city. Tired of having his provost guard running all over town after the miscreant soldiers, he rounded up many of the city's worst "doves" into one area, which soon was called "Hooker's Division" and prostitutes, "hookers."

Houses

A pure brothel as distinguished from a dance hall or saloon offering girls "out back" could be called a cathouse, whorehouse, resort, bawdy house, sporting house, stockade, chicken coop, disorderly house, joint, dove hotel, bagnio, bird cage, palaces of sinful pleasure, wine rooms, mansion, cottage, nunnery, skirt factory, female boardinghouse, cribs, box houses, or the more up-market bordello or parlor house. There was also a real pecking order to the various establishments.

Parlor houses were the top of the line. They were elegant affairs, with opulent furnishings, music and excellent liquor. Only the most refined and beautiful women worked in them. They were the prettiest and most accomplished women in the business. In many cases they were considered more cultured and beautiful than the young society ladies of the town. Only wealthy and important men visited such houses and the

Parlor house ladies were the "pick of the trade." Stonehouse Collection

experience was as much for the company of the ladies as for sex. Parlor houses were never located in the tenderloin district but rather in more upright areas of town. These houses were very much part of "respectable" society although kept in the shadows. A visit to one was much like a visit to an upper crust private home. When a gentleman arrived he was escorted to the ornate parlor by the madam. If he had no special girl in mind, she would either select one for him or allow a choice between those available. The girl then entertained the gentleman with clever conversation in the very plush and ornate parlor while he enjoyed fine wine or liquor. On occasion she might further entertain him with a musical instrument. The atmosphere was always highly dignified and any hint of commercialism was kept to the absolute minimum. When the time came for the man and girl to retire for a furtherance of activity, the madam discreetly collected the required compensation.

Brothels were a step down from the parlor house and usually resembled a hotel, or apartment over a store or saloon. The fees were much lower and girls less cultured and attractive. It could be as small as a rooming house or immense depending on the needs of the trade and temper of the times. Usually located in the tenderloin, they could also be at the edge of town. Some brothels did approach parlor houses in appearance, but were a distinct decrease in class.

Box houses, also known in some areas as variety theaters, were the next step down the chain. Typically they had a small stage at one end and a long bar at the other. Tables for drinking, gambling, watching the show or chatting up the girls were in the center. Curtained cubicles or "boxes" surrounded much of the perimeter of the room. The "pretty waiter girls" who solicited drinks and "services" from the customers provided the action. Once a deal was struck the girl and her customer retired to the nearest cubicle. In many instances the girls were outfitted with gaudy costumes designed to highlight their attributes. The stage was used by various performers and traveling "artists" most performing lewd skits to entice the audience. Many of the female performers were also available for private performances in the cubicles. Sometimes the "pretty waiter girls" performed spicy dances or tried to sing.

The bottom of the food chain were the girls that worked the "line." They occupied small cribs or shanties in the worst area of the tenderloin or near construction or lumber camps; anywhere there were large numbers of men. Cribs were usually about four by six feet; similar to the corncribs they were named after. It was just enough space for a cot, washbasin and chair. The women didn't live in the cribs, rather they rented them for a fixed fee. In some cases the girls were from the higher trade working their way down as their skills deteriorated. The term "line" referred to the procession that often formed outside their door.

The critical element in the trade was the madam. She filled many roles to both customer and girls; counselor, medical advisor, confidant, banker and contributor to numerous local charities. The girls of course were the madam's prime stock in trade and a good madam at least at the upper level of the trade, in parlor houses and upper tier bordellos, managed them for long term viability, taking care of their every need. She also taught her charges all the skills needed for success, including smoothing the rough edges off those lacking proper social grace or breeding. On a less obvious point, it was critical she taught the girls not to recognize or speak to a customer in public regardless of their earlier intimacies. It was important a man's public life be kept separate from his private entertainments.

The madam had to be a good businesswoman to survive and prosper. She needed to negotiate the best prices with the local grocer and spirits provider as well as milliner to assure her clients were well fed and girls stylishly attired. Above all it was necessary to work with the local authorities to assure the appropriate "fines and fees" were promptly paid to correct people to avoid business interruption.

It was critical madams maintain a reputation for scrupulous honesty in her dealing with customers, girls and local citizens. There was no quicker road to ruin for a madam than dishonesty. Madams usually served an apprentice as doves before moving into management. It was a business that called for experience from the "bottom up."

The best advertising was word of mouth from well-satisfied customers. Sometimes "steerers," men who circulated through theaters, dance halls and train stations, "steering" men to their employers. Business cards were also used.

Inside the Joints

The real action of course was in the lower class establishments. The presence of so many working women in many districts often led to fights. It was not uncommon for men to carry their drinks out to the street to watch two doxies rolling around in the mud locked in deadly combat.

One old sailor remembered there were women in all the gathering places, "lots of them." They would sell the man beer and whisky and get them feeling pretty good and then take them upstairs or into a back room and "get all their money."[6]

Bouncers were always on hand in the bigger bars to "take care" of drunks and men whose money was gone. Customers usually came off the worse for wear in any encounter.

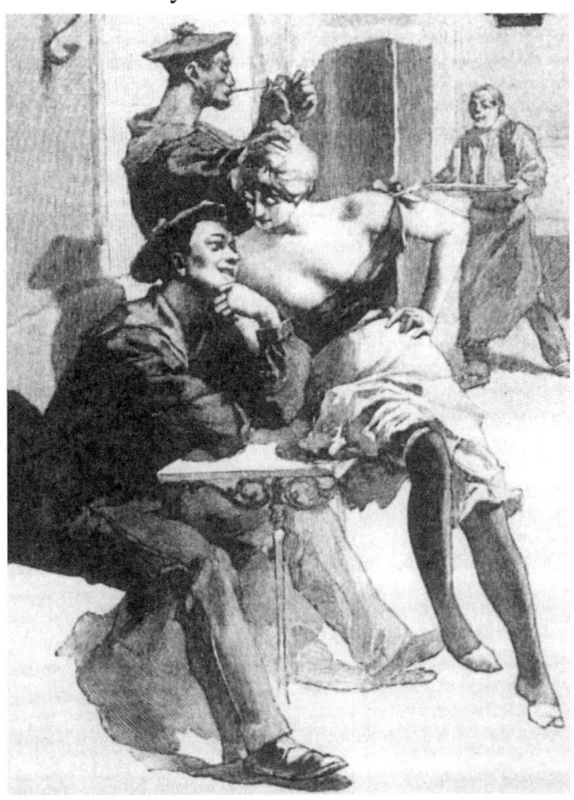

Sailors and the women always mixed easily.

Observers remarked that a sailor with cash in his pocket hated to drink alone and everyone in the room, male and female, would be invited to raise a glass with him. Soon he would be "three sheets to the wind" and easy prey for a girl to usher him to bed, or elsewhere.

Card playing was popular in many of the honest sailor saloons and it was usually for small stakes, often drinks as opposed to cash. It was usually jovial, without rancor but should trouble breakout the landlord or bartender was ready to break-up the fight. Invariably the sailor tossed out on the street would be the one without money. Business after all, is business!

The girls in the saloons were usually heavy drinkers but were not permitted to become drunk in daytime. If the bartender noticed a girl becoming intoxicated, he substituted water for gin. The girls needed to keep their wits to be able to exploit every opportunity offered by the sailor. In some houses all of the income earned by the girls went to the landlord who in turn provided them with food, clothing and lodging. In others they paid the landlord a fixed rate.

Boarding Houses

Boarding houses were also important to the sailors, both for a short stay between boats and as a place to lie over during the long winter months. Not all Lake sailors stayed over for the winter, some sailed saltwater, often going to the Gulf coast and returning to freshwater in the spring. Others went off to the lumber camps. Especially skilled men could usually find work in a shipyard.

In 1883 room and board for the winter in Milwaukee ranged from $35-$45. When a smart sailor got off his last boat for the season he marched up to his selected boarding house, plunked down his money and the landlord in turn guaranteed his lodging until the spring. Weekly charges ran $2.50-$3.00.

Landlords were not overly concerned whether the sailor could pay cash for the winter lodging when a sailor stayed "on the cuff." They knew they could get their money from the first trips of the season. It often took sailors until July 4 to earn enough to pay their boarding house bill. Responsibility for paying the bill often fell to the shipmaster, who held his wages until it could be paid.[7]

Many bars had boarding houses attached and vice versa. Landlords encouraged drinking since it helped to peel the sailor from his money. This was always the object of the land sharks. If the sailor got too boisterous in his celebrating and carted off the jail by the local police, so much the better for the landlord. He was already paid for his lodging whether the sailor used it or not.

In some communities facilities were opened to provide sailors "good and cheap board and lodging and other comforts and conveniences without being brought into contact with the demoralizing influences of the bar…" In 1874 Friendly Inns were established in Cleveland, Buffalo and Troy, New York (on the Hudson River). Board and lodging cost $4.00 a week, considered at the time, comparable to the cheapest of the dives. Part of the arrangement included writing and reading rooms, a notable extra for a sailor's boarding house.

A notice in the *Buffalo Commercial Advertiser* for July 24, 1874 encouraged, "Shippers, boat captains and all others desiring male help would find it their advantage to call in the Friendly Inn, as it is intended to make it the rendezvous of sober, steady men. No charge is made for furnishing help. Captains who desire to see the social states on their men improved, should advise them to go to the Inn, corner of Canal and Commercial, Lloyd and Pearl Streets."[8]

TO SEEKERS OF HEALTH AND PLEASURE.

Grand Pleasure Excursion for the Season of 1874

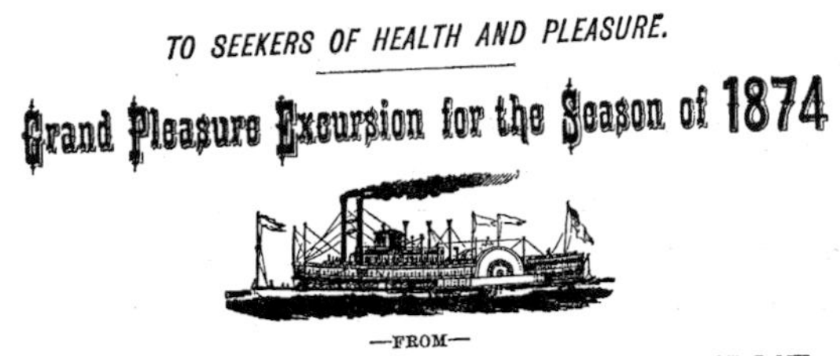

—FROM—

BUFFALO, ERIE, CLEVELAND AND DETROIT,

TO DULUTH AND ST. PAUL,

PASSING THROUGH

LAKES HURON AND SUPERIOR.

To Continue during the Summer Months.

A Daily Line of Steamers will run from **Buffalo, Erie, &c.**, to **Saut Ste. Marie, Marquette** and **Duluth**,—Connecting with Cars on the **Lake Superior & Mississippi Railroad**, running to **St. Paul, Minn.**

From **St. Paul** Steamers run Daily on the Mississippi River, during the season of Navigation, to **La Crosse, Prairie du Chien, Dubuque** and **St. Louis**,—Connecting with the Lines of Railroad running to **Milwaukee, Chicago** and **Detroit**,—thus furnishing a Round Trip of over *two thousand miles*, by land and water, through one of the most healthy and interesting regions on the Continent.

DULUTH TO BISMARCK, DAKOTA,

VIA

NORTHERN PACIFIC RAILROAD

This new and Health-Restoring Line of Travel, by means of steamers on the Upper Lakes of America affords an extended Excursion of 1,650 miles from Buffalo to Bismarck, Dakota—connecting with Steamers on the Red River of the North, and on the Upper Missouri, extending for 1,200 miles. further to Fort Benton, Montana—forming altogether the

GRANDEST EXCURSION IN THE WORLD.

Steamships from Buffalo served the entire Great Lakes. Stonehouse Collection

Buffalo

Buffalo was perhaps the most notorious port on the Great Lakes. An old-timer remembered the waterfront as "pretty bad but an exciting place to stay." Key to the city was the Erie Canal completed in 1825, which opened the Great Lakes to the world and by virtue of the produce of the Midwest, made New York City into the most important port in the country. The stubby

Canal boats and lake vessels mixed in Buffalo. Stonehouse Collection

canal boats carried the goods from the Great Lakes to the vast and expanding markets in the east and returned with both products and immigrants to "grow" the Midwest. The bustling 363 mile long waterway ran from Albany on the Hudson River to Buffalo, making the city the critical transfer point between the canal boats and Great Lakes vessels. Its population boomed from roughly 6,300 in 1830 to nearly 16,000 in 1835! Over

61,000 passengers passed through the city in 1833, most boarding Lake ships and heading west. The initial boom deflated with the Panic of 1836 but recovered and continued until about 1850 when the quickly developing railroads began to eat into the Erie Canal-Great Lakes connection.[9]

Lest the reader get entirely the wrong idea, there were acceptable hotels in town suitable for a family moving west. Places like Miles Jones' Steam-Boat Hotel and Farmer's Home all offered reasonable lodging. But make no mistake; Buffalo was a wide-open town where virtually anything went. In the years before the Civil War, Buffalo was also a major station on the Underground Railroad. Once across the Niagara River, fugitive slaves were free. Some however stayed in Buffalo and added to the population.

The district where the canal met the Great Lakes was a swampy hunk of territory known locally as the "Flats." Initially such swampland was considered virtually useless, but when the canal came through, development happened nearly overnight. While there was only one Erie Canal, a large number of minor canals, slips and lagoons developed in the area. Soon a host of waterfront industries including warehouses for transshipping freight, stables for the horses and mules that pulled the canal boats, grain elevators, shipyards and docks as well as a large number of "service" industries–gambling halls, bars and brothels, were all crammed tightly into the Flats. The area was also called as the Hooks, Five Points, Canal Street Badlands, Canal District or Canal Street.

Since the canal was really a massive open sewer, the area was an appalling breeding ground for disease and infection. All of the waste generated from people and activity packed around the canal ended up in the still waters of the ditch. Cholera as well as various unidentified fevers were common and bodies were often hauled away during night to avoid needlessly exciting people.

Winter was a hard time to be in the Buffalo flats. Sailing on the lakes was finished until spring and ice melt, as was work on the canal boats. If a sailor was out of money, he could try for jail time or else practiced begging and thievery until spring.

The area was a terrible fire-trap and two major blazes raged through the Flats, one in 1851 and the second in 1853. In each instance, business owners quickly rebuilt. All the fires really did was clear away some old buildings, making room for ones that would be bigger, better and more profitable. It was urban renewal by another name.

The women usually worked from the back of the saloons or perhaps from rooms on the second floor if there was one. Their names were nothing if not colorful. The Creole, Humpy McFarland, Polack May, Bert Black, Frosty-Face Liz, English Lena, The Bluebird, Tonawanda Jane, Soapy Kate and Pug-Nosed Cora all working at separating sailors from their money.

The working women were not usually the raving beauties as depicted by Hollywood. One old-timer described them as "toothless hags, so skinny, blotched and battered that Macbeth's witches are beauties compared with them; girls young in years but old in crime and corruption; middle-aged women in faded finery and vile habits–these are the representatives of the feminine sex that you see on Canal Street."[10]

Responding to an 1856 inquiry from crusader W.W. Sanger, the mayor proclaimed there were officially 87 houses of prostitution, 37 houses of assignation, 272 public prostitutes, 81 private prostitutes, 31 kept mistresses for a population of 75,000. That works out to be one for every 195 men, women and children! And remember, these are the "official" numbers and certainly do not include "free-lancers" or women the police did not know about.[11]

The most notorious saloon and sailor boarding houses were centered on Canal Street at the foot of Main Street and along Commercial and Ohio Streets. The area could be extremely dangerous for sailors that weren't very careful. Men often carried "Spanish shivs," long thin knives easy hidden in a boot or sleeve. Razor sharp, shivs could slice a neck open in a flash loosing a flood of blood. More than one sailor ended up robbed, murdered and dropped through a trap door into the canal. Such stories were not just tall tales. Crime ran rampant. Some villains were caught. Many were not.

One sailor witnessed just such a murder. He was passing by a saloon when a strange noise attracted his attention and he entered the dive. The front door banged shut behind him and locked as a group of men lugged away a bleeding and beaten victim. The unconscious man was dragged to the rear of the saloon where a trap door was opened and he was quickly dumped into the Canal. Strangely the witness was allowed to leave. Although he read the newspapers closely for several days afterward, he never saw a mention of the murder.[12]

An old schooner captain named Cole interviewed in the *Buffalo Express* in 1894 had vivid memories of the Flats. "Buffalo was a hard place in those days. A life didn't count for much and the lower part of the city was a mighty bad place. There were worse dens and joints round Canal Street then than one would believe." He said the city had no real police and the ones they had just left well enough alone. Cole spoke about a particularly notorious underground den. "I went ashore one day and my mate was with me. I had a roll of money with me but I never thought of it. The mate proposed to get a drink in the place by Old Mother Cary's. I went in. I was young then and did not know the town very well. After we had the drink he said let's go in here, Cap. I looked and he opened a trap in the back of the saloon. I thought I might as well see what was there, so I followed him. We went down and got in a passageway that led about 50 feet. Then we came to a heavy oak door about four inches thick. The mate rapped a peculiar knock on the door and it opened. Inside was a room about 12 feet square. In one end was a bar with five or six black bottles stuck up on it and at the other end was a table where three men sat playing cards. The door closed behind and I knew I was trapped. I had heard of the place. It was one where they fed drugged drinks to the suckers they got in there and then they poked them out through the slide with a stone round their necks and when they were found it seemed as though they had committed suicide. I knew where I was and I thought I was a goner. The door was bolted on the other side and I heard it slip into the catch. Well, sir, I began to buy them drinks. I made it out that I was an awful drinker and said that I could drink the whole lot of them drunk. I poured out big tumblers of the stuff and poured them down my neck on the outside, instead of inside. When I got out I was fairly wringing with poor whisky. They drank the stuff and got paralyzed. I pretended to be boiling drunk and pretty soon everyone of the crowd but the bar tender was stiff. I made him take drinks with me till he got pretty well under. Did you ever see one of them Spanish knives? We all used to have them in those days. Stuck up your sleeve you know and bound round your wrist with a thong. I took this out and grabbed the bartender–I was a husky lad in those days–and told him I would cut his throat if he did not open the door. He finally gave the signal and I got out of the place soaked with whisky. Spent $7 for those drinks I bought the cusses, but I was mighty glad to get out, I tell you. You see the mate knew I had money and he got me in there."[13]

One of the most popular Buffalo hangouts of the 1880s and 90s was Boney's Concert Hall on Canal Street. It reportedly had a bar 60-70 feet long staffed by a dozen bar tenders and 25-30 "working girls" who had rooms upstairs. Over 50 tables were scattered around on a sawdust-covered floor and a stage was on the wall opposite the bar. Other Canal Street hangouts were Hank Haley's Star Theater, Big Nell's, John O'Mara's, the Orley Theater, Kilcounse's Saloon, Big George Fix's Saloon and Boardinghouse, London Jim's Soup House on lower Main, the Alhambra and Drebolt's on Commercial. A bar called Jimmy Cody's was in the basement and illuminated by weak and smoky oil lanterns and what little light came through nearly opaque deadlights in the sidewalk above. Diebold's Saloon, although smaller than some of the big joints like Bonney's, had its stories. The rooms on the floor above Diebold's were rented out to all comers. Apparently two of the boarders got into an argument and bet who could do a better job of blackening his girlfriend's eye. It is not remembered which of the men won but certainly the girls lost!

Concert hall entertainment could be varied, running from traditional burlesque, singing, dancing, boxing and wrestling to two not very bright contestants trying to gouge each other's eyes out with sharp thimbles. It wasn't the Ed Sullivan Show!

The Flats developed a worldwide reputation. Foreign visitors making the "grand tour" of America in the 1870s and 1880s wanted to see (for the men, experience) the famous tenderloin district. A trip to America wasn't complete without including the Flats on the itinerary. It was claimed 60 percent of the buildings on Canal Street were bordellos and 30 percent were saloons during this period.

The Fourth of July was always a special holiday in the district and the celebration started early and ended late, if at all. There is a legend that on July 4, 1881, an entertainer named Kitty O'Neill danced naked on a foot wide pedestal in a Canal Street joint for over an hour. Witnesses claimed the place was so packed with wide-eyed and bedazzled men that if one passed out from drink he couldn't fall because of the tight packed crowd![14]

The old canal passed directly along the back areas of many of the bars and canal boats often moored behind the saloons. The canal boat crews frequently came ashore barefoot and the lake sailors made fun of them There was a fierce rivalry between the two groups and fights between lake and canal men were common and bloody affairs. While the canal men worked on boats, they were not considered sailors by the true deepwater men. It was said that all a lake sailor had to do was yell "low bridge" and all the canal men would instinctively duck and a fight automatically ensued. In spite of such natural animosity, many new men were recruited for the Lakes from the canal sailors. In the spring

"Liverpool men" or saltwater sailors often arrived at Buffalo to ship out on the Lakes for the better pay and conditions further adding to the nautical mix of humanity. Both groups were usually paid off when they reached the city, so money jangled heavy in their pockets when they headed for their favorite joints.

Fights would start over the most trivial items. An argument whether Admiral Dewey was a Republican or Democrat was enough to spark a street brawl. During one fracas the police hauled off an angry bartender who had a customer flat on the floor and was viciously kicking in his face. A jury turned the bartender loose when it learned the victim had refused to pay for drinks. Surely such treatment was only fair for such a crime!

One sailor thought enough of the women of Buffalo to compose a popular ditty or verse of the type sailors commonly sang in saloons when required to entertain or buy drink. Obviously other ports could be substituted for Buffalo.

When first I went to Buffalo
And was walking down the street,
A pretty little damsel
I happened for to meet.

She was a fair one, fol-a-de-lie-do,
She was rare one, fol-a-de-o-lay.

If ever you go to Buffalo
Be sure you are reefed down'
It was there I got my main yard sprung,
It was there I got aground.[15]

Another ditty ran:

Aye learn to drink and learn to chew,
Learn to curse 'till all is blue.
Lose your pants in Buffalo,
And call yourself a sailor.[16]

A popular capstan chantey was "The Buffalo Maid." Sailors commonly sang it when the capstan was used to raise the anchor, haul the vessel into position to load cargo or other heavy lifting. As in all chanteys, the chantey man decided the length, especially by detailing the progress with the "maid." In this version it has been localized to Buffalo, but other ports were also substituted.

In Buffalo I met a maid
  Mark well what I do say
In Buffalo I met a maid
  And she was mistress of her trade
I'll go no more a-ro-o-vin' with you fair maid!

A-ro-vin', a-ro-vin',
  Since ro-vin's been my ru-I-in
I'll go no more a-ro-o-vin' with you fair maid!

I touched that maid beneath her chin
  Mark well what I do say
I touched that maid beneath her chin
  She says, "young man, won't you come in?"
I'll go no more a-ro-o-vin' with you fair maid!

I bought her meat, I bought her wine
  Mark well what I do say
I bought her meat, I bought her wine
  Says she, "young man, you're my kind."
I'll go no more a-ro-o-vin' with you fair maid!

I put my arm about her waist
  Mark well what I do say
I put my arm about her waist
  Says she "young man, you're in great haste."
I'll go no more a-ro-o-vin' with you fair maid!

I took that maid upon my knee
  Mark well what I do say
I took that maid upon my knee
  Says she, "young man, you're rather free."
I'll go no more a-ro-o-vin' with you fair maid![17]

Polite society usually ignored the Flats, referring to it only when absolutely necessary and then as the "infected district." Only when Flats activities migrated into "better" neighborhoods did the upper crust society become concerned. Considering the Flats were for a long time, the center of Buffalo's economy (legitimate and otherwise), such a hands off attitude is difficult to understand.

The Flats of course was tied to the viability of the Erie Canal and when it declined as the result of increased competition from the growing railroads, the Flats suffered too. What once was a vibrant mix of lake and canal, became a backwater, just a pale reflection of what once was.

The Pan American Exposition in Buffalo in 1901 was a tremendous draw for people of all sorts. Stonehouse Collection

Eventually reform forces gained in power and threatened the existence of the Flats. In 1902 an anti-saloon league, an association of more than a hundred churches and temperance organization, went to war with the city's vice establishments. The anti-vice group was inspired by a couple of factors. While the traditional battle against vice in any form motivated the crusade, so did the troubles with the Pan-American Exposition in 1901. The exposition was an opportunity to show Buffalo off to the world. While the city fathers had one perception of the exposition, namely focusing on progress and enlightenment, the lords of the Flats looked at an entirely different set of opportunities. Tourists did flock to Buffalo. Many went to the exposition. Others took the opportunity to see shows of a different kind. One story claims that a group of nymphs from New York City journeyed to Buffalo to handle the needs of the visitors. However when they reached Canal Street the local talent attacked the interlopers with vigor. The police eventually sorted the mess out and the sent the interlopers packing back to New York.

Some of the denizens of the district spent time in the Erie County Penitentiary, which was conveniently located close to the canal. It was a dark, dank and disreputable place and there was no attempt to rehabilitate inmates. The miscreants were there to do their time and that was it. However, if a vessel captain was short a crew, he could pay the prisoners fines and thus "recruit" him for work. Writer Jack London spent 30 days in the pen after being convicted as tramp in June 1894. One of the men London met in the pen was an early version of the "Birdman of Alcatraz" except instead of studying birds, when a bird flew into his cell, the "Birdman of Buffalo" popped it into his mouth and ate it, feathers included!

In the 1920s and 30s, the more expensive sporting houses were spread along Niagara Avenue in the Johnson Park area. Most of the customers arrived by taxi and the drivers were well experienced in making the run with out of town visitors. Less expensive joints were on Oak, Elm, North and South Division Streets. Many were disguised as cigar shops or soda fountains. Surprisingly perhaps the cheaper houses during this time closed around midnight while 10 p.m. was the rule in the more sedate Rochester. Of course such trade could not flourish without the protection of prominent men. Everyone needed "connections" and Buffalo was no different. It was claimed that at one time a police captain owned the best house in town.[18]

A variety of organizations operated in the area to try to redeem the lives of the residents including the American Bethel Society, Charity Organization Society, Salvation Army, Christian Homestead Association and Women's Christian Temperance Union among others. While all did good work, they were trying to climb a very steep hill.

Oswego

Oswego enjoyed a fine reputation as a sailor's town. Most of the establishments were located in the an area also known as the "Flats," north of West Cayuga Street and east of West Second Street, bounded by the lake and Oswego River. This part of town was the oldest and once the main business district. As the city expanded, the center moved south along First Street and the older buildings on the Flats became saloons and bawdy houses. Many small shacks in which sailors lived were also erected there. By any stretch of the imagination, the Flats were not a place others went into after dark.[19]

Oswego sailors had a reputation of being among the toughest on the Lakes. In one incident a group of Oswego sailors were attending a Chicago picnic arranged by a group of "Dutchmen." Seeing one of the Dutchmen carrying a watermelon, an Oswego man grabbed the watermelon and challenged, "What does a Dutchmen know about watermelons?" A brawl ensued from which the Oswego men emerged victorious, watermelon intact.[20]

Port Huron

While never considered outstanding as a sailor's town, the area around Quay Street and the Atlantic Hotel had many of the usual entertainments. Saloons and boarding houses lined the main street and "houses" were common.[21] The vessel traffic up and down the St. Clair River was tremendous, a parade of sail and steam the entire season.

Cleveland

The Cleveland waterfront was always a rough place but in the 1860s-1890s, it was especially so. Shipyards and ore and coal docks were on the old riverbed near Whiskey Island. Nearby were freight warehouses. Most of the unloading was done by manual labor using picks and shovels, wheelbarrows, carts and mules. Deck hands, stevedores and shipyard workers were all tough customers ready to "mix it up." Drinking and brawling were accepted methods of stress relief. Fighting was especially vicious and there were no holds bared. Biting off ears and noses, kicking and stomping were as commonplace as a roundhouse right. On paydays the local saloons, whores and other ner-do-wells directed their total efforts to relieving the men of the cash. Shanghaiing was not unusual. Neither was floating face down in the Cuyahoga River. Local operators included Elephant Bill, Mother Loverly of Third Street, Chicken Smith and Hickory Nut Mary.[22]

Popular spots included the Merchant's Hotel at the west end of the Main Street bridge, Heller's Row on west Ohio Street and the Seneca Street House. Harry Rye's Saloon on River Street was unique. The owner put a donkey in the bar room that begged for free beer and in turn got drunk to the amusement of all.[23]

An example of a "high class" hotel and saloon that catered to ship's officers and owners was the American House on Superior Avenue. Other sailors called it to the "lumber doodle house."[24]

A madam called, "Deaf Meg" kept a sporting house up on Factory Street hill. Sailors considered it a "pretty low type of place." Molly Mason's on Mandrick Street and Mattie McGowan's on Factory Street hill were considered much better. Others on Hamilton Street catered to a "layer or so above the bottom." Those on Haymarket and Canal "took on all comers."[25]

Efforts were made to address a sailor's religious needs. A Brother Jones had a floating Bethel moored on the east branch of the river behind a ship chandlery. Other gospel ships operated on the lakes, some moving from port to port.

The Detroit waterfront. Stonehouse Collection

Detroit

The Detroit sailor joints were mostly around the region west of Jefferson and First and Second Streets. Lower Larned Street was well known for its many sporting houses. The old waterfront boasted a number of "snug harbors" where sailors could "tie up" for the winter or lay over between ships.

A song popular in Detroit warned the local girls of the "ways of sailors."

> Come you girls of Detroit,
> And take advice of me.
> And never let a sailor lad,
> And reach above your knee.
> He'll double reef your mainsail girls,
> And down your tops'l too.
> No storms can throw him off his work,
> And him you'll surely rue![26]

Popular hangouts included Baltimore Red's at the corner of West Jefferson and First, a two story red brick building combining dance hall and sporting house; the Wagner Hotel Saloon at West Jefferson and Second and Drummond's Dock at the foot of Front Street; the Golden Dollar and Silver Dollar Saloons on Monroe, Jimmy Owen's, Jimmy Duck's and Mike Doud's.

The old Potomac Hotel at the corner of Atwater and Beaubian was another lively saloon and boarding house. At times up to 100 sailors stayed there during the winter months including the likes of "Billy the Bum" Boushaw, "Johnny the Whistle" famous for whistling through his nose and "Patty the Piker." The Potomac gave its name to an entire section of town. The Franklin and Atwater Streets east of Brush, was known to the police simply as the "Potomac." It was thought of as kind of a sub-cellar for the underworld of the city. The police paid close attention to this seething pit of depravity.[27]

The Potomac took it's name from an early Civil War song, "All Quiet Along the Potomac."

> "All quiet along the Potomac, they say,
> Except now and then a stray picket
> Is shot, as he walks on his beat, to and fro,
> By a rifleman hid in the thicket.
> Tis nothing–a private or two now and then
> Will not count in the news of the battle;
> Not an officer lost–only one of the men,
> Moaning out, all alone, the death rattle."

After a night's activity, it was common for the police to simply report, "all quiet along the Potomac." In later years the area was largely taken over by bootleggers and rum runners. The battle between civil authority and miscreants continued to be waged.[28]

The call to "promenade the bar" seems to have been unique to Detroit. It required the men to take the "ladies" to the bar and treat them to a drink.[29]

Detroit was equally as dangerous as other ports. It was said, "many a good man went floating down the river at night without a vessel." In an era with minimal police reporting and no coordination among law enforcement authorities, the true number of "floaters" taking the current to Lake Erie will never be known.

The waterfront was populated by a large number of deep-water sailors, tug men and longshoremen. Often they divided into rival gangs. When the inevitable clashes occurred many of the ruffians ended up in the local hospital. The gangs were also occasionally hired by various political parties to assure that caucuses and other voting affairs were run "right." The mere presence of such toughs often kept honest citizens from questioning the long accepted practice of stuffing ballot boxes etc.[30]

During prohibition it was claimed one of Detroit's most famous madams was known as "Silver-Tongue Jean," for reasons best not described. During this period the Grand Circus Park area had more than two hundred bordellos. It was said the side streets of Woodward Avenue had hundreds of girls hanging out their windows trying to attract customers. Some of the larger houses went through three shifts of women a day. Costs were always hard to track but during World War I, $1 or $2 was the going rate with inflation raising it up a dollar in the 1920s. Elite establishments charged $5. World War II bumped the prices upward with $5 becoming average.[31]

Bay City

When the lumberjacks came in from the woods, Bay City was awash with money. Throughout the long, cold winters the jacks slaved in the woods, felling the mighty white pine that would build America's cities. When spring came and log drives were over, it was into town for bath (maybe), a shave (could be), but definitely a long session with whisky and women! It was time to "put on a toot" and the town was waiting and willing to entertain them. The men had upwards of $200 cash in their pockets and they were anxious to make up for lost time. As many as 5,000 jacks could "hit" town in a single wave!

Whisky or women were not allowed in the lumber camps so the jacks had a strong hankering for both. Although the men worked hard all week, they did have Sunday off and reading (or just looking at) old magazines was popular. There is a tale, true or not, about a young woman who made a fortune going through the camps (and jacks) selling "magazine subscriptions," but this was certainly an exception!

The crowd of jacks headed for the Third Street Bridge where saloons, gambling dens and bordellos stretched out for a third of a mile, an area some called "Hell's Half Acre." As the men approached the joints many of the girls called them by their names. Scotty Maguire's Alhambra was a popular destination, offering liberal amounts of booze, gambling and women. Others were the Do Drop Inn and Idaho Saloon on Water Street. All were waiting to help the men spend their money. Today economists call it more politcly "recirculating" assets. From the 1870s-1880s the white pine in the forest around Bay City was wooden gold and the lumber companies were in a race to see who could mine the most. Bay City was important as a location for lumber mills and shipping operations. The docks were piled high with lumber and shingles destined for all the ports of the Great Lakes. The lights in the tenderloin burned constantly and wild music was continuously in the air. Often the melody was accompanied by the sounds of fighting as men decided who was the tougher "bull of the woods."[32]

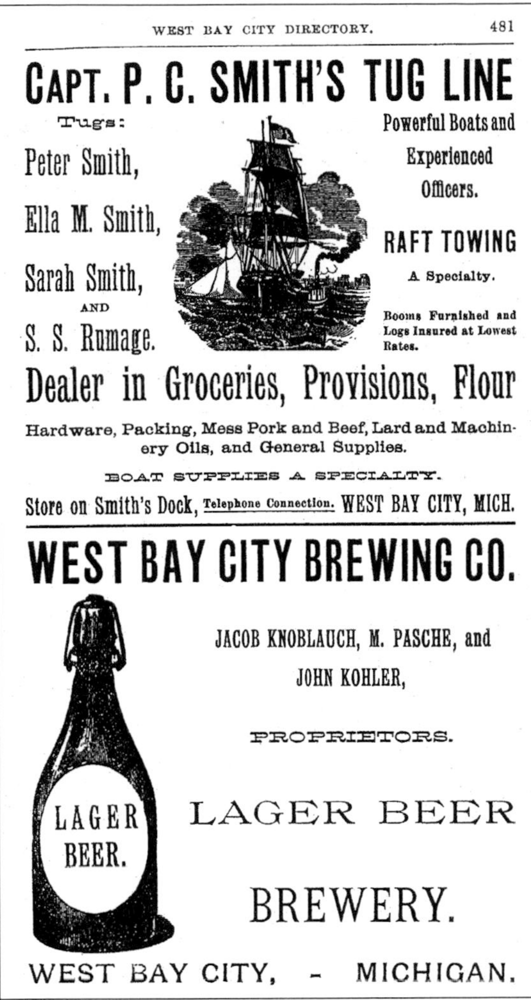

Bay City, Michigan. Stonehouse Collection

During 1880-1900 West Bay City was also known as the "Wooden Shipbuilding Capital of the Great Lakes." In thc latc 1880s the industry employed roughly 1,600 men, all every bit as thirsty and hungry as the jacks and sailors.[33] But for all the men, regardless of occupation, Bay City was where they got the booze, (among other things). Since Michigan passed a law in 1855 outlawing the manufacture and sale of liquor, technically it wasn't available in the state. Prohibition was the law of the land. However, it was a law largely ignored. It was not until 1875 that the legislators finally figured out what the will of the people was and repealed the repulsive legislation. "Outlaw whisky! Why you might as well outlaw breathing!"

The economic depression of 1873 hit the lumber operations hard with a rippling effect into the local red light district. At the time there were 25 sawmills with 1,500 workers in the city and another 11 just across the river. When the economy turned sour, the effect was devastating. Half of the saloons and bordellos closed. Perhaps even worse for the trade was the "Red Ribbon Movement," an early anti-drinking campaign urging men not to imbibe and to wear a red ribbon in testament to their adherence. It was much like the colored ribbons worn in today's society to mark all kinds of silly politically correct social issues. For a while the Red Ribbon movement enjoyed success, but like all efforts by zealots, it was doomed to crash on the rocks of human frailty. When the 1880s rolled around the economy was recovering, the need for lumber growing daily and the jacks were back it the woods. As one jack put it, "Ya can take this damn red ribbon and tie it around yer nose for all I care! There's pine in the woods and my two-bitters' ich'n to start sing'n!" Cutting in the woods meant cutting up in town and soon the Third Street red lights were back it business. Thirty hotels, 37 saloons, 2 liquor stores and 80 places with "pretty waiter girls" were available for all comers. As the lumber piles on the docks grew, so did the number of vessels coming into port and sailors added their influence to the mix.[34]

A collection of Bay City dives called the Catacombs operated near the north side of the Third Street Bridge near where the lake steamers moored. The name came from the various runways and alleys connecting it to other buildings, harkening to the subterranean dens of Paris or Rome. It was reputedly the toughest place on the Saginaw River. The first floor was level with the river while the second floor, with three different saloons, one known as the Steamboat Saloon, was level with the bridge. A thirsty man could get whatever he wanted, fine liquor, varnish remover (rot gut whisky) or if necessary, a swig from the infamous "black bottle" or service from a "pretty waiter girl" at a charge of 50 cents and up. The

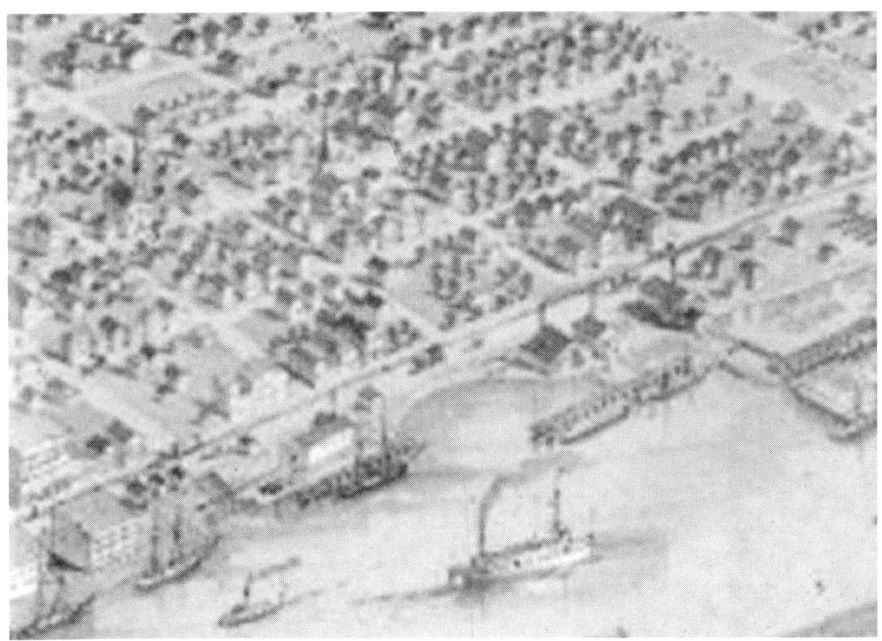

Between sailors, shipyard workers and lumber jacks, Bay City was a "rip-roaring" town. *Stonehouse Collection*

top floor had a variety theater and "wine room," where the girls could entertain their clients. One critic complained the room was the "receptacle of rotten moral, corruption, impossible to even... hint at." The acts presented on the stage were, "suited to the vilest and most depraved taste." The spectators of course were the judge of quality. If the audiences approved of the show, they threw money on the floor. Like vivacious Kitty Leroy, the entertainers performed both on stage and in private, for a fee. When her stage time was finished, she retreated with her customer to one of the "box seats" on either side of the stage. A plank walkway ran from the bottom level of the catacombs to other bars filled with pretty waiter girls. Small, dark apartments were everywhere. All of the stairs were covered with brass to prevent undue damage from the jacks' calked boots. Forty saloons were within 300 feet of the Catacombs, allowing for a full range of tastes and service.[35]

Another major complex stood on the south side of the bridge. A two-story building, it had a saloon on the first level and two in the upper floor. Pretty waiter girls were everywhere too!

There were bartenders who adulterated their whiskey with all kinds of things to "stretch" it out. For example according to one old-timer this was best done by taking a half barrel of whiskey and adding some fine cut chewing tobacco, perhaps a little pepper and gunpowder for a better bite. Fill the barrel with water, and the result is a new barrel of the finest Kentucky bourbon! Well, maybe not, but a drunken lumberjack or sailor didn't know the difference.

If the red light district seemed a little crude it was because the customers were "hard" on things. In one instance they were happily dancing with the local gals and just having a great old time, ripping and stomping to their heart's content. With a screech and crash the entire dance floor collapsed, sending everyone into the basement. After the victims sorted out their miscellaneous injuries, broken bones, bruises and related bumps and scrapes, those that were able just took off for another dance hall to continue the evening.

The Bay City Police were not hired for their legal knowledge or criminal rights sensitivity. What counted was the ability to "lick the tar" out of any man who refused to obey the officer's instructions. Recruits for the force came from the lumber camps, sawmills and shipyards. They were strong and dangerous and took no guff from anyone. Tough cops were an absolute necessity to keep any kind of order in the city. Tough police however did not imply the force constantly battled the "forces of evil." In 1875 the town marshal owned a brothel where it is claimed he spent the majority of his time. This gives a whole to meaning to the phrase, "I'll be in my office." He also collected "protection" money from other landlords and their women. If they didn't pay, then their joints were raided.[36]

Although the joints were not often raided since reasonable arrangements had been made with authorities, when a raid was conducted it often turned into a "Keystone Cops" fiasco. When a resort was attacked by the police it was usual for the girls and their customers to flee to the upper floors and push planks from the windows over the alley and across to the windows on the opposite building. Everyone then scrambled across the plank to safety, dropping the planks into alley so the frustrated police could not follow. If a girl was caught during a raid the fine for what was called "resorting" was a maximum of $5.00 and the opportunity to leave town under suspended sentence. Considering that just across the bridge was West Bay City, which was a separate town from Bay City and it had a considerable number of joints too, leaving town was not a great inconvenience.[37]

At times Bay City seemed of two minds about the saloons and resorts. Many certainly liked the money spent in the community and various civic leaders had a direct business involvement, but there were those goody-two shoes objecting to such entertainment. Local newspapers sometimes published items complaining of the area, occasionally even printing the names of various community members caught "in delicate circumstances" with a pretty waiter girl during a raid.

There were many saloons with their own "variety shows" along the river as well as "whores by the hundreds." A big husky woman known as "Gentle Annie" was well known as the "boss of the river."[38] Many dance hall floors were covered in sawdust. It did a great job of soaking up spilled beer, missed tobacco squirts (tried to hit the spittoon but the windage was off) and even blood when the customers got to brawling. Accordions, bagpipes, fiddles and melodeons provided music. It didn't make much difference as long as it was loud. When the men fought, it was fierce and no holds barred. They didn't know who the "Marquis of Queensbury" was and didn't give a splinter about his rules. Eye gouging, kicking, biting was all OK, but no knives or firearms were the rules they followed. The loser often ended up with a bad case of "logger's smallpox" from being kicked in the face with calked boots. It was all just part of the fun! They would fight over anything; a girl, an insult or just for the pure unmitigated joy of it. Sometimes it was just a couple of men and other times it could be a hundred in a massive brawl. Local men admitted some of the most dangerous men in town were the French-Canadian sailors, many spending their winters in the woods working as lumberjacks and sailing during the shipping season. Molded by both worlds, they were considered the toughest men in town.

Saloons like the St. James were open seven days a week. The Lord may have rested on the seventh day, but not fun-loving jacks and tars! Cassie Hawkins, remembered as a "real good looker woman" by one old timer, ran the highest-class resort in town. She charged $5 for her girls and everyone said they were worth every nickel. The going rate other places was 50 cents to $2.00. Cassie was considered a true beauty in the tradition of Lillian Russell mold. Polly Dickson was popular at the Bark Block until she died of typhoid in the late 1880s. Mag Snay was another Catacomb favorite, known as Bay City's answer to Calamity Jane of Wild West fame. Reportedly she once drove down Water Street in her fancy carriage and intentionally ran a man down. Whether he failed to get out of her way or she was "gunning" for him isn't known. When Mag was on the streets, honest men (or otherwise) needed to stay well clear. Paddy the Pig, Annie Cup O'Tea, Morphine Lou, Kissing Jennie and Paddy the Racker were all remembered as Catacombs girls. During the long winters in the woods the jacks must have dreamed fondly of a roll with Paddy the Pig![39]

During this period drugs such as morphine and cocaine were available "over the counter" in a variety of dubious concoctions, which lead to increased addiction. Many of the prostitutes were very likely "hooked" into the game through such easy availability.

Like some of the infamous Buffalo bars, the bodies of "rolled" sailors were supposedly dropped through a trap door into the river.[40] It is more likely more men died trying to use the sanitary facilities. The toilets were constructed on planks over the river, and instead of cutting a hole in the seat, which was clearly too much work, the men just leaned over. It is probable some just leaned too far and literally fell into the river and drown. No one at the time, sailors or jacks, knew how to swim.[41] Regardless of the reason, finding a body bobbing along in the river sailing for Lake Huron wasn't cause for particular comment.

Of course there were legitimate hotels in town. The Republic on Fourth and Saginaw Streets was a favorite winter home for Great Lakes captains. Considered a luxurious establishment for Bay City, it's bar won a gold medal for beauty at the 1893 Exposition in Chicago. There were many cheap hotels too usually providing only a shared room and mattresses stuffed equally with straw and ticks. The pretty waiter girls stayed in boarding houses. There were 18 located along Water Street and Woodside Street alone. It was common in city directories to list the girls as "waiters," "domestics," "servants" or "seamstresses."

Bay City also had a floating saloon. Built on a scow barge named the *Ida May*, in 1889 it was anchored just off the beach in front of the summer resorts. It enjoyed a brisk business and there was a " continual procession of sailing and rowing boats to and from the floating saloon, where they lingered with the ardent at long and short intervals."[42]

The ladies of the night were not just employed in the tenderloin district establishments. Several private homes, some closer to mansions, in residential neighborhoods were converted into parlor houses catering to more affluent businessmen. They were invariably both discrete and expensive. While everyone knew what went on, they were well kept and presented no special difficulties to either police or neighbors.

As the timber was harvested, the red lights in Bay City dimmed but never went out. There were still the shipyard workers as well as other industrial men looking for a good time. A concerted effort was made with the end of World War I to close many of the places down. It was never entirely successful and it can be argued that the trade, although much subdued, continues to this day.

Saginaw

Although more of a mill town than a sailor's town, Saginaw did have a considerable amount of nautical activity as the lumber ships and tugs worked the trade. During its heyday in the 1870s and 80s many considered it one of the most hell-raising place on earth! It was not uncommon for 5,000 lumberjacks to be in town, each with a seasons worth of cash burning a hole in his pocket. Mix in a healthy crew of sailors and a powerful brew was cooking! The men wanted booze and broads and not necessarily in that order. Saginaw was ready to supply both!

Belle Stevens ran the best house in town but it was a parlor house not suited for the common folk. The shipping owners and lumber barons were her clientele as well as those of Saginaw's leading citizens that could seek relaxation without setting the local gossips wagging. The working men headed for dens run by Ma Smith, Emma Keys and Carrie Lee. Ma Smith had between 12-20 girls and when she was briefly forced to relocate to an island in the middle of the river, she duly increased her rates to cover the additional expense. Warden Bordwell ran a joint with the high-sounding name Opera House on the corner of Jane and Washington Streets but the only singing was by the working girls. It was a typical box house, with a bar on one wall and concert stage on another. Tables and chairs for drinking and gambling occupied the center of the room. Two smaller "wine rooms" were off to the side. The waitresses made initial contact with the customer in the main room, brought him to the wine room for further negotiation and eventually closed the deal in one of the small "tasting" rooms or boxes off the wine rooms. Bordwell took a percentage of every drink his waitresses sold as well as their action. It was a very profitable enterprise. When he died in 1895 he left an estate of $15,000, a very large sum for the times.[43]

When the lumber industry died in the 1890s, so ended Saginaw's heyday as tenderloin town. The town slipped quietly into oblivion, just a fond memory to the old jacks and tars.

Chicago

A fugitive slave from San Domingo named Jean Baptiste Point du Sable was the first non-native to settle in what is now Chicago in 1779. Soon a small settlement had grew up around his original plot which was purchased in 1804 by trader Jonathan Kenzie. The federal government soon established Fort Dearborn at the juncture of the Chicago River and Lake Michigan to protect travelers moving west, but in 1812 local Indians largely wiped out the garrison. Rebuilt two years later, it provided critical protection for the growth of the early city. Chicago expanded from the river outward in a haphazard fashion. While the original 1829 plat was logical, the pressure of the rapid growth soon overwhelmed it. Cheap hotels, bars, saloons and all matter of dens sprang up to service the legions of immigrants streaming west as well as the crews of the ships carrying them. Since the river was the basis for the city, it all took on a distinctive nautical flavor. As the city grew, so did crime in all of its guises. The first of many reform movements blossomed in 1834. It failed, as did every crusade since, causing one wag to claim, "Chicago is unique, it is the only completely corrupt city in America." The Illinois and Michigan Canal opened for navigation in 1848 and the railroad soon followed. Chicago quickly became the countries major inland shipping center. Until the sandbar at the mouth of the Chicago River was dredged in 1854, bringing a vessel into the river was nearly impossible. Once the dredging was finished, although it would be a near constant requirement, the city blossomed into a major port. Two years later the steamer *Dean Richmond* cleared the city bound directly for Europe. A new era had begun.

During the 1830s-1850s Chicago was often visited by deadly disease. Smallpox, dysentery, cholera and unidentified fevers infected thousands of people. The cause was a combination of immigrant steamers bringing ill passengers and the Chicago River. As the population increased, the use of the river as an open sewer grew in proportion which increased the propensity for illness and death.

By 1838 disorderly houses were common and by 1849 it was claimed there were more gambling halls for its population than in New York City. The Civil War provided a "decadence" boost for the city as Mississippi gamblers migrated north and numerous "war widows" opened houses (many which developed into expensive parlor houses) on the second floor of buildings downtown. Many of the madams became important figures in the social life of the city.

By this time the Chicago political machine had a firm grasp on the red light trade. Payoffs were common and expected. Everyone and everything had its price. From the cop on the beat to the mayor, all were participants in the scheme. The basis of everything was maintaining control through elections and in this the Chicago politicians were unchallenged. On

Election Day the ward and precinct captains made certain everyone voted including, if the records are to be believed, George Washington, Thomas Jefferson, and James Madison. The machine gathered up anyone it could find and marched him to the polling stations complete with false names and addresses. Votes were counted, counted again or if necessary dumped into the river!

One source estimates that by 1867 there were 1,300 hookers in the city. Randolph Street in the middle of downtown between State and Dearborn was lined with bordellos, dance halls and saloons. The devastating Great Fire of 1871 burned out most of the city, including this nest of sin and for a short period it was hoped by the local reformers that it was gone forever, but it came back bigger and better than ever! Chicago was sometimes called the Paris of the Great Lakes but not because of its architecture or art museums. Rather it was a reflection of the city's depravity and moral decadence.

In the 1870s a tenderloin district was located between Sangamon, Halstead, Lake and Monroe streets. The pride of the district was the Diddle Briggs brothel on Halstead. The most popular girl was a midget named Julie Johnson who reportedly gave exhibitions with an African American nearly three times her height and more than double her weight.[44]

When the city recovered after the fire and the railroads converged on the area, the opportunity for "adult entertainment" increased dramatically. The opening of the 1893 Columbian Exposition in the Jackson Park area provided an unparalleled need to provide all the fair goers wanted and the city responded with vigor. Tenderfoots arriving to "see the sights" were escorted to the red light area also known as the Custom House district by "runners" and naive young women were often recruited directly from the trains into the bordellos. Others arrived thanks to the smooth charm of con-men that lured them to the city from small towns with promises of romance and exciting city life. The Custom House district was thought comparable to San Francisco's infamous Barbary Coast. Generally speaking, it was bordered by Harrison, Polk, Dearborn and Clark Streets but constantly shifted, as new businesses were established and old ones closed. Famous madams included Lizzie Davenport, Emma Ford, Flossie Moore and May Hastings. It was claimed the most renowned bordello at this time was Carrie Watson's on South Clark Street. She was said to be a woman of unusual charm and grace who ran an elegant house with the help of sixty "hostesses." Vina Fields, who normally used 40 women, doubled her stable for the fair![45]

By 1895 the south end of State Street gained the title of "Whiskey Row" due to the large number of saloons, bars, dope dens, cheap theaters and arcades as well as a drink called a "Mickey Finn." This special libation was a mixture of red-eye whiskey and knock out drops. The drugged drinker was hauled out to a nearby alley, robbed and left for dead. Supposedly it gained its name from one Mickey Finn, a bartender who specialized in its use. A morality crusade in the 1905-07 period caused most of the joints to pack up and move but only into other areas of the city.

The whole tenderloin district outdid itself to entertain the tourists. The big concert house saloons threw open their doors with music and girls flowing out into the streets. Gambling tables ran continuously. Beer flowed in rivers and champagne bubbled forth like fountains. Doves beckoned men from windows, trying to entice customers inside.

As part of the 1893 Fair the U.S. Life-Saving Service operated a demonstration station complete with scheduled lifeboat and Lyle gun drills. The eight surfmen were the responsibility of Keeper Henry Cleary, not only for training but also certainly to keep them "out of trouble." For lifesavers from the wilds of the Michigan coast, the temptations must have been extraordinary and Cleary's vigilance constant.

Not all establishments in the area were high class. There were a fair number of places that specialized in drugging and robbing the patron. Some were referred to as "panel" houses. While the customer and lady of his choice were cavorting on the bed, an accomplice of the house would sneak into the room through a hidden panel in the wall, rob the customer's wallet and slink back out. The customer had little basis for complaint since he was alone with the girl and the door was locked. One police office claimed $150 million was "lifted" in 1893 alone by this simple method of thievery.[46]

In 1894 Chicago was shocked by the publication of a book by English social reformer William T. Stead titled, *If Christ Came to Chicago*. It was a scathing inditement of the city's sin industry. He listed the addresses of bordellos, saloons, gambling dens and included very detailed maps. While Stead intended it to provoke the city to change its ways, the actual result was nearly the reverse. Many people purchased it as a guidebook to find the best places and the first 70,000 copies were sold out in a day! Regardless of the popularity of Stead's book the best guide was the popular *Sporting and Club House Directory* authored anonymously. It was considered a must have for men desiring to explore the city's

Many out of town visitors to the Chicago tenderloin district were "led astray" and sandbagged by "gay birds." Stonehouse Collection

attractions without being robbed or attacked. Many of the male students from Northwestern University in nearby Evanston had their first "liberal" educational experience in the tenderloin houses.

The city wasn't so shocked by Stead's 1894 indictment to miss a good business opportunity. When the Grand Army of the Republic held their national encampment in Chicago in 1895 they were greeted by the *Souvenir Sporting Guide* listing four "theaters" and 28 bordellos, all eager to serve the old soldiers. Many of the dove hotels had personal listings. One enticed, "While seeing the sights boys do not fail to drop in upon Miss Elsie at 828 Grayson Street and you will be royally entertained. Everything connected with her establishment is first class."[47]

Finally in 1903 sufficient municipal reform pressure was exerted to drive the Custom House district businesses south toward Twenty-Second Street and Wabash. This is Chicago, and such enterprises may shift a bit, but certainly not close. The South Side Levee as it came to be known, was one of the largest in the city and developed in part during the 1893 Worlds Fair. Not only was it a center of normal vice activities, it was also the axis of a white slavery ring stretching south to St. Louis. Temptations like the House of All Nations, Little Green House, Ed Weiss' Capitol, Bed Bug Row, Bucket of Blood and Freibergs Dance Hall provided entertainment for all comers. Some of the dens were low end with the girls going for as little as a dollar a "roll."

There were honest bars like Hinky Dink Kenna's the "Workingman's Exchange." No women or gambling were allowed but the bar did serve the largest schooners of beer in Chicago, one pint, nine ounces for nickel with a huge free lunch thrown in too. The long wooden bar ran two inches short of 100 feet long! There was a unique tradition of sorts at the Workingman's Exchange. Every night a number of drifters and bums slept upstairs in a dive called the "Alaska Hotel." In exchange for lodging, they cleaned the bar in the morning and when finished each received a powerful "eye opener." Under the bar was a large barrel into which all of the dripping and "leavings" were dumped while the saloon was open. Think of it as an early form of what in college was called a "garbage can social." Each saloon cleaner received a mug of this concoction, enough to warn off the staggers and shakes until the free lunch was laid out at noon.[48] The ward boss and owner of the bar took care to treat his patrons well, whether they had money or not. Come election day each voted as told, marching in mass from polling place to polling place. Have things really changed in Chicago?

The district was also the home of the elegant and sophisticated Everleigh Club on South Dearborn. Housed in a twin brownstone mansion and run by the Everleigh sisters, Ada and Minna, it was said to be the most luxurious bordello west of New York and Chicagoans were justly proud of it. The mansion was decorated to the height of Victorian luxury, well suited to impress its very exclusive clientele. Mahogany and walnut paneling, heavy tapestries, gold-framed nude paintings, $650 gold cuspidors, gilded bathtubs, silk curtains, solid silver dinner service, gold trimmed china, all added to the rich and lavish atmosphere. Brochures advertising the club circulated all over the Midwest. The fees matched the décor: $10 for admission, $12 for a bottle of wine, $50 for dinner, $50 for an evening with a hostess. An evening of enjoyment could easily conclude with a $500 bill, certainly far beyond the wildest dreams of simple sailors. But for vessel owners of course it was another matter entirely. Captains of industry, notable politicians and occasional European royalty were all repeat customers. In a gesture of civic responsibility, state legislators were always entertained for free. Reputedly the establishment had fifty bedrooms and 90 ladies, the cream of the crop, were available to help the guest relax. One room was said to have a waterfall, another a gold trimmed piano worth $15,000 and orchestras played refined arias as the evening progressed. A dozen parlors were decorated in various themes such as; the silver parlor, gold parlor, rose parlor, or Japanese throne room. The Blue Room was decorated with collegiate pennants and pillows emblazoned with risqué Gibson Girls illustrations. All were intended for group activities and were sound proof. A "never on Sunday" policy was strictly followed. Everyone needed a day of rest, especially the hard working staff of the Everleigh House. The sisters accumulated a large fortune only quitting the trade when police pay-offs became intolerable. Minna later estimated the sisters paid over $100,000 in protection money during the dozen years the club operated. She further claimed the entire district paid over $15 million since it moved to the 22nd Street area (as of 1911). Eventually the sisters retired to New York and lived in style and comfort.[49]

It was said Mary Hastings operated the most debauched houses in the Levee. She claimed there was nothing her doves would not do. They would satisfy all customers regardless of the demand. Since her four houses were all $5 establishments, she was almost at the top of the pecking order, just below the Everleigh House.

"Hinky Dink" Kenna and "Bathhouse" Jim Coughlin were the bosses of the Chicago tenderloin for many years. Stonehouse Collection

John "Bathhouse" Coughlin and Michael "Hinky Dink" Kenna were two First Ward politicians known as the "Lords of the Levee." They ran the tenderloin for nearly 40 years, 1897-1938, managing the vote as well as accepting the required payoffs for official protection. Perhaps they are most remembered for the remarkable First Ward Balls they ran, first at the Seventh Avenue Armory and later at the Coliseum. Initially they were intended as fundraisers for charity but once the pair realized the money to be made, they became the charity! Called by the newspapers the "annual underworld orgy," it was required that every madam, pimp, gambler, and general crook buy at least one ticket, while the owners of the saloons and bordellos purchased them by the handful. Not only did the underworld attend, but also the chiefs of police and political elite! In many cases these worthies were escorting a galaxy of nymphs, all fitted out in their finery. Everything and anything went at the balls. No costume was too risqué or activity unacceptable. The lowest of the low and highest of the high all mixed together. Female impersonators, tramps, cardsharps, young bloods, politicians and police all danced with rare abandon. Drunken throats bellowed ribald songs and shouts for favorite doves. People were packed so tightly that drunken women who had collapsed were passed overhead until they reached the outside. Most balls ended in a riot but arrests were rare. A typical take for Bathhouse and Hinky Dink ran to $50,000! When the ball was held in the Chicago Coliseum as many as 15,000 people attended, many spilling over into nearby streets and alleys. In 1908 a crusade lead by a local Baptist do-gooder minister (who had apparently attended an earlier ball and pronounced it "unspeakably vulgar and immoral") forced the mayor to refuse to issue a liquor license preventing the ball from happening. So ended a special Chicago tradition.

One thing Chicago did very well was study the "problem" of sin in the city. They never really did anything about it but they did investigate it! The 1911 report of the Vice Commission of Chicago claimed annual profits from prostitution in the city exceeded fifteen million dollars. It also concluded that 5,000 full-time prostitutes were actively working in the city but could make no estimate of the numbers of women working only part-time. The report identified 1,012 "houses, flats and hotels and saloons used for immoral purposes" but since their investigators could not cover the entire city, the commission knew there were many more. Taking math a step further, the commission estimated 15,180 men were "serviced" every day making a total of 5,540,700 for the year! Remember, this report is examining the situation before gangsters like Al Capone arrived on the scene to "organize" things![50]

The commission noted the houses were not all confined to the various tenderloin districts in the city. A number were being established in residential districts. Many of the girls working the houses were transient, living in nearby towns and coming to the city at different times to earn money then returning home. Others worked in city department stores, mills or factories and worked the street to earn easy money. One department store manager actually ran his own bordello, recruiting his store employees to work the second "job." New girls were recruited through word of mouth. Customer advertising was generally simple. Madams distributed business cards to customers, as did the girls. One Dearborn Street house produced an elaborate booklet describing in glowing terms the comforts to be found inside the "sumptuous" house. It claimed no one need, "feel the chill of winter nor heat of summer" in this place. The actual sights and sounds of the tenderloin districts were usually the best advertising. Flashing lights, raucous music, enticing girls, all helped to sell the area to customers, especially to visitors not familiar with it. An effort to protest one of the districts by having a crusade parade through it backfired dramatically. After marching through the sin district, the marchers, young and old alike, realized that this was a pretty "interesting" place and remained after the march to see what it was all about. One witness claimed, "the saloons never did such a large business nor were the houses so crowded with men and boys."[51]

One crusader said soliciting was a constant activity on all the streets from the river to Chicago Avenue. Nearby hotels rented rooms by the hour or night as needed.[52]

How much money a girl could make was of course dependent on what type of establishment she worked in. If she was at the Everleigh Club, the sky was the limit. If she was at a 50-cent house, $100 a week was possible. One woman claimed to have "entertained" 60 men in a single night at 50 cents each![53]

During this time Chicago was well provided with saloons. The commission claimed there were 7,152 in the city, a ratio of one for every 300 people![54] During the 1880s and 1890s about a quarter of the council seats were held by saloon owners.[55] One wag claimed the easiest way to end a city council meeting was to stand in the door and yell, "Your saloon is on fire!" In 1900 approximately half of the Democrat Party precinct captains were saloon keepers and in 1886 saloon license fees provided 12% of the city's tax revenue.[56]

Chicago also had a villainous gang of African American females who preyed on visitors to the worst part of the south side levee. Said to be Amazonian in size, they were feared even by the police.[57]

The south Clark Street area in Chicago had many sailor saloons and bawdy houses. An especially popular one was the Sans Souci run by "Olaf the Swede." Roughly translated as "without care," Sans Souci was also the name of French king Louis XIV's summer palace. Other popular places were Starboard Jack's and the Fort Dearborn. Another saloon known as Steamboat Bill's, featured a 150-foot long bar, dwarfing the one at the Workingman's Exchange.[58]

Chicago was certainly as tough as any of the Lake ports. One old-timer stated, "The old sailors were a bad lot. I've seen many of them floating in the Chicago River filled up on whiskey from the night before. The police wagon would come down and fish them out with a pike pole and take them away and nothing would ever be in the newspaper about them, who they were or nothing."[59]

One of the oldest red light districts was known as the "Sands," located near the present site of the *Chicago Tribune* building, on the north side of the river. In the early days it was filled with lumber yards and the army of workers and sailors needed ready "refreshment" provided by a host of houses of ill-fame, saloons and gambling dens. As long as the action did not come to far south, into areas populated with "respectable" people, everything was acceptable. Eventually reform pressure caused the various establishments to be torn down and the occupants moved to less desirable areas.[60]

A variation to the typical land bound brothel was also available in Chicago. An official report noted, "Excursion boats have been used for immoral purposes, because of the ease with which the cabins may be obtained for short periods." Gambling machines were generally available on all the boats.[61]

The commission noted, "There were two classes of boats on the lake, those that carry the holiday crowds and those which cater to the regular vacation traffic. The excursion boats, as a rule, carry an element, which is more or less disorderly. The other boats are less frequented by this element. There are several classes of these disorderly groups on the holiday boats: first, girls who are evidently professional or semi-professional prostitutes, together with young men whom they find easy to attract; second, the class of young men who make these excursions trips for the purpose of seeking out girl recruits…"[62]

"The boats running between Chicago and Milwaukee, Chicago and St. Joseph, Grand Haven and Michigan City are the worst. The staterooms are rented over and over again. The boys carry whiskey in their suitcases or buy it at the bar. They are soon drunk and the trip becomes an orgy. The commission sent its investigators to take a close look at the situation. Their shamuses were detailed in reporting, "the facts, just the facts." For example, aboard the Grand Haven run they noted, "In No. 66 were four men. Two girls visited the room during the trip. In 61 there was one girl. Four men visited her at different times. No. 68 was occupied by two girls and two young men."[63]

In order to provide some degree of subterfuge to the business, the ship borne activities were sometimes called "floating poolrooms." In 1906 the newspapers announced the Detroit steamer *John R. Stirling* was purchased by Chicago interests to run as a floating poolroom against the popular steamer *City Of Traverse*. The vessel was obtained for $20,000 from the Great Lakes Engineering Works and another $10,000 invested to refurbish her for the new trade. A cabin was added on the upper deck and with other modifications; she was planned for a capacity of 1,500 people. A landing point was established in the Chicago River, east of the Rush Street Bridge. The *Sterling* was formerly the freight steamer *Vanderbilt* that ran for many years between Chicago and Buffalo.[64] During the time the *City Of Traverse* was in Chicago her owners paid $1,700 a month in graft to operate from the city.[65]

The 1939 Century of Progress Exposition provided another major boost to the Chicago vice trade. Millions of people came to see the sights and many explored fully what the city had to offer.

A sailor ending up in a Chicago jail was in a bad fix. They were considered among the worst in the nation. Stead commented about one police station, "Behind the iron bars of it's underground cages are penned up night after night scores and hundreds of the most dissolute ruffians of both sexes that can be raked up in the dives of the levee." And that, "They resemble the cages of wild beasts in a menagerie." An open gutter at the back provides the only sanitary accommodation. Into to this criminal stock pot of the city the homeless tramps were thrown to stew in their own juice together with the toughs and criminals and prostitutes, the dehumanized harvest nightly garnered by the police of the district.[66]

In the mid-1880s a sailors mission was run on Grand Avenue. The proprietor was Malcolm McNeil, a veteran sailor of 27 years experience. It was intended to be a refuge for destitute men in addition to the normal mission work.[67] Such sailor's missions were common in many of the larger lake ports.

Chicago is also given credit for inventing the mirrored bedroom. The innovation was installed in Madam Emma Duvall's French Elm bordello in the early 1890s.[68]

Milwaukee harbor circa 1880. Stonehouse Collection

Milwaukee

The sailor district in Milwaukee was located in the lower end of the Third Ward and the upper end of the Fifth Ward along South Water Street, Lake and River Streets as well as the network of alleys throughout the area. Jack McCarthy's and McCloud's were popular establishments.

By 1898, a local newspaper was lamenting the passing of the colorful sailing ship era. "The old Whale Club now closed at 6:00 p.m. and only mild gambling was permitted. The Shipmates Association was now known for its library of 800 volumes instead of the bar." Sailors had become respectable, the result of the trade of sail for steam.[69]

Fairport

As late as the 1940s Fairport sported the infamous "dirty dozen" houses of ill fame. Well known over the Lakes, some mariners looked forward to a quick trip to the Ohio port. One old sailor said, "You were on the water so long, you almost had to have them."[70]

Kingston

This Ontario port had numerous sailors' hangouts as well as a few for the higher class of client. Known as "gentlemanly resorts" they included Cicolari's, L'Hoists and Dumble's all on Princess Street. The sailor joints were less in the public view.[71]

Toronto

This fair Canadian city, originally called York, was no slacker in terms of vice, holding its own with many America ports. The first European settler in the area arrived in 1780. Others quickly followed necessitating the construction of a jail in 1798. When two crooks were convicted for robbing a tavern, they were not given jail time; one was lashed and the other had his hand branded. By the 1830s Lombard Street was well known as the red light district and reformers were complaining about bawdy and gambling houses on every corner. One was even owned by a police magistrate.[72]

Generally Toronto was merely a large trading village until 1850 when the British (remember, Canada was a British colony) gave up the imperial trading route through Montreal to the St. Lawrence as part of the general discarding of colonial trade protection. This forced Toronto to focus south to the United States and the Erie Canal in nearby New York State for trade. Railroads soon arrived and as they were connected to the U.S. system, Toronto grew into a major manufacturing area. Schooners and steamers flocked to the docks to transport the goods necessary to grow the city and sailors by the hundreds swaggered across her streets. City population swelled with Irish fleeing the potato famine, going from 23,000 in 1848 to 30,000 in 1850. As elsewhere, the Irish were not welcome and often were driven out of the city as soon as they arrived. The Toronto fathers complaining, "They fill our poorhouses and our prisons and are as brutish in their superstitions as Hindus." They arrived by steamer in batches of 300-600 at a time. Many were sick with various fevers and all were weak and largely without skills. Clashes between Orange Protestant and Green Catholic Irish were inevitable and deadly resulting in six major riots between 1852-1858. Crime increased dramatically.

A spectacular, although very unlikely riot, occurred in July 1855. It seems a circus from the U.S. had come to town and after the performance the clowns visited a bordello on King Street leading to a fracas with some local citizens. (Every time I think of red-nosed clowns with orange hair and floppy flat feet cavorting with the soiled doves I can only laugh. Hollywood could not invent a better scene!) Two of the citizens were hurt in the melee and since both were members of the city fire company, their compatriots swore vengeance on the clowns. (Picture the firemen with their oversize boots, red suspenders and bouncing helmets, chanting, "Get the clowns–get the clowns," you get the idea!) The following day a group of Torontonians attempted to wreck the circus but the troupe battled back and held their own. When the fire company arrived to take its vengeance, it was more than the circus folk could handle. Although the clowns escaped, (did they run off in a little clown wagon?) the firemen toppled

Many services were provided for sailors in the city's dock area.
Stonehouse Collection

the wagons and set them on fire. The police stood by watching the amazing scene and order was only restored when the Army arrived. When 17 rioters were finally arraigned in court, none of the police could remember seeing any of them at the riot. This led a local newspaper to comment that the fireman, police and saloonkeepers were all in cahoots.[73]

In the early days Canadian justice could be ruthless. Conviction of any of 120 different crimes could result in the death penalty. In wasn't until 1865 that hanging was limited to murder, rape or treason. Other penalties included branding, whipping or confinement in the stocks. Lynching was not unheard of either. When a farmhand murdered his stepson by burning him alive in the fireplace, outraged citizens lynched him from a tree just outside the city.

Vice continued to be a part of the city. In the early 20th Century an official Canadian inquiry noted, "It will be sufficient for present purposes to say that nearly all of the so-called massage parlors investigated were houses of prostitution and worse, - worse standing for things abominable and unspeakable... it is even impossible to give the details of the treatment given by the women to the men."[74]

Ashland

Association with the infamous dens in the lumber town of Hurley sometimes tainted (or polished) Ashland's reputation. It seems that around 1890 a number of articles on "stockades" in the lumber country appeared in the Chicago and Milwaukee newspapers claiming Hurley was the center of white slaving. At the time Hurley was part of Ashland County and it is easy to see how ill informed readers confused the port of Ashland and Hurley.

While Hurley was certainly a wide-open lumber town with all of the typical attractions, its black reputation may not be entirely deserved. The tale is based on the gullibility of the press and goes something like this: "I think it was in 1886 that Hurley was first advertised as an outlaw's paradise. At that time a young lady representing Elmira, N.Y. arrived on the scene to write up the great mining camps. This reporter met a couple of well-dressed men (gamblers) who were very nice and fluent talkers. They told her great stories of lawlessness and goings on which should be aired in the press and the poor tenderfoot swallowed the whole story and when the next issue of the *Telegram* arrived it was filled with lurid matter telling that a lot of innocent girls were enticed to Hurley and kept in stockades guarded by vicious bulldogs. Other papers, not to be outdone by the *Telegram*, proceeded to have almost daily stories of Hurley's inequities." All that said, Hurley was a wide-open town but certainly didn't have women locked in stockades and guarded by bulldogs! Gambling was also popular with roulette, craps, poker, and faro, all available along the infamous Silver Street. Lumberjacks and iron miners from the Gogebic Range all enjoyed the virtues of Hurley.[75]

Hurley had its share of popular girls, and the most admired was Lottie Morgan, at least that is what she called herself. Beautiful and cultured, it seemed she belonged in one of the high class parlor houses in Chicago instead of a rough and tumble north woods village. She was particular who she did business with however and invariably had only the best men in town as her customers. When murdered in April 1890, she was thought to be in her late twenties.

A passerby discovered Lottie's lifeless body behind a saloon. Her skull was smashed and it was surmised the murder weapon was an old axe found nearby. Since its blade was covered with blood and hair, it was surmised this was the murder weapon. Later examination showed she had also been shot. Although the police investigated thoroughly, they never tracked down her killer. There was speculation she was murdered because she knew too much about a recent bank robbery or that she was blackmailing some important man over their "dalliances."

In spite of her occupation, or perhaps because of it, Lottie was given a magnificent funeral, the best Hurley could provide. Held at the city opera house, everyone that could attend did. One newspaper estimated a third of the mourners were women. The Reverend C. C. Todd spoke eloquently on her behalf as did the reverends F. A. McGraw and Burrows. But the service was not all "churchy." When it was announced that the mourners will rise and sing Lottie's favorite hymn, a man yelled out, "Bet on the Red" and another called, "Keno!" A solemn occasion need not be a sad one! After the service a large number of carriages conveyed the hearse to the cemetery and Lottie was laid to her final rest.[76]

Unlike many vice cities, Hurley continued well into the 1980s although much was driven out of easy public view. Regardless of Hurley's excesses, however, Ashland was hardly as pure as the driven snow. Mix sailors, sawmill workers and lumberjacks and the result is a perfect recipe for a red light district. In it's heyday Ashland was a rip-roaring center of action. Charlie Charlier's dive was acknowledged as an infamous hangout where everything a man wanted was available. Molly Cooper was well known as a pioneer Ashland madame whose fame spread far and wide. At one time during the 1890s she ran two different bordellos and was highly regarded by all who knew her except the extremist reformers who finally forced her from town in 1904. Once she left, Ashland became the boring little town it is today. Her memory isn't dead however. The Hotel Chequamegon, the classiest place in town, has named it's bar "Molly Cooper's Drinking Establishment" in her honor.[77]

Marquette

The streets surrounding the Lower Harbor were well populated with saloons catering to the needs of sailors as well as dock wallopers, iron foundry and lumber mill workers. It was a wide-open town as long as the recreational activities did not bother the town's best families. Houses of ill fame were fine as long as they were on the outskirts of town, or in the sailor's district but not where polite society would gather.

For reasons that are not clear, the local paper took delight in following the exploits of a local hooker named "Dutch Mary." The November 23, 1878 issue of the *Mining Journal* stating, "Dutch Mary is back again and is as sinful as ever, though her term of one year in the house of correction ought to have been enough to make her see herself as others see her. Once

Marquette was a fine sailors town. Stonehouse Collection

she was pure as the driven snow and know her but to love her, but she fell. The love and respect of husband, children, friends and acquaintances were all forfeited in a maddening desire for drink and today she is a pitiful wreck on the great sea of life, with tattered rigging drifting about in search of a tow. Poor Mary! Hers is indeed a worse fate that that of Mary who had the lamb."[78]

A year later the paper noted "Dutch Mary" arrived in town the early part of the week and immediately commenced operations on the unsuspecting youth of this community as only Mary, with her laughing brown eyes and pretty winning ways knows how to do. She was waited on by under sheriff Dolf and advised to desist but heeding him not she was taken into custody and given quarters in the county jail. On examination before Justice Hardy she was fined $2.00 and costs and advised to quit town. She took his advice but didn't pay the fine. She's a goner but not forgotten."[79]

While Mary was treated with a degree of forbearance and humor, dishonest operators received the full force of the law. The same day Mary was dealt with, the newspaper noted a hooker named Russell was arrested along with her "sweet-scented male demirep named Dalley." The woman was charged with keeping a "disorderly house" and Dalley with robbing a customer of $70. Such behavior may be tolcrated in

Chicago, but certainly not in Marquette! After pleading guilty, she was required to post $500 in bonds for good behavior for a year and Dalley incarcerated for trial.

The city's favorite fallen woman, Dutch Mary was still in business in June of 1880. "With her pretty winning ways and gallant airs (she) continues to captivate and entangle the unwary sailor boy and dock walloper who may chance to come within the radius of her bewitching smiles."[80]

Dutch Mary and Russell were not the only practitioners of the oldest profession in the city by any means. In October of 1880 complaints were made about a house near Arch and Spruce streets, considerably removed from the waterfront, that "a certain female of African extraction keeps a disorderly house." The problem wasn't that the house was there as much as the customers were causing too much racket and were disturbing the neighbors. The newspaper threatened that unless the brawls and quarrels stopped; the police would be forced to act. Apparently all parties concerned took note and things quieted down.[81]

In June 1882, the police raided a house in the "Rolling Mill" section of town and arrested two women. As in other cases, it was less that the house was operating, than it was an irritant to the neighborhood. Mrs. Emily Bly was described as an "old offender from somewhere up the road" and Miss Anna Whitcomb as "a lass who served an apprenticeship in vice under the older hags tutelage." Both were fined $25 and costs and instructed to leave town. The newspaper duly noted the "lonely gentlemen" who arrived at the house as "supplicants for the boon of a nights shelter under Emily's roof." It threatened to reveal their names in a future issue.[82]

Less than a month later the police raided a house on the edge of town and arrested two men and five women. The owner was charged with running a disorderly house and fined $35 and costs while a bartender and five "soiled doves" received fines of $5 each.[83]

The local campaign against the oldest profession continued into the fall when Kate Moore, an "incorrigible sinner against the good morals of the community" was arrested and charged for her "chronic contempt for law and decency." Fined $50, she was given ten days to leave the county or be sent to the state prison.[84]

In August 1882 a woman was found in the harbor lying partly in the water and partly ashore. For a while it was thought she was dead, the victim of suicide. Later it was discovered she was only dead drunk. Identified as a dove from "some location up the road" it was surmised she had taken too much whisky and deciding on ending it all, walked out into the lake. Discovering the water too cold, she reconsidered and collapsed on the beach.[85]

The county sheriff raided two houses of ill fame south of the city in the fall of 1883, apprehending seventeen soiled doves. Five were found hiding in a loft above a kitchen in a space two feet high between roof and rafters. Several sporting men were also caught, but as they were married and stalwarts of the community, their names were not published. The owners of the houses were charged with keeping a disorderly house and placed under a $200 bond pending trial. The girls were typically charged between $5-$12 and released. The local paper commended the sheriff for working hard to keep such activities "within bounds."[86]

In May 1894 a nymph named Della Hammell was arrested for running a disorderly house on Third Street. Hauled before the judge, she paid a $35 fine. The police thought she would "quiet down" after the arrest but apparently she continued to attract attention. When they raided her house a second time, several customers piled out of the doors and windows, heading for the hills. Della was again arrested and paid $100 fine.[87]

Rumors of impropriety by members of the well to do set were commonplace in the local bars. One claimed fat steel industrialists chased naked countesses and opera singers on horseback across the hills and glades of the nearby Huron Mountain Club, a resort catering to the richest of the rich.[88] Was it truth or just jealous envy? Strange things have happened in the north woods, so who knows for certain.

Fights among sailors were commonplace and the police did their best to manage the troublemakers. In July 1880, "John Mellen, wheelsman on the tug *Niagara* who got into a little fracas with one of the crew named Charles Campbell some two or three weeks ago and came near to putting an end to said Campbell's earthly career by hitting him on the head with a capstan bar (think of a baseball bat eight feet long and six inches round) and causing him to go into dry-dock (hospital) for repairs was arrested... and hauled before Judge O'Keefe."[89]

In 1882, "Three drunken sailors from the *Arizona* cruised about town with more sheets to the wind than they were able to carry with safety yesterday afternoon and in consequence they ran afoul of officer Donavan on Superior Street. The officer hailed them in the language of the law, ordering them to wear about and tack for the city lock-up, kindly offering to tow them that safe harbor of refuge for distressed mariners. The tars manifested a disposition to keep on their course, regardless of the consequences, when the officer called on bystanders to assist him and with their aid the cantankerous trio was removed to quarters in the cooler. They were maudlin drunk and just as ugly as drunk. A couple of them drew knives and might have made vicious use of these were they not promptly disarmed. They will come up before his honor of the recorder's court today for a hearing, whence they will probably be convoyed to the county jail to do service for a term in beautifying the county property."[90]

Lake captains weren't immune from pugilistic activity. In June 1881, two captains who were also brothers-in-law came to blows over the merits of seeing the world through a bottle. The temperance man tried to convince the other of the error of his way but only received "chin music" for his trouble. Responding with his fists, the temperance captain was hauled before the local judge and fined $5 for his lack of restraint.[91]

Marquette's Lake Street was a sailor's district and had the reputation of being one of the worst locales in town. The local paper called it a "dark and bloody ground." One Friday morning in August 1883, two local toughs, known only as McGraw and Dwyer, went "at it" in front of O'Brien's saloon to the great amusement of large crowd of "brother bums." Which Irishman won isn't recorded and the police didn't bother arresting either for disturbing the peace. The cops simply thought each fighter had been punished enough![92]

The city's ore docks were dangerous places to work. Not only in terms of crooks and other disreputable characters preying on mariners, but also general environmental hazards. More than one dock walloper or ore trimmer were run down by trains or slipped and fell to his death. Drunken sailors slipped into the water when navigating back from the saloons and subsequently drown in the harbor. Finding a "floater" was a common event, barely worthy of mention.

Just being down at the docks could be dangerous. In November 1871 the judge fined a vessel captain $5 for firing bullets from his revolver at a target on the ore dock. Watching out for trains was one thing, but dodging errant bullets was quite another.[93]

Fayette

The Upper Peninsula iron port of Fayette on Lake Michigan's Garden Peninsula may have been small, but it still had it's own tenderloin district. The Jackson Iron Company of Negaunee started the village as a company town in 1867. The company owned everything, all houses, stores, hotel, opera house, machine shops, etc. and some claimed the people too. The surrounding forest had large supplies of hardwood, needed to make charcoal as well limestone for building and flux. It also had Snail Shell Harbor, a deepwater bay perfect for the construction of docks for lake schooners. Iron ore was shipped down from the Lake Superior mines and using the locally produced charcoal and limestone flux, was smelted into pig iron, which was then shipped by vessel to market. Fayette soon became the second largest producer of charcoal iron in Michigan in the 1870s-80s.

The developers of Fayette laid it out to preclude any bars or resorts within the town limits proper but enterprising saloonkeepers soon built their establishments just over the boundary line. The result was in town everyone could pretend to be of high moral standard but when they wanted to raise a little hell, it was just a short walk down the road. For sailors from the schooners moored at the wharf loading iron, it wasn't quite as convenient as some places, but then it felt good to stretch your legs anyway. One of the worst of the operators was a man named Jim Sommers. His resort, located about a mile out of town, was known as the Hole in the Ground and was considered the worst of the lot. A tall wood fence was erected around his building to keep the inmates from running off and it was claimed many were held against their will. Finally rebelling against Sommer's wicked treatment of his doves, a group of local citizens nearly beat him to death, leaving him lying on the lonely beach to die. The mob then marched to his resort and burned it to the ground and distributed what cash they could find to the girls. Sommers recovered from the beating and was last seen making his way in a rowboat across Little Bays de Noc.[94]

By the late 1880s Fayette was dead. The hardwood forest needed for charcoal had been harvested and the market for iron largely died. As steel became the material of choice, old Fayette faded into history.

Manistique

When George Orr and his Chicago Lumber Company founded Manistique they went to extraordinary lengths to prevent the introduction of sin. Theirs would be a clean town. There would be no saloons, cribs, dance halls or other decadent attractions! How wrong they were!

To prevent the introduction of such establishments the company refused to sell land for such use and all deeds for property sold, included a morality clause governing its use. But since no good deed will go unpunished, somehow a small tract was not included in the land the company owned and it was this piece that ended their dream of a sinless

Manistique's jacks and tars made it a busy place. Stonehouse Collection

city. Roughly two blocks square, it soon became a small tenderloin offering all the excitement the lumberjacks, mill workers and sailors looked for. The major player in the tenderloin was saloon keeper Dan Heffron who made certain there was always enough whiskey to keep a man's whistle wet and "lov'n" available in the back rooms to keep him satisfied. As business increased, Heffron recognized a good opportunity and had his brother Denis join him. When Denis was elected county sheriff, wide-open Manistique got wider. Anything went! Overwhelmed by the effort, the Chicago Lumber Company finally gave up trying to regulate morality, more "joints" set up shop until there were roughly 29 bars in a town of 3,000 population giving a ratio of one bar per 103 customers, including women and children! When the timber began to run out, the mills moved on and the town's purer citizens exerted control, which left men like Dan Heffron in potential trouble. Indicted for running a disorderly house, he was only moments away from conviction when on a prearranged signal a sleigh came past the front of the courthouse at a fast clip. Dan ran out the door, jumped into the sleigh as the driver whipped the horses to full gallop. Soon a second sleigh filled with police was in hot pursuit. Just in the nick of time Heffron's sleigh dashed in front of a moving locomotive and escaped. When the big timber was mostly cut over the good days in Manistique ended and in a fever of morality, many of the saloons and cribs were closed. Eventually blended into the past.[95]

Escanaba

Escanaba owes its existence to the Civil War. Realizing that running a rail line from the Lake Superior iron mines south to a Lake Michigan port was a great idea, the work was put in motion and completed in 1863. Initially it was planned to run it further to the north at Masonville, but when a problem developed with property owners, it was rerouted to what would become Escanaba. Iron ore from the Marquette mines was hauled to the docks by train and loaded on schooners and steamers for the trip to the lower lakes steel mills. The first sawmill in the area arrived in 1838 at Flat Rock on the Escanaba River and the area soon became a major center for the lumber industry. The forests were not far from town and the logs were rafted down the river to the mills that dotted the banks. The cut lumber was then shipped out on a collection of sailing and steam vessels. The most powerful impact on the town was undoubtedly the lumberjacks. Like Bay City and Saginaw, when they hit town with money in their pockets from a long winter in the woods, it was "Katy, bar the door." The good and respectable folk stayed inside where it was safe. Ludington Street boasted it's share of saloons each filled with men stomping around in steel calked boots and flannel shirts. They drank, gambled, fought and whored, in whatever order seemed best at the time. The tenderloin district was down on Thomas Street near the rail yards. It was said the doxies were available twenty-four hours a day for a fee of anywhere from fifty cents to two dollars. One house boasted doves at $5 a roll, a price

Escanaba was a busy place in the 1890s for ships and sailors.
Stonehouse Collection

calculated to keep the low life out! Although only two blocks long, the Thomas Street tenderloin for size was as vibrant as any on the Great Lakes. When the sailors hit the streets the action only got hotter! The houses continued to function until 1942 when the city closed them to allow construction of a new ore dock.

Houghton and Hancock

The twin cities of Houghton and Hancock were also well supplied with "joints." Between the thousands of copper miners and sailors, the need for the services offered by the saloons and houses was great.

It is said that some of the high class parlor house nymphs drove through town in fancy carriages sophisticatedly dressed in silk gowns holding dainty parasols over their heads. Small dogs sat comfortably on their laps.

It is interesting to note that the first person apprehended under the White Slave Traffic Act (Mann Act-1910) was a madam escorting five prostitutes from Chicago to a brothel in Houghton. The arrest occurred at Chicago's Union Station.[96]

Green Bay

The following 1869 newspaper item shows the different ways the needs of customers could be served. "Shipwreck at Green Bay–During the southeast gale on the 14th, the small schooner *Art Palace*, commanded by "Commodore Peg-Leg," and used as a floating bagnio (brothel), anchored off Cedar River, in Green Bay, but dragged until she struck upon the rock strewn shore, when she filled with water. The craft will probably prove a total loss. The captain and crew of the vessel, the latter consisting of a half a dozen model artistes, succeeded in reaching the shore and were at last accounts, leading a gypsy life in the woods at Cedar River."[97]

Duluth

Duluth always had a fair share of hookers and joints to cater to the needs of sailors, dock workers, railroad men and traveling businessmen. The Hotel St. Francis was a popular place for the upper end doves while various less reputable places handled the lower end trade.

Like many cities, Duluth still has a fair sized hooker trade. In 2002 Duluth Police conducted three sting operations netting 50 people in connection with the various aspects of the business. Old traditions die-hard. [98]

Superior

From it's very beginning Superior has always been a wide-open town. Duluth tended to be upscale and money, Superior working class and customer focused. Combining railroads, flour mills, grain elevators, ore and coal docks, lumber mills and shipyards provided a powerful economic vitality, which meant men with money to burn. When the boys weren't working, they often headed for the bars and bordellos of Superior. During the darkest days of Prohibition longshoremen headed for the docks stopped at local bars for an "eye opener." Even today it is claimed by some that in the early morning local restaurants are filled with various pimps, gamblers, hookers having a meal before calling it quits for the day. Business goes on.

In the old days places like Edna's Bordello on John Avenue, Rose's Bordello on 3rd and Tower, the St. Paul Rooms, Indian Sadie's, Madame Sax's and the Arcade House all were popular houses. There were many others. The Spotted Dog Saloon in West Superior was especially infamous.

In the 1940s and 50's 3rd Street from Ogden to Grand was filled with small cottages and was called "window tappers row", "chippies" or "hookers hideaway". The common theme came from the way the gals would sit in their windows and watch the parade of men pass. They

Superior, Wisconsin was the most wide open port on the big lake.
Stonehouse Collection

tapped the glass to attract a customer's attention. If a man showed interest the woman would come out and escort him inside.

Periodic crackdowns had mixed results. It seems that whenever the local police received word of a state raid, they telephoned ahead to the joints warning what was coming. The system worked fine for all concerned. The State Police did their duty by raiding Superior, the local police supported the state with extra detectives and officers, local customers had plenty of time to get clear and avoid apprehension and the bordellos had only a minor business interruption.[99]

Activities were not always confined to dry land. In some instances they were carried on in the small "bumboats" that moored alongside a freighter during short stops. The boats provided a basic selection of snacks, candies, etc. needed by the crew. If their needs were more personal there was a curtained area in the forepeak available, or so say the sailor's tales.

Others

Portage Avenue in the Michigan Soo had a fair number of establishments catering to the needs of sailors. The Minnesota Iron Range ports, especially Two Harbors was especially well known. In its heyday this little lake port had 22 saloons and dance halls. Some sailors called the district "Whisky Row." Knife River also had an excellent reputation. Hammond, Indiana and Calumet were well stocked with houses too. In short, wherever sailors went, there were entrepreneurs willing and able to market their wares.

Great Lakes BITS AND PIECES

Lightkeeper's Cavort

Different men responded to the long isolation of lightkeeping in different ways. Some "went over the edge." Others went "wild" when finally given a chance to return to civilization. The following item from an 1879 *Marquette Mining Journal* illustrates the problem. "The Light on the west side of the entrance to Rock Harbor, Isle Royale, has been extinguished and will not be relighted (sic) until there is something in the way of commerce there to warrant it. It will be seen elsewhere that the occupation of another former lightkeeper of a light at Isle Royale is gone–unless perchance–they have a lighthouse department in the Wisconsin State prison. When he got loose from the island William went cavorting about very much like a seven year old colt who had been pastured with sheep all his life and had never before seen any of his kind of the opposite sex but though he was less fortunate–they don't send colts old or young to the penitentiary."[1]

A further dispatch provided the details. "Captain William Stevens, former keeper of the lighthouse on one of the Siskiwit Islands, Isle Royale and who has lately been stopping in this city, has either been having a "bad job put upon him" or else he has been acting exceedingly naughty. Early in the month the captain left this city for Milwaukee, taking with him all his money and remained away so long that his wife became alarmed and called the collector of customs stating her fears that something dreadful had happened to him and it appears that her fears were well founded. The captain hadn't been knocked down and robbed of his wealth, neither had he fallen among thieves or gamblers, but what was worse, he had succumbed to the fascinations of a fair damsel he met at one of the cream city hotels and forgetful of the wife who had shared with him the solitude and privation of his lonely life in the watery wilds of Isle Royale, had actually married the Milwaukee charmer. The circumstances of his marriage in Milwaukee are related in a special dispatch to the *Chicago Times* of the 19th. A telegram from his wife here brought him home and he remained here about a week departing the day before the denonment (sic) came in the Chicago papers before giving out that he had been waiting here nearly a week for a boat to take him to Duluth. In the meantime wife No. 2 had started for Marquette and was expected here on Monday but learning at Escanaba that her gay deceiver had gone south the day before, she turned back in pursuit and probably ere this has had her digits in his hair. The young woman's name is Sophia Farner and she hails from Cincinnati. Steven bought her a number of costly presents but after a few days left her, ostensibly to go to Duluth but came it appears, direct to this city and from here he wrote to the Milwaukee woman advising her to return to her home in Cincinnati and saying that he would send for her to come to him after a while. There are those who express the belief that the whole thing is an attempt at blackmail. Certainly Stevens, if guilty, displays anything but ordinary good sense in again venturing back into the vicinity of his amatory exploit, though it is possible the attraction may be more than he can possibly resist. If the *Times* correspondent tells a true story, Captain William Stevens is in a fair way to attain the peace and quiet of a solitude to which that of a lighthouse on a small Lake Superior island bears no comparison."[2]

The records do show that Stevens was the keeper at Isle Royale Light on lonely Menagerie Island from October 26, 1875-August 9, 1878 when he transferred to the Portage Lake Ship Canal Station. His wife (number 1), simply listed in the records as Mrs. M., was his assistant keeper at Isle Royale Light during the same period. He remained at the Ship Canal Light until August 20, 1879 when he is shown simply as "resigned."

Lake Ontario Ship Turns Slaver

A vessel built on the Great Lakes wasn't necessarily trapped on the Lakes forever. Intending to spend their days working one trade sometimes ships found them selves engaged in entirely different endeavors. The small 400-ton propeller *Ontario* was built in 1846 at the mouth of the Genesee River at Rochester, New York by George Steers. When she was sold to eastern merchants, she became the first Great Lake built steam vessel to leave the Inland Seas. She proved a good ocean vessel, normally running between Boston, New Orleans and other ports. She was reported to have sailed as far as San Francisco. What makes her unique as a Great Lakes vessel was her journey to the west coast of Africa to pick up a cargo of slaves and their subsequent transport to Cuba. As she approached the island a Spanish warship intercepted her and to avoid capture, the captain ran the *Ontario* onto a deserted island. He escaped but what happened to the human cargo was not reported. She was converted from propeller to sail in 1853, so it is assumed she was a sailing vessel when involved in slaving. From Great Lakes freighter to high seas slaver–quite a change in fortune![3]

Anything For a Bet

There is little good that comes of gambling, especially with men's lives and the tale of the tug *Lamont* well illustrates the point. The incident takes place in Lake Michigan between Pentwater and Ludington, Michigan in March 1880. It seems that two tug owners, Captain Lamont of the *Lamont* and the master of the *Gem* had a bet as to which vessel was faster. The race would be from the ferry wire (used to haul a ferry across the river) at Pentwater and the ferry wire at Ludington and return to Pentwater, a total distance of 25 miles or so. The wager was set at $25. When race morning arrived, the lake was running high and the captain of the *Gem* tried to convince Captain Lamont to postpone it until calmer weather. Captain Lamont refused, taunting the captain as "a coward" and that the *Gem* was "an old pepper box." On signal, the race started and clouds of billowing black smoke boiled from the stacks as both tugs raced past the harbor breakwaters. The *Gem* reached the lake first with the *Lamont* close behind. On the open lake it looked like both vessels would be swamped by the waves but after a few minutes it appeared they would weather the seas. After about a mile and a half the *Lamont* turned back for Pentwater. In response the *Gem* blew her whistle twice. Apparently stung by the celebratory whistle, the *Lamont* turned for Ludington again and was soon lost to sight. Apparently she capsized soon after being lost to view. Three men died with her, Captain Lamont, his 13 year old son George and engineer Palmer Hill. Lamont left a large family and Hill a wife. It was suspected Captain Lamont was drunk when he made the challenge to the *Gem* and when he sobered, was unwilling to back down.[4]

A Deep Diver

The rule of finder's keepers does not apply to underwater salvage, as a Detroit diver found out to his regret.

"Some time ago Mike Donovan was arrested at the insistence of the Michigan Central Railroad Company for carrying off a ton or more of pig iron which had fallen into the river near the company's dock while a vessel was being loaded and which Donovan had recovered by diving for it. Yesterday his case came on for trial before Police Justice Haug and Donovan set up the defense that he thought he had the right to the iron. He said he had dove and recovered iron in times past and sold it and supposed it was all right."

"Then you think anything you find in the bottom of the river is yours, do you?" asked the complainant's lawyer.

"Yes," answered Donovan.

"Suppose you were to find a silver brick?"

"A silver brick?" and Donovan's eyes sparkled.

"Yes."

"Why, I'd raise it!"

"How deep can you dive?" asked Justice Haug, "and how long can you remain underwater?"

"I can dive thirty or forty feet and remain under three minutes and over."

"Without any diving apparatus?"

"I put cotton in my ears, that's all."

The justice held that while Donovan was doubtless ignorant of the law and might have had no intention of stealing, he was never the less guilty and assessed a fine of $20 or thirty days in the house of corrections.

As Donovan was leaving the courtroom he turned to George Tuite, who was the principal witness against him and said; "I'll pay the fine for you my young fellow, when I get out."[5]

Working the Line

The U.S.-Canadian border may be the longest undefended border in the world, but just don't cross it! A case in point is the Canadian seizure of a U.S. vessel in 1947. "Seizure by the Canadian government of a 140-foot, three-masted full-rigged schooner *J.T. Wing*, for alleged violation of the Canadian Coastwise Law, was announced Wednesday by the Collector of Customs at Amherstburg. Whether the officials will confiscate the only full-rigged commercial craft seen in these waters in many years depends on a report expected from Ottawa Thursday. If the alleged violation is proved, the craft can be confiscated of a fine levied against the owner, Grant H. Piggott of Windsor."

"Piggott bought the ship in 1935 to be used as a training ship for boys seeking adventure sailing under canvas and for commercial use, he said Wednesday night. According to Canadian customers officials, the alleged violation occurred last Saturday when the schooner stopped in Detroit and unloaded some cedar posts for a local lumber concern. Because the ship's billing disclosed that the cargo was consigned from Manitoulin Island in Georgian Bay, to Amherstburg and Kingsville, the law was violated, officials pointed out. Under the Canadian law a cargo cannot be unloaded at an American port when it is billed from one Canadian port to another, officials said. Or cargo cannot be billed between two Canadian ports on ships of American registry. The schooner *Wing* is of American registry, it was claimed."

"We unintentionally violated the coastal laws," Piggott explained. "We unloaded some of the 25,000 cedar posts at the foot of the Rivard St. and then proceeded to Amherstburg. We hope we can straighten up the matter when we get together with customs officials." "It was ignorance of the law as the *Wing* has been engaged in hauling pulpwood and posts all summer between Georgian Bay, Wisconsin and from Drummond Island, Michigan to Goderich, Ontario."

"Piggott said that the skipper of the ship, Captain George A. Fisher, would confer with him in his offices Thursday morning and give him a complete report on the ship's activity. Besides Fisher, the schooner carries a crew of three men and five boys who are undergoing training."

The schooner, originally named *J.O. Webster*, was launched in Nova Scotia in 1921. She was engaged in the rum-running trade in the prohibition era, carried mahogany logs from East Africa to the New England states and once was wrecked on the Florida coast.[6]

The trouble was eventually cleared up and the old *Wing* continued to sail the lakes ending up in a bone yard at Detroit's Belle Isle. She was purposely burned in the 1950s to clear space for the then new Dossin Great Lakes Museum. Certainly this was an ironic fate for such a fine old vessel.[7]

Credit Can be Dangerous

It is fascinating to learn that the first white inhabitant in Menominee County wasn't, or better explained, actually was an African-American whose name is lost to history. Tradition tells us that a black Indian trader and his Canadian voyager employee were trading near the present day site of Peshtigo in the late 1700s. Fortune did not smile of the pair however.

It seems he had extended credit to the local Indians who understood the concept, came in regularly, drew goods and later returned with payment. It was a satisfactory arrangement for all. However a band from Sturgeon Bay failed to grasp the concept of credit sales and the need for ultimate payment. When they came across the bay to trade, he insisted on payment for the earlier provided goods. After the Indians reluctantly paid with furs, he refused to advance further credit, demanding payment on receipt.

The Sturgeon Bay Indians responded by "lifting" the scalps of both trader and voyageur and plundering the trading post. There is also a persistent rumor that a large cache of silver remains buried near the post.[8]

Smuggling

Smuggling has long been an activity on the Great Lakes. Before the War of 1812 the U.S. Brig *Oneida* captured the British vessel *Scourge* for smuggling on Lake Ontario. Originally built as the Royal Navy schooner *Lord Nelson*, the miscreant was quickly brought into the U.S. fleet. On August 8, 1813 she was sunk at the mouth of the Niagara River by a sudden squall.

The schooner *Florence*, which sailed on Lake Superior in 1846, was seized by Canadian authorities in the spring of 1847 for smuggling. Officially condemned by the court, she was sold to cover costs.

The "Disappearing" Rifles

Some smuggling tales are truly strange. During the early days of World War I a home guard force called the Legion of Frontiersmen formed in Edmonton, Canada. It was a quasi-military association of Canadian patriots, Boer War and various imperial campaign veterans intent on serving their country and the greater British Empire.

Of course a military force needs arms for simple drill as well as fighting so their leader duly requested a supply from the army. The request was denied. The Mayor of Edmonton tried to us his influence but the army still refused to issue them. After all, soldiering was for the professionals. These amateurs would only get underfoot and perhaps even hurt themselves if we gave them rifles! This flawed attitude of superiority was common among the professional soldiers around the world, at least until the shooting started!

The Legion decided if the official way didn't work there always was the unofficial method. They would just buy the rifles. They duly contacted a company in New York City that agreed to sell 1,000 45/70 caliber "Peabody Breech-loading" single shot rifles, including bayonets, for $3.85 each.

The unit placed an initial order for 60 rifles, which were shipped via transcontinental Grand Truck Railway freight in November 1915. The shipment never arrived and after a great deal of correspondence between the Legion and New York, it was finally determined that Canadian Customs had seized them as contraband! Livid over their own government's lack of patriotism, the Legion went to work behind the scenes and the contraband rifles disappeared from the Custom shed at the border. Using a method still unknown, the Legion smuggled the rifles across Lake Superior to Port Arthur where it was apparently intended to send them to Edmonton by rail. When Customs realized the rifles were missing from their shed, they realized the probable destination and wired Port Arthur to have the rifles seized again. One step ahead of the authorities, the Legion made the rifles "disappear" again. How the rifles finally reached Edmonton isn't known, but they did.

After the miffed customs men were finally convinced the Legion were the good guys and not some subversive German plot to seize Edmonton with the New York rifles, the unit was allowed to keep the weapons. Doubtless some heavy political intervention was applied to call off the customs dogs. The rifles never saw combat. Their entire career was spent as home guard training rifles and it seems after the Great War they seemed to disappear, only to reappear in time to help train units for World War II. The best explanation seems to be that when the unit was disbanded in 1920, one of the members was given the rifles to take care of in the event they were ever needed again.[9]

Smuggling continues on the Great Lakes today. For example, on August 25, 2002 the Detroit News reported that 22 Caribbean stowaways were found by authorities aboard the cargo ship *NST Challenge* after it docked in Detroit. Because of the sheer numbers, a U.S. Immigration and Naturalization Service supervisor believed it was part of a smuggling operation. The ships owners were fined $10,000 per stowaway as well as appropriate INS costs relating to the investigation.

A Leaky Border

The U.S. and Canada have nearly always been close allies, at least since the War of 1812, and we do share the longest undefended border in the world. Every year nearly 200 million people and billions of dollars worth of goods and services pass easily between the two nations. But all of the people and material are not always the kind the other wants.

As expected, illegal drugs are a major substance smuggled both ways across the border. From Canada to the U.S. popular drugs include marijuana, precursor chemicals, methamphetamine, heroin and cocaine.

From the U.S. to Canada includes LSD, steroids, cocaine, hashish, marijuana and other illicit drugs. As both U.S. and Canadian authorities discovered to their chagrin during Prohibition, the boarder is thousands of miles long and includes dense forest, many lakes including the Great Lakes and numerous rivers. A considerable amount is virtually unmarked and unguarded, open for the enterprising smuggler. Areas occupied by Indian reservations are particularly difficult to police.

Canada and the U.S. work closely in joint border initiatives to improve coordination to stop smuggling. It is clearly in the best interests of both nations to do so. It is believed organized crime groups are behind the smuggling effort in both countries.[10]

Firearms

Canada is largely a disarmed nation. Without a constitutional guarantee as provided in the Second Amendment to the U.S. Constitution, Canadian citizens have no right to "keep and bear arms." Smuggling in firearms is especially lucrative since they are so scarce; anyone having one has immense relative power. An armed criminal in Canada knows he is the "king of the street." He can commit all matter of crime without fear of running into an armed citizen. The major source of illegal firearms is the U.S. They are usually obtained from U.S. dealers or gun shows and smuggled into the country. In some cases U.S. citizens are used to purchase the weapons legally and send them across the border in small numbers, perhaps in the three to five weapon range.

In some rare instances weapons have been purchased aboard and shipped into Canada then smuggled into the U.S. In one instance over 23,000 surplus World War II M-1 Garand rifles were obtained overseas and shipped into Canada with the intention of bringing them into the U.S under false documents.[11]

Diamonds

When large deposits of diamonds were discovered in the Northwest Territories in 1991 it opened up entirely new opportunities of illegal trade. The new deposits vaulted Canada into fifth place among world diamond producers.

Diamonds are always an attractive commodity to criminals since they are high value and small in size. Traded the world over, they are small in size and easily smuggled. The terrorist Al Qaeda network may be using them to bypass international banking controls. There is also the very real likelihood of "blood" or "conflict" diamonds being smuggled into Canada, mixed with production from the Northwest Territories and introduced into the legitimate world market. Conflict diamonds are from regions of the world, notably west Africa, where violent civil wars are raging. As profits from local diamond mines have been known to finance such civil wars, the world diamond industry has refused to handle the diamonds. Bringing them into Canada and either mixing with domestic production or smuggling them into the U.S., the world's largest diamond market, is commonly done.[12]

Tobacco

Because of restrictive Canadian taxes, tobacco in all it's various forms is often smuggled into Canada from the U.S. Some Canadian tobacco products are legally exported (tax free) then smuggled back into the country as are illegal foreign brands.

Alcohol

Nearly 70 years after Prohibition the alcohol market in Canada continues to be supplied by a variety of methods identical to the "good old days." Cross border smuggling, theft of product from warehouses and trucks and moonshining are still the "modus operandi." In a Prohibition role reversal most of the bootlegged booze comes from the U.S. The Canadian market is attractive to the rumrunners because of the extreme federal and provincial taxes. If untaxed American liquor can be slipped into Canada the profit is considerable, certainly enough to bc worth the risk of apprehension. The booze comes in via criminal gang operations as well as tourists entering with more than the approved amount.

Much of the illegal substances, drugs, tobacco, firearms, diamonds and liquor, enter Canada through marine terminals, safely hidden away in steel shipping containers. Shipping the containers to Great Lakes ports, U.S. or Canadian, is an easy and effective way of bringing the material directly into the heartland of North America. Like their U.S. counterparts, customs officers can only examine a small percentage of the containers. What is hidden away undetected in the others is unknown. Of course good and timely intelligence of what illegal products are arriving from where is critical and the U.S. and Canada as well as other civilized countries work closely together in a continuing struggle against criminal forces.[13]

END NOTES

Murder

[1]*Marquette Mining Journal*, July 20, 1889.

[2]*Detroit Post and Tribune*, August 24, 1883.

[3]*Oswego Palladium*, New York, November 1, 1875

[4]*Chicago Inter-Ocean*, May 12, 1882.

[5]DePere File, Stonehouse Collection.

[6]*Oswego Palladium*, August 10, 1881

[7]*Duluth Evening Herald*, September 5, 1904.

[8]*Saginaw Weekly Courier*, December 4, 1879.

[9]"Certified Copy of Record of Death, Edward S. Morrison," dated July 10, 1908, *Flint Daily Journal*, June 15, 20, 1908, *Port Austin News*, June 18, 19, 1908,

[10]*Green Bay Advocate*, June 29, 1854.

[11]Jack Edwards, "The Castles of Seul Choix," *Great Lakes Cruiser Magazine*, July 1995, pp. 32-39.

[12]Leslie E. Arndt, *By These Waters*, (Bay City, Michigan: *Bay City Times*) 1876, pp, 148-150.

[13]Jack Edwards, "The Mystery of Sand Point Lighthouse," *Great Lakes Cruiser Magazine*, June 1995; *Escanaba Ironport*, March 5,13, April 10, 1886; *History of the Upper Peninsula of Michigan*, (Chicago: The Western Historical Company, 1883), pp 246-247.

Mutiny & Barratry

[1]*Detroit Free Press*, August 9, 1889.

[2]*Detroit Free Press*, September 30, 1905

[3]*Oswego Commercial Times*, May 22, 1860

[4]*Detroit Post and Tribune*, April 28, 1883

[5]*Detroit Free Press*, October 27, 1883.

[6]W. O. Stubig, "Shanghai on the Great Lakes," *Inland Seas*, Spring, 1946, pp. 130-131.

[7]Interview, Captain Edward C. Beganz, October 14, 1993.

[8]James P. Barry, Georgian Bay, *The Sixth Great Lake*. (Erin, Ontario: Boston Mills, 1995), p. 99.

[9]*Detroit Free Press*. October 23, 1906.

[10]*Detroit Post and Tribune*. October 16, 1883.

[11]*Detroit Free Press*. August 23, 1900.

[12]Ivan Walton Collection, Bentley Historical Library, University of Michigan; *Saginaw Weekly Courier*, August 3, 1882.

[13]*Chicago Inter-Ocean*, August 5,11, 12, 14, 14, 26, 27, 1874; July 26, 29, 1875.

[14]*Detroit Free Press*, October 21, 1888.

[15]Lakeland File, Stonehouse Collection.

Rum Running

[1]Edward Behrs, *Prohibition, Thirteen Years That Changed America* (New York: Arcade Publishing, 1996), pp. 40-44; Norman H. Clark, *Deliver Us From Evil* (New York: W.W. Norton and Company, 1976), pp. 82-85.

[2]http://www.walkervilletimes.com

[3]John Kobler, *Ardent Sprits and the Rise and Fall of Prohibition* (New York: G.P. Putnam's Sons, 1973), p. 25.

[4]Ardent, p. 222

[5]Henry Lee, *How Dry We Were, Prohibition Revisited* (Prentice-Hall: Englewood, New Jersey, 1963), p. 72.

[6]http:// www.walkervilletimes.com

[7]Lee, *How Dry*, p. 203

[8]http://www.walkervilletimes.com

[9]Mabel Walker Willebrandt, *The Inside of Prohibition* (Indianapolis: Bobbs-Merrill Company, 1929), p. 150-151.

[10]http://www.walkervilletimes.com

[11]Treasury Department, *Rum War at Sea*, (Washington, DC: U.S. Government Printing Office, 1964), pp. 12-13

[12]Ardent, p. 338

[13]Kobler, *Rise and Fall*, pp. 214-215, 223.

[14]Ardent, p. 271

[15]Lee, *How Dry*, p. 53.

[16]Ardent, pp. 272-275, 278

[17]Prohibition, pp. 153-154

[18]Lee, *How Dry*, p. 219

[19]http://www.walkervilletimes.com

[20]RG 26, NARA

[21]HYPERLINK "http://www.walkervilletimes", http://www.walkervil-letimes.com

[22]Paul R. Kaviett, *The Violent Years, Prohibition and the Detroit Mob*, (Fort Lee, NJ: Barricade Books, 2001), p. 58

[23]*Scandals of Prohibition Enforcement*, Prepared by the Association Against the Prohibition Amendment, No. 4. (Washington, DC: March 1, 1929), p. 17.

[24]*Scandals of Prohibition*, p. 17.

[25]Willebrandt, *Inside*, pp. 73-74

[26]Willebrandt, *Inside*, pp. 71-72

[27]John C. Cahalan, Jr., "Rum-Running at Detroit." *The Commonwealth,* (August 21, 1929): p. 402.

[28]Cahalan, "Rum-Running," p. 402

[29]Lee, *How Dry*, p. 110

[30]Willebrandt, *Inside*, p. 63-64

[31]Lee, *How Dry*, P. 173-174

[32]HYPERLINK "http://www.walkervilletims.com" http://www.walke-rvilletimes.com

[33]HYPERLINK "http://www.walkervilletimes.com" http://www.walke-rvilletimes.com

[34]HYPERLINK "http://www.walkervilletime.com" http://www.walke-rvilletime.com

[35]Willebrandt, *Inside*, pp. 66-67

[36]John M. Mills, *Canadian Coastal and Inland Steam Vessels, 1809-1930* (Providence, Rhode Island: Steamship Historical Society of America, 1979), p. 120.

[37]*Violent Years*, pp. 55-56.

[38]*Canada Liquor Crossing the Border*, Prepared by the Association Against the Prohibition Amendment, No. 2, (Washington, DC: July 1929), pp. 2-3.

[39]http://www.spsbe.jhu.edu/evrgreen/egjournal/duke.cfm

[40]Andrea Gutsche and Cindy Bisaillon, *Mysterious Islands, Forgotten Tales of the Great Lakes*, (Toronto: Lynx Imges, 1999), pp. 76-79

[41]HYPERLINK "http://www.kwic.com/~pagodavista/schoolhouse/lore/dresden.htm" http://www.kwic.com/~pagodavista/schoolhouse/lore/dresden.htm

[42]HYPERLINK "http://www.cityofbayvillage.com/history/main/com" http://www.cityofbayvillage.com/history/main/com

[43]HYPERLINK "http://www.geocities.com/MotorCity/Downs/3548/facility/willard.html" http://www.geocities.com/MotorCity/Downs/3548/facility/willard.html

[44]HYPERLINK "http://www.americanmafia.com/Allan_May_10-4-99.html" http://www.americanmafia.com/Allan_May_10-4-99.html; Cleveland Plain Dealer, June-August, 1921

[45]*Prohibition*, pp. 255-245.

[46]Willebrandt, *Inside*, pp. 67-69

[47]*Mysterious Island*, pp. 44-45

[48]HYPERLINK "http://www.erieyachtclub.org/membership/history.html", http://www.erieyachtclub.org/membership/history.html

[49]http//klark.org/schlitz/history.php

[50]http//klark.org/Schlitz/history.php

[51]Treasury Department, *Rum War at Sea*, (Washington, DC: U.S. Government Printing Office, 1964), pp. 124-125

[52]C. W. Hunt, *Booze Boats and Billions*, (Toronto: Billa Flint Publishing, 1988), pp. 295-296)

[53]*Milwaukee Journal*, May 17, 1930; RG 26, NARA

[54]Clarence R. Pickering, *The Early Days of Prohibition*, (New York: Vantage Press, 1964), pp. 131-133.

[55]John Mills, *Canadian Coastal and Inland Steam Vessels 1809-1930*, (Providence, Rhode Island: Steamship Historical Society of America, 1979); *Marquette Mining Journal*, November 23,24, 27, 29, December 4, 1920; January 5, 10, 17-22; April 14; November 28, 1921; November 15, 1922; Arbutus File, Fosburg Collection.

[56]*Superior Evening Telegram*, February 16, 1978; *Ashland Daily Press*, October 13, 1927.

[57]*Canada Liquor Crossing the Border*, *No. 2*, Prepared by the Association Against the Prohibition Amendment, Washington DC, July 1929

[58]Allan S. Everest, *Rum Across the Border* (Syracuse, New York: Syracuse University Press, 1978), p. 159

[59]www.walkervilletimes.com

[60]U.S. Coast Guard. *Record of Movements, Vessels of the U.S. Coast Guard*, 1790-December 31, 1933. Washington, DC: Treasury Department, 1989.

[61]Ardent, p. 307

[62]Ardent, p. 268

[63]Everest, *Rum*, p. 76.

[64]Everest, *Rum*, pp. 90-91

[65]RG 26, NARA, online

[66]Ardent, p. 309

[67]*Early Days of Prohibition*, p. 57

[68]*Early Days of Prohibition*, pp. 27-31

[69]Several Coast Guardsmen were murdered by a rum runner off the Florida coast in 1927. Two years later the murderer was executed by hanging on a gallows built in the aviation hanger at the Fort Lauderdale Coast Guard Station.

[70]Ardent, pp. 289-291

[71]Lee, *How Dry*, p. 205

[72]U.S. Congress, Senate. Committee on the Judiciary. The National Prohibition Law. 69th Congress. Ist Session, 1926, pp. 649-652.

[73]http://www.brownandwilliamson.com/index_sub2.cfm

[74]http://college.hmco.com/history/readerscomp/rcah/html/ah_071600_prohibitiona.htm

Piracy

[1]*Detroit Post and Tribune*, November 15, 1877.

[2]*Detroit Post*, August 3, 1885

[3]Mikel B. Classen, "Escanaba Buccaneer", *Great Lakes Pilot*, n.d., "Captain Seavey Remembered," unidentified article, Tom Powers, *Michigan Rouges, Desperados and Cut-throats*, Freide Publications, Davison, Michigan, 2002.

[4]Ivan Walton Collection, Bentley Historical Library, University of Michigan.

[5]*Cassier's Magazine*, April 1899.

[6]*Oswego Palladium*, December 30, 1876.

[7]Ivan Walton Collection, Bentley Historical Library, University of Michigan.

[8]Elizabeth Whitney Williams, *A Child of the Sea*, Detroit: J.E. Jewett, 1905, pp. 197-198; "Strang File," Stonehouse Collection.

[9]Mansfield, *History of the Great Lakes*, Chicago, 1899.

[10]*Buffalo Emporium*, August 12, 1837.

[11]*Schenectady Cabinet*, September 26, 1848.

[12]Bradley A. Rogers, *Guardian of the Great Lakes*, the U.S. Paddle Frigate *Michigan*, University of Michigan Press, 1996; Dave Swayze, "A Great Lakes Pirate Ship. . . or Not" unpublished manuscript.

[13]Basil Lubbock, *Bully Hayes, South Sea Pirate* (Boston: Charles E. Lauriat Company, 1931), p. 5.

[14]Frank Clune, *Captain Bully Hayes, Blackbirder and Bigamist* (London: Angus and Robertson, 1971), pp. 5-6.

[15]Lubbock, *South Sea*, pp. 13-17.

[16]Clune, *Captain Bully Hayes*; Lubbock, Bully Hayes.

[17]Carl A. Norbery, "Biography of the Schooner *C.H. Hackley*, Lumber Hooker-Trader-Pirate Ship." *Inland Seas*, Winter 1981, pp. 244-251.

[18]Margaret Beattie Bogue, *Fishing the Great Lakes, An Environmental History 1783-1933*, (Madison, Wisconsin: University of Wisconsin Press, 2000), pp. 33, 52.

[19]Annual Report, U.S. Lighthouse Service, 1893.

[20]*Fishing*, pp. 144-145

[21]*Fishing*, pp. 230-231; *Record of Movements, Vessels of the U.S. Coast Guard, 1790-1933*, (Washington, DC: Commandant, U.S. Coast Guard, 1989), p. 277.

[22]*Two Rivers Chronicle*, April 18, 1905.

[23]Richard G. Lilliard, *The Great Forest* (New York: Alfred A. Knopf, 1947), pp. 159-161

[24]William B. Greeley, *Forest Policy* (New York: McGraw-Hill Books, 1953), p. 135.

[25]Lillard, *Great Forest*, pp. 161-162.

[26]Lillard, *Great Forest*, p. 165.

[27]Greeley, *Forest Policy*, pp. 146-147.

[28]Lillard, *Great Forest*, pp. 167-168.

[29]Donald L. Cannery, *U.S. Coast Guard and Revenue Cutters, 1790-1935* (Annapolis, Maryland: U.S. Naval Institute Press, 1995), p. 22.

[30]Bradley A. Rodgers, *Guardian of the Great Lakes, The U.S. Paddle Frigate Michigan* (Ann Arbor: University of Michigan Press, 1999), pp. 48-51.

[31]Greeley, *Forest Policy* pp. 139-140.

[32]Rodgers, *Guardian*, pp. 53-55.

[33]There is some conflicting information regarding the dates of the *Michigan* action. All agree it was the fall of 1853.

[34]Greeley, *Forest Policy*, p. 148.

[35]Greeley, *Forest Policy*, p. 151-155.

[36]Stumpage is the right to cut trees on defined land.

[37]Lillard, *Great Forest*, p. 169.

[38]Lillard, *Great Forest*, p. 170.

Sailors Ashore

[1]Thomas P. Lowry, M.D., *The Story the Soldiers Wouldn't Tell, Sex in the Civil War* (Stackpole Books, 1994), p. 211

[2]Walton, box 4.

[3]Ivan Walton Collection, Bentley Historical Library, University of Michigan, box 7.

[4]Walton, box 4.

[5]George B. Catlin, *The Story of Detroit* (Detroit: *Detroit News*, 1930), p. 64.

[6]Walton, box 4.

[7]*Buffalo Commerce Advertiser*, July 24, 1874.

[8]http://intotem.buffnet.net/bhw/erie-canal/infected/infected.htm

[9]Walton, box 4.

[10]William W. Sanger, M.D. *The History of Prostitution, Its Extent, Causes and Effects Throughout the World* (New York: Eugenics Publishing Company, 1939), p. 608.

[11]Walton, box 4.

[12]Walton, box 6.

[13]Walton, box 4.

[14]Walton, box 4.

[15]Walton, box 7.

[16]Walton, box 5.

[17]Walton, box 5.

[18]Charles Winick and Paul M. Kinsie, *The Lively Commerce, Prostitution in the United States*, (Chicago: Quadrangle Books, 1971), pp. 124-125, 134,145, 156-157, 240-241.

[19]*Oswego Palladine-Times*, May 17, 1943.

[20]Walton, box 4.

[21]Walton, box 7.

[22]Richard J. Wright, "History of Shipbuilding in Cleveland," *Inland Seas*, Spring, 1957, pp. 71-72.

[23]Walton, box 7.

[24]Walton, box 4.

[25]Walton, box 7.

[26]Walton, box 7.

[27]Walton, box 7.

[28]Catlin, *The Story*, 579.

[29]Walton, box 7.

[30]Catlin, *Detroit*, p. 579.

[31]Winick and Kinsie, *The Lively*, p. 136, 150.

[32]Bay County Historical Society File

[33]Rodney H. Mills, Jr., "Glory Days in West Bay City," *Inland Seas* (Summer 2002), p. 114-115.

[34]Raymond J. Herek, "Bay City's Wilderst Era, the Shanty Boys and the Catacombs." Bay City Historical Society, n.d.

[35]Herek, "Bay City's,"

[36]Manuscript, Bay County Historical Society, n.d.

[37]Manuscript, Bay County Historical Society, n.d.

[38]Walton, box 7.

[39]Manuscript, Bay County Historical Society, n.d.

[40]Stewart H. Holbrook, *Holy Old Mackinaw* (New York: MacMillian, 1938) p. 189.

[41]Herek, "Bay City's"

[42]*Bay City Times*, July 9, 1889.

[43]Unidentified manuscript, Bay County Historical Society.

[44]http://members.aol.com/Kschessler/wizzo.html

[45]Lloyd Wendt and Herman Kogan, *Bosses in Lusty Chicago* (Bloomington, Indiana: Indiana University Press, 1943), pp. 80-81.

[46]Richard Lindberg, *Return to the Scene of the Crime: A Guide to Infamous Places in Chicago*, (Nashville, Tennessee: Cumberland House, 1999), pp. 1-9, 15, 27-3175, 364-372.

[47]Catlin, *The Story*, p. 175

[48]Wendt and Kogan, Lusty, pp. 375-338.

[49]HYPERLINK "http://www.seanparnell.com/Bar%20Reviews/Gone/Everleigh.htm" http://www.seanparnell.com/Bar%20Reviews/Gone/Everleigh.htm; Wendt and Kogan, Lusty, pp. 284-285.

[50]Vice Commission of Chicago, *The Social Evil in Chicago, a Study of Existing Conditions With Recommendations by the Vice Commission of Chicago*, (Chicago: The Vice Commission of Chicago Inc.1911) p.p. 69-73

[51] *Social Evil in Chicago*, p. 79.

[52] Joanne J. Meyeroweitz, *Women Adrift, Independent Wage Earners in Chicago, 1880-1930*, (Chicago: University of Chicago Press, 1988), p. 110.

[53] *Social Evil in Chicago*, p. 97.

[54] *Social Evil in Chicago*, p. 108.

[55] Donald L. Miller, *City of the Century* (New York: Simon and Schuster, 1996), p. 145.

[56] Miller, *City of the Century*, p. 146.

[57] Miller, *City of the Century*, p. 508.

[58] Walton, box 7.

[59] Walton, box 4.

[60] Lindberg, *Return*, p. 75.

[61] *Social Evil in Chicago*, p. 216.

[62] *Social Evil in Chicago*, p. 215.

[63] *Social Evil in Chicago*, p. 216.

[64] *Detroit Free Press*, July 1, 1906.

[65] Wendt and Kogan, *Lusty*, p. 295.

[66] Stead, *If Christ*, pp. 18-21.

[67] *Chicago Tribune*, January 27, 1895.

[68] HYPERLINK "http://members.aol" http://members.aol.com/Kschessler/wizzt.html

[69] Unidentified Clipping, February 13, 1898.

[70] Beganz, interview

[71] Daily British Whig (Kingston). May 10, 1856.

[72] HYPERLINK "http://www.torontocityofdreams.com.sincity.htm" http://www.torontocityofdreams.com.sincity.htm

[73] http://www.russianbooks.org/crime/cph4.htm

[74] "Report, Social Service Committee," Toronto, 1915, p. 17.

[75]Guy Burnham, *The Lake Superior Country in History and Story* (Ashland, Wisconsin: *Ashland Daily Press*, 1930) P. 357.

[76]John Bartlow Martin, *Call It North Country* (Detroit: Wayne State University Press, 1986), pp. 180-183.

[77]http://216.239.37/104/search?q=cache:d-FSUxf6dfEJ:www.assured-publications.com/ihs-p

[78]*Mining Journal* (Marquette, Michigan), November 23, 1878.

[79]*Mining Journal*, October 11, 1879.

[80]*Mining Journal*, June 19, 1880.

[81]*Mining Journal*, October 9, 1880.

[82]*Mining Journal*, June 17, 1882.

[83]*Mining Journal*, July 1, 1882.

[84]*Mining Journal*, October 21, 1882.

[85]*Mining Journal*, August 19, 1882.

[86]*Marquette Mining Journal*, November 24, 1883.

[87]*Weekly Mining Journal*, May 26, 1894.

[88]Martin, *Call it North County*, P. 247

[89]*Marquette Mining Journal*, July 3, 1880.

[90]*Marquette Mining Journal*, June 17, 1882.

[91]*Marquette Mining Journal*, June 18, 1881.

[92]*Marquette Mining Journal*, August 25, 1883.

[93]*Marquette Mining Journal*, November 11, 1871.

[94]Tom Powers, *Michigan Rogues, Desperatos and Cut-throats* (Davison, Michigan: Freide Publications, 2002) p. 112.

[95]Martin, *Call It North Country*, pp. 138-139.

[96]David J. Langum, *Crossing Over the Line, Legislating Morality and the Mann Act*, (Chicago: University of Chicago Press, 1994), p. 48.

[97]*Detroit Free Press*, August 20, 1869.

[98]www.startribune.com/stories/1282/3943357.html;

[99]Alex O'Kash, *Waterfront* (Keadney, Nebraska: Morris Publishing, 2002), 2000.

Bits and Pieces

[1]*Marquette Mining Journal*. October 25, 1879.

[2]*Marquette Mining Journal*. October 25, 1879.

[3]*Oswego Daily Times*. October 14, 1856; Mansfield, *History of the Great Lakes*, Volume 1, (J.H. Beers and Company: Chicago, 1899), p. 869.

[4]*Detroit Post and Tribune*, March 15, 1880.

[5]*Detroit Tribune*, August 17, 1886.

[6]*Detroit Free Press*. November 4, 1937.

[7]http://www.boatnerd.com/swayze/trivia/23.htm

[8]*History of the Upper Peninsula of Michigan*, p. 473. *Lake Superior News*, May 13, 1848.

[9]http://www.frontiersmenhistorian.info/canada4.htm
http://www.boatnerd.com/news/archive/8-98.htm

[10]http://www.usdoj.gov/ndic/pubs07/0794/intro.htm

[11]http://ww.cisc.gc.ca/AnnualReport2002/Cisc2002/contraband2002.html

[12]http:// Annual Report

[13]http:// Annual Report

BIBLIOGRAPHY

Books

Allen, Clifford, editor, *Michigan Log Marks*. East Lansing, Michigan: Michigan State College,1941.

Arndt, Lesile, E., *By These Waters*. Bay City, Michigan: Bay City Times, 1876.

Asbury, Herbert, *Gem of the Prairie*. New York: Doubleday, 1940.

The Great Illusion, an Informal History of Prohibition. New York: Doubleday, 1950.

Barry, James, *Georgian Bay, the Sixth Great Lake*. Erin, Ontario: Boston Mills, 1995.

Behrs, Edward, *Prohibition, Thirteen Years That Changed America*. New York: Arcade Publishing, 1996.

Bennett, James O'Donnell, *Chicago Gangland, the True Story of Chicago Crime*. Chicago, 1929.

Burnham, Guy M., *The Lake Superior Country in History and in Story*. Ashland, Wisconsin: Paradigm Press, 1996.

Bogue, Margaret Beattie, *Fishing the Great Lakes, An Environmental History 1783-1933*. Madison: University of Wisconsin Press, 2000.

Burnham, Guy, *The Lake Superior Country in History and Story* (Ashland, Wisconsin: Ashland Daily Press, 1930.

Cameron, Jenks, *The Development of Government Forest Control in the United States*. Baltimore: The Johns Hopkins Press, 1928.

Cannery, Donald L., *U.S. Coast Guard and Revenue Cutters, 1790-1935*. Annapolis, Maryland: Naval Institute Press, 1995.

Catlin, George B., *The Story of Detroit*. Detroit: *Detroit News*, 1923.

Chisholm, Barbara and Gutsche, Andrea, *Superior Under the Shadow of the Gods*. Toronto: Lynx Images, 1998.

Clark, Norman H., *Deliver Us From Evil*. New York: W.W. Norton and Company, 1976.

Clune, Frank, *Captain Bully Hayes, Blackbirder and Bigamist*. London: Angus and Robertson, 1971.

Evans, Hillary, *Harlots, Whores and Hookers, A History of Prostitution*. New York: Dorset Press, 1979.

Everest, Allan S., *Rum Across the Border*. Syracuse, New York: Syracuse University Press, 1978.

Granlund, Nils Thor, *Blondes, Brunettes and Bullets*. New York: David McKay Publishing, 1957.

Greeley, William B., *Forest Policy*. New York: McGraw-Hill Books, 1953.

Haynes, Roy A., *Prohibition Inside Out*. New York: Doubleday, 1926.

History of the Upper Peninsula of Michigan. Chicago: The Western Historical Company, 1883.

Holbrook, Stewart H., *Holy Mackinaw*. New York: MacMillian Company, 1938.

Hunt, C. W., *Booze, Boats and Billions*. Toronto: Billa Flint Publishing Company, 1988.

Langum, David J., *Crossing Over the Line, Legislating Morality and the Mann Act* (Chicago: University of Chicago Press, 1994.

Lillard, Richard G., *The Great Forest*. New York: Alfred A. Knoff, 1947.

Lindberg, Richard, *Return to the Scene of the Crime; a Guide to Infamous Places in Chicago*. Nashville: Cumberland House, 1999.

Lowry, Thomas P., M.D., *The Story the Soldiers Wouldn't Tell, Sex in the Civil War*. New York: Stackpole Books, 1994.

Lubbock, Basil, *Bully Hayes, South Seas Pirate*. Boston: Charles E. Lauriat Company, 1931.

Kaviett, Paul R., *The Violent Years, Prohibition and the Detroit Mob*. Fort Lee, New Jersey: Barricade Books, 2001.

Kobler, John, *Ardent Spirits and the Rise and Fall of Prostitution*. New York: G.P. Putnam's Sons, 1973.

Mackey, Thomas C., *Red Lights Out–A Legal History of Prostitution, Disorderly Houses, and Vice Districts, 1870-1917*. New York: Garland Publishing, 1987.

Mansfield, John, *History of the Great Lakes*. Chicago: J.H. Beers, 1899.

Martin, John B., *Call It North Country*. Detroit: Wayne State University Press, 1886.

Meyeroweitz, *Women Adrift, Independent Wage Earners in Chicago, 1880-1930*. Chicago: University of Chicago Press, 1988.

Mills, John M., *Canadian Coastal and Inland Steam Vessels 1809-1930*. Providence, Rhode Island: The Steamship Historical Society of America, Inc., 1979.

Miller, Donald, *City of the Century*. New York: Simon and Schuster, 1996.

Nelson, Derek, *Moonshiners, Bootleggers and Rumrunners*. Osceola, Wisconsin: Motorbooks International, 1995.

Pickering, Clarence R., *The Early Days of Prohibition*. New York: Vantage Press, 1964.

Powers, Tom, *Michigan Rogues, Desperados and Cut-Throats*. Davison, Michigan: Freide Publications, 2002.

Rodgers, Bradley A., *Guardian of the Great Lakes, The U.S. Paddle Frigate* Michigan. Ann Arbor: University of Michigan Press, 1999.

Sanger, William W., M.D., *The History of Prostitution, Its Extent, Causes and Effects Throughout the World*. New York: Eugenics Publishing Company, 1939.

Stead, William T. *If Christ Came to Chicago*. Chicago and London, 1894.

Treasury Department, *Rum War at Sea*. Washington, DC: U.S. Government Printing Office, 1964.

Van Every, Edward, *Sins of America as "Exposed" by the Police Gazette*. New York, 1931.

Vice Commission of Chicago, *The Social Evil in Chicago, a Study of Existing Conditions With Recommendations by the Vice Commission of Chicago*. Chicago: The Vice Commission of Chicago, 1911.

Wendt, Llyod, *Lords of the Levee*. New York: Garden City Publishing, 1943.

Willebrandt, Mabel, *The Inside of Prohibition*. New York: Current News Features, 1929.

Williams, Elizabeth Whitney, *A Child of the Sea*. Detroit: J.E. Jewett, 1905.

Winick, Charles and Kinsie, Paul M., *The Lively Commerce, Prostitution in the United States*. Chicago: Quadrangle Books, 1971.

Newspapers

Ashland Daily Press
Bay City Times
Buffalo Commerce Advertiser
Buffalo Emporium
Chicago American (1901-40)
Chicago Inter-Ocean (1890-1906)
Chicago Tribune
Daily British Whig
Detroit Free Press
Detroit Post and Tribune
Detroit Post
Detroit Tribune
Duluth Evening Herald
Escanaba Ironport
Flint Daily Journal
Green Bay Advocate
Lake Superior News
Milwaukee Journal
Mining Journal
Oswego Commercial Times

Oswego Daily Times
Oswego Palladine-Times
Oswego Palladium
Port Austin News
Saginaw Weekly Courier
Schenectady Cabinet
Superior Evening Telegram
Two Rivers Chronicle
Weekly Mining Journal

Reports

Annual Report, U.S. Lighthouse Service, 1893.

Canada Liquor Crossing the Border, No. 2, Prepared by the Association Against the Prohibition Amendment, Washington, DC, July 1929.

Herek, Raymond J., "Bay City's Wildest Era, the Shanty Boys and the Catacombs." Bay County Historical Society, n.d.

Record of Movements, Vessels of the U.S. Coast Guard, 1790-1933, Washington, DC: Commandant, U.S. Coast Guard, 1989.

Reforming America With a Shotgun, No. 15. Prepared by the Association Against the Prohibition Amendment, Washington DC, November 1929.

Report, Social Service Committee, Toronto, 1915.

Scandals of Prohibition Enforcement, No. 16, Prepared by the Association Against the Prohibition Amendment, Washington, DC, March 1, 1929.

U.S. Congress, Senate. Committee on the Judiciary. The National Prohibition Law. 69th Congress. Ist Session, 1926.

Collections

Bay County Historical Society

Arbutus File, Fosburg Collectin

Depere File, Stonehouse Collection

Lakeland File, Stonehouse Collection

Record Group 26, National Archives and Records Service

Walton Collection, Bentley Historical Library, University of Michigan.

Unidentified Manuscript, Bay County Historical Society, Bay City, Michigan.

Internet

HYPERLINK "http://www.boatnerd.com/news/archive/8-98.htm" http://www.boatnerd.com/news/archive/8-98.htm

http://www.boatnerd.com/swayze/trivia/23.htm

HYPERLINK "http://www.brownandwilliamson.com/index_sub2.cfm" http://www.brownandwilliamson.com/index_sub2.cfm

http://www.cisc.gc.ca/AnnualReport2002/Cisc2002/contraband2002.html

HYPERLINK "http://www.cityofbayvillage.com/history/main/com" http://www.cityofbayvillage.com/history/main/com

http://www.college.hmco.com/history/readership/rcah/html/ah_071600_prohibition.htm

HYPERLINK "http://www.erieyachtclub.org/membership/history.html" http://www.erieyachtclub.org/membership/history.html

http://www.frontiersmenhistorian.info/canada4.htm

HYPERLINK "http://www.geocities.com/MotorCity/Downs/3548/facility/willard.html" http://www.geocities.com/MotorCity/Downs/3548/facility/willard.html

HYPERLINK "http://intotem.buffnet.net/bhw/erie-canal/infected/infected.htm" http://intotem.buffnet.net/bhw/erie-canal/infected/infected.htm

HYPERLINK "http://klark.org/schlitz/history.php" http://klark.org/schlitz/history.php

HYPERLINK "http://www.kwic.com/~pagodavista/schoolhouse/lore/dresden.htm" http://www.kwic.com/~pagodavista/schoolhouse/lore/dresden.htm

HYPERLINK "http://members.aol.com/Kschessler/wizzo.html" http://members.aol.com/Kschessler/wizzo.html

http://www.russianbooks.org/crime/cph4.htm

http://www.seanparnell.com/Bar

HYPERLINK "http://spsbe.jhu.edu/evergreen/egjoournal/duke.htm" http://spsbe.jhu.edu/evergreen/egjoournal/duke.htm

HYPERLINK "http://www.torontocityofdreams.com.sincity.htm" http://www.torontocityofdreams.com.sincity.htm

HYPERLINK "http://www.usdoj.gov/ndic/pubs07/0794/intro.htm" http://www.usdoj.gov/ndic/pubs07/0794/intro.htm

HYPERLINK "http://www.walkervilletimes.com" http://www.walkervilletimes.com

Interview

Captain Edward Beganz. October 14, 1993.

Journals

Cahalan, John C., "Run Running at Detroit." *The Commonwealth*. August 21, 1929.

Cassier's Magazine. April 1899.

Classen, Mikel B., "Escanaba Buccaneer." *Great Lakes Pilot*, n.d.

Edwards, Jack, "The Castles of Seul Choix." *Great Lakes Cruiser Magazine*. July 1995.

Edwards, Jack, "The Mystery of Sand Point Lighthosue." *Great Lakes Cruiser Magazine*. June 1995.

Norbery, Carl A., "Biography of the Schooner *C.H. Hackley*, Lumber Hooker-Trader-Pirate." *Inland Seas*. Winter 1981.

Staubig, W.O., "Shanghai on the Great Lakes." *Inland Seas*. Spring 1946.

Tydings, Millard E., "Suppressed Prohibition Killings." *Plain Talk*. November 1929,

Unidentified Author, "Captain Seavey Remembered."

Wright, Richard J., "History of Shipbuilding in Cleveland." *Inland Seas*, (Spring, 1957): pp. 71-7

ABOUT THE AUTHOR

Frederick Stonehouse holds a Master of Arts Degree in History from Northern Michigan University, Marquette, Michigan, and has authored many books on Great Lakes maritime history. *Went Missing, Unsolved Great Lakes Shipwreck Mysteries, Lake Superior's "Shipwreck Coast," Dangerous Coast: Pictured Rocks Shipwrecks, The Wreck Of The Edmund Fitzgerald, Great Lakes Lighthouse Tales, Lighthouse Keepers And Coast Guard Cutters, Women And The Lakes, Untold Great Lakes Maritime Tales, Final Passage, True Shipwreck Adventures, My Summer At The Lighthouse, A Boy's Journal* and *Cooking Lighthouse Style, Favorite Recipes From Coast To Coast* are all published by Avery Color Studios, Inc.

He has also been a consultant for both the U.S. National Park Service and Parks Canada, and an "on air" expert for National Geographic Explorer and the History Channel as well as many regional media productions. He has also taught Great Lakes Maritime History at Northern Michigan University and is an active consultant for numerous Great Lakes oriented projects and programs. Check frederickstonehouse.com for more details.

His articles have been published in *Skin Diver, Great Lakes Cruiser Magazine* and *Lake Superior Magazine*. He is a member of the Board of Directors of the Marquette Maritime Museum and a member of the Board of Directors of the United States Life Saving Service Heritage Association.

Stonehouse resides in Marquette, Michigan.

Other Fred Stonehouse titles by Avery Color Studios, Inc.

- *Pirates, Crooks and Killers, The Dark Side Of The Great Lakes*
- *Blood On The Water, The Great Lakes During The Civil War*
- *November: The Cruelest Month, Great Lakes Wrecks*
- *The Wreck Of The Edmund Fitzgerald, 40th Anniversary Edition*
- *Steel On The Bottom, Great Lakes Shipwrecks*
- *Women And The Lakes, Untold Great Lakes Maritime Tales*
- *Went Missing Redux, Unsolved Great Lakes Shipwrecks*
- *Final Passage, True Shipwreck Adventures*
- *My Summer At The Lighthouse, A Boy's Journal*